More Than the Sound of Many Waters

More Than the Sound of Many Waters

Faith Through the Pathways of the Sea

CHRISTINE GRAEF

RESOURCE *Publications* · Eugene, Oregon

MORE THAN THE SOUND OF MANY WATERS
Faith Through the Pathways of the Sea

Copyright © 2016 Christine Graef. All rights reserved. Except for brief quotations in critical publications or reviews, no part of this book may be reproduced in any manner without prior written permission from the publisher. Write: Permissions, Wipf and Stock Publishers, 199 W. 8th Ave., Suite 3, Eugene, OR 97401.

Resource Publications
An Imprint of Wipf and Stock Publishers
199 W. 8th Ave., Suite 3
Eugene, OR 97401

www.wipfandstock.com

PAPERBACK ISBN: 978-1-5326-0235-1
HARDCOVER ISBN: 978-1-5326-0237-5
EBOOK ISBN: 978-1-5326-0236-8

Manufactured in the U.S.A.   OCTOBER 10, 2016

The Holy Bible, English Standard Version Copyright © 2001 by Crossway Bibles, a publishing ministry of Good News Publishers.

Poetry by contributors of the Refugees and Human Rights Student Poetry Contest, 2015, used by permission.

Mightier than the thunders of many waters, mightier than the waves of the sea, the Lord on high is mighty! (Ps 93:4)

THE SECOND COMING

W.B. Yeats 1919

Turning and turning in the widening gyre
The falcon cannot hear the falconer;
Things fall apart; the centre cannot hold;
Mere anarchy is loosed upon the world,
The blood-dimmed tide is loosed, and everywhere
The ceremony of innocence is drowned;
The best lack all conviction, while the worst
Are full of passionate intensity.
Surely some revelation is at hand;
Surely the Second Coming is at hand.
The Second Coming! Hardly are those words out
When a vast image out of Spiritus Mundi
Troubles my sight: somewhere in sands of the desert
A shape with lion body and the head of a man,
A gaze blank and pitiless as the sun,
Is moving its slow thighs, while all about it
Reel shadows of the indignant desert birds.
The darkness drops again; but now I know
That twenty centuries of stony sleep
Were vexed to nightmare by a rocking cradle,
And what rough beast, its hour come round at last,
Slouches towards Bethlehem to be born?

Contents

Illustrations | viii

Part 1   The Sand of the Sea | 9

Chapter 1 | 11

Chapter 2 | 25

Chapter 3 | 39

Part 2   The Light of Life | 57

Chapter 4 | 59

Chapter 5 | 70

Chapter 6 | 81

Part 3   A New Song | 95

Chapter 7 | 97

Chapter 8 | 110

Chapter 9 | 119

Part 4   The Sea of Glass | 133

Chapter 10 | 135

Chapter 11 | 149

Chapter 12 | 167

Illustrations

Asylum applications pending at the end of the month in the EU Member States | 183
Source: Eurostat

Great Ocean Conveyor Belt | 184
Source: Woods Hole Oceanographic Institute

PART 1

The Sand of the Sea

BEFORE

By Jackson Hunter

Grade 8, J.H. Putman, Ottawa, ON 2015[1]

    i can remember when
    she told me that she once
    loved to paint
    the tales of our lives
    with only the brightest colours,
    but i suppose that was
    before
    our world became grey

    i can remember when
    he whispered to me
    that he used to
    plan
    what our lives
    could become
    after

---

1. UNHCR Canada, "Refugees and Human Rights Poetry Contest."

we finally returned home

i can remember when
i used to write poetry
back when my words would
craft tales of bliss
and drift off the pages like smoke
but i guess that was

Before
i left

Chapter 1

Do you not fear me? declares the LORD. Do you not tremble before me? I placed the sand as the boundary for the sea, a perpetual barrier that it cannot pass; though the waves toss, they cannot prevail; though they roar, they cannot pass over it (Jer 5:22)

ARIAS OF WIND CROSS the ocean tossing waves to wash up pebbles and shells, raining down tiny grains of quartz crystals on the ocean floor, taking hundreds of patient years to pile into a new bay. Even the mighty rocks are scooped and smoothed, every cave and tiny niche sought to fill. Their thunderous overtures are resisted by the sand, sending the crashing waves to sweep powerfully back into itself.

The sky accompanies the drama with interludes of sapphire, tints of lavender, dappling with clear blues, blushing with rose and laden with opaque grays playing a cantata across the ripples like notes of an intimate song. The chords combine to draw the weary from every land to come look out across the water, needing to see a beyond that lifts from tired thoughts.

So awestruck were the prophets and singers of the Bible, they were inspired to write of God's presence, deeper than the ocean, higher than the heavens guiding the waves, powerful to save beyond our horizons.

> Some went down to the sea in ships, doing business on the great waters; they saw the deeds of the Lord, his wondrous works in the deep. For he commanded and raised the stormy wind, which lifted up the waves of the sea (Ps 107:23–25).

Covering two-thirds of earth's surface, cradling 97 percent of all water, most of the hundreds of trillion gallons of ocean are still an unexplored mystery beyond the sight of man. An underwater landscape of high

The Sand of the Sea

mountain peaks and low trenches hidden several thousand feet below is where most all of God's creations live. The waves rise and fall, scaling the heights of praise and sinking so deep it is out of the reach of light's presence. Restlessly churning in the clouded storm and quieting in the gladness of morning, the tide stirs a whisper in us, a seed of knowing that we cannot lift ourselves from the depths that toil to claim us. Clamoring with unquenchable thirst, steeped in infinities of blessings, leaving treasures on our shore and returning undreamt hope at our feet, this visible, tangible, untamed liquid challenges us to let go of the shore. There must be a power that can save.

> O God of our salvation the hope of all the ends of the earth and of the farthest seas (Ps 65:5).

When God prepared the boundaries of the ocean, he made sand forceful enough to impede navigation, fill in harbors, emerge chains of islands from the water's depths, and hold back the sea. Yet sand is gentle enough to imprint a child's footstep and blanket the eggs of a mother turtle to keep them protected and unbroken.

For thousands of summer seasons, female Kemp ridley turtles ride the waves to the shallows of the Gulf of Mexico, congregate as they wait for night and sink their toes into the soft white sand. Making their way to the dunes, they dig through the dry surface sand with their front claws, scoop the damp sand into a nest to lay a clutch of ping-pong ball size eggs, breathing hard and grunting from the contractions. Flinging sand over the eggs with their back flippers, they pat it down, lay it flat with their underside and hide their young in the sand.

Exhausted, they turn to the ocean. The ocean's heartbeat powers earth, its perpetual currents guiding lives, determining weather, and the plentitude of food on land. Wave upon wave call and the scent of the salt sea air bids to the turtles. Moving slowly they throw sand behind them to conceal the nest's location. Again later that night or several times between April and August they ascend from the rolling crests, up the beach, leaving eggs to incubate where the embryos can breathe air, trusting the sun to monitor the ratio of males and females of their offspring. If the temperature drops below 85.1 degrees Fahrenheit, the hatchlings will be male.

Nestled on the Gulf a female turtle gained strength after incubating for two months in the sheltered darkness. She pecked at the egg with a knob on her head, cracked the shell and scooped away at the sand. Hiding

Chapter 1

under the sand with all her siblings, they waited a couple of nights. Then suddenly they all began to dig and wiggle their way out of their chambers at the same time, climbing on top of the discarded egg shells to give them traction as they made their way up to breathe the humid breeze coming in from the ocean.

Environmentalists stood around watching her, their papers and pens in hand, speaking of the risk of extinction to the black, two-inch-long baby turtle, listed as Critically Endangered by the International Union for Conservation of Nature and Natural Resources. Facing staggering obstacles to reach adulthood in the billowing waves, only about one in a thousand will survive.

But the word that marked her coming when God created her to wake and see the canopy of countless stars shining from millions of miles away was faith. The environmentalists named this little one *Emunah*, meaning faith in the Hebrew language, because every life is called to be transformed, urged to walk, to fly, to swim, as God has called. God promises this. God ordained this.

On the third day of creation he said, Let the waters below the heavens be gathered into one place, and let the dry land appear; and it was so. God called the dry land earth, and the gathering of the waters he called seas (Gen 1:9).

This was the first immersion of water. The earth was unformed and void. Darkness was over the face of the deep and the Spirit of God hovered over the water. Out of a submerged world came land and life. God saw that it was good (Gen 1:10). The whole ocean glowed with light. It was pristine and undefiled.

Water gathered by nature is the water used for the *mikveh*,[1] the Hebrew immersion that brings new life out of baptism. The Talmud speaks of the spirit of God over the waters, referring to the spirit of Messiah directing all movement to replenish creation and restore its purity to its original strength.

In the shallows where our feet are bounded by the land, Jesus found his disciples and said, "Follow me." Gazing out at a new beginning, the men in Galilee were swept by the current of his majesty and said, "I will" and followed. Others in the crowds just curious about his teachings fell away. Still others came only for the bread Jesus fed them. The ones who followed and said "I will" tasted the righteousness and thirsted for more, knowing

1. Luft, Mikveh.

the dangers of the tossing waves were not reason to cling to their shorelines. Some grow old and white-haired, wrinkled and still saying yes. Some are taken from this life still young. Knowing there will be a cross to take up, a death requirement because life was no longer about them, all were certain about who it was they followed.

> If I take the wings of the morning and dwell in the uttermost parts of the sea, even there your hand shall lead me, and your right hand shall hold me (Ps 139:9–10).

As the cleansing waters degraded with mankind's fall, the world's young began to be effected more than ever before. Seventy percent of the world's 6.8 billion people live in countries under severe restrictions to serve the risen Lord.[2] Children represent 2.2 billion of this population, heavily targeted for their own faith or the faith of their parents and community.[3]

Mixed flows of humanity move with the ocean across the globe as poverty, violence, and persecution strike like a tsunami that has pulled out its tides, left the land quieted, only to be gathering its unseen power into a terrible force that within seconds knocks down entire towns. Snapshots emerge of a new people group. A three-year-old boy looks out from a tent in the Za'atari refugee camp in Jordan where he is living with his parents and five siblings. A two-year-old arrives from a Syriain Domiz camp in northern Iraq after fleeing from town to town with his family of four for an entire year. The tent they receive is the first home he has known since he was one-year-old. A woman crosses into Lebanon and becomes the 1 millionth refugee at a UN center. Another woman in Greece clings to her family photo album, the only keepsake she has of family still in Syria where they ran a small village shop. A man holds a photograph of his wife, a memory of happier times. They fled Syria twenty days after his wife gave birth, walking two hours to reach the border where they paid a smuggler $1,100 to get them into Iraq.

When Jesus led the way into the baptizing water, a bright cloud overshadowed him and a voice from heaven said, "This is my beloved son in whom I am well pleased. Listen to him" (Matt 3:17). The invitation crossed all the world's ocean for souls to follow and be restored to God's original pristine creation. The willing who said "I will" may be the native youth running up the mountains of the Andes with the message of salvation, a

---

2. Pew Forum on Religion and Public Life, "Global Restrictions on Religion."
3. UNICEF, "State of the World's Children 2011: Adolescence—An Age of Opportunity."

CHAPTER 1

Pakistan prisoner beaten and held in a dark cell, or a speaker who God lifted to give a national voice on North American radio. It may be the woman of yellow skin sneaking a Bible into her country, the red skinned singer playing praise on a water drum, the brown skinned dressed in lively colors knelt in prayer as gun fire explodes nearby, or the white skinned in the UK gathering coats and shoes for the thousands of refugees seeking a safe shore to proclaim their faith. All crossed over a deep vast ocean of unknown currents to be where Jesus is needed, all adopted by the Lord who said, "Follow me." It would bring mockery, loneliness, and the burdens of others.

> And there arose on that day a great persecution against the church in Jerusalem, and they were all scattered throughout the regions of Judea and Samaria, except the apostles (Acts 8:1).

They went everywhere and preached the word of God "and the crowds with one accord paid attention to what was being said" (v6). Skilled in seamanship, they adjusted their sails knowing that the sea will never rest but it is Jesus who paints the winds.

UNHCR's annual 2015 Global Trends Report: World at War found worldwide displacement has reached its highest level in recorded history. The number of people forcibly pushed from their homes by the end of 2014 had risen to a staggering 59.5 million, compared to 37.5 million a decade before, and likely to worsen. Half of the refugees are children.[4] The young are experiencing imprisonment, torture, murder and kidnappings, being burned alive, and watching entire families be executed. Torn from home to relocate in places of unknown languages, refugees and asylum seekers climb wire fences, stow away in airless containers, taking to sea in leaking boats moving across the ocean with their stories of courage and tragedy, some with families, others alone, all putting their lives at risk on the high seas.

Comfort my people, God told Isaiah. God does not want anyone to live and die without knowing he is willing to cleanse them from every trespass. With us in our suffering, he especially cares about eternal suffering.

"I have loved you," says the Lord. But you say, "How have you loved us?" (Mal 1:2). After God spoke to his people through Malachi, he withdrew from speaking for a quiet four centuries as heaven gathered readiness for a new birth. The next voice to speak was John the Baptist at the rushing waters of the Jordan River. It was the first commandment of the New

---

4. UNHCR, "Worldwide displacement hits all-time high."

Covenant, calling "Prepare the way of the Lord," on a sliver of land chosen by God. From this land all the families of earth would be blessed. The rushing waters of this baptism would plow paths through the wilderness and cover over all wrongs leaving no trace that it was ever there. The Lord would fill in valleys to lift us from the shadows so that we can see him. He lowers mountains and removes them from paths to make the way straight so we can reach him. A way in the sea, a path in the mighty waters, he will bring down the army and quench enemies like a wick (Isa 43:16–17).

The water pumps life around the planet, circulating through interconnected currents, spinning out in turbulence, gathering in complex patterns that bring the deep up to the surface and the shallows down to the deep. Reaching to every shore to touch every story, the baptism goes on creating a congregation crossing denominational, cultural, and political differences. The shores return accounts of the baptized, carrying the heritage of immersion across the seas. Jesus everywhere is saying, "Follow me."

Sinking the past out of sight and upwelling new life in dreams being told in places of extreme injustice and hopelessness, unbelievers are asking what it means for them. In Guinea someone speaks of a man in white appearing in a dream, calling to him with outstretched arms. In Malaysia a Muslim saw her parents, who were Christians, celebrating in heaven. Jesus appeared in a white robe and said, "If you want to come to me, come!" She did. A man from west Africa saw a religious Muslim in hell, and a poor Christian, who could not even give alms, in heaven. A voice explained that this was not because of the alms, but the faith in Jesus. Among the Tausugs, the Philippines' largest Muslim group, a man dreamed of Jesus slaying a huge dragon in a duel. He had the same dream the next night and began finding answers in the Bible. There are stories from Turkey. There are stories from Iraq. In Egypt a Muslim was looking at the gospels when a strong wind swept the room and a voice said, "I am Jesus Christ, whom you hate. I am the Lord you are seeking." He made the decision to follow Jesus.

God's inspiration in visions from the beginning of the Bible through to Revelation leads his people into one body. Jacob dreamed and was shown a ladder set up on the earth that extended all the way to heaven where the Lord stood above it (Gen 28:12–13). The dream may be a call placed on a life. In Gibeon the Lord appeared to Solomon in a dream by night and God said, "Ask what I shall give you" (1Kgs 3:5). Paul was on his way to Damascus when a light from heaven shone around him and those who traveled with him. They fell to the ground and he heard a voice speaking in his Hebrew language, "Saul, Saul, why are you persecuting me?" (Acts 26:14–16). Sometimes God sends a warning. God came to Laban the Syrian in a dream by night, and said to him, "Take heed that you speak not to Jacob either good or bad" (Gen 31:42). God spoke to Joseph telling him to take Mary as his wife, take Mary and Jesus to the land of Egypt, and when to return to Israel after the death of Herod (Matt 1:20). Jesus showed John the vision of Revelation, the completion of repairing the world, to warn the Israelites that the antichrist is false.

Bill Bright, director of the mission agency Campus Crusade for Christ, wrote, "We are experiencing an amazing phenomenon. Muslims in particular are having dreams and visions confirming the reality of Christ."[5] After a radio program reported that Jesus had appeared to many Muslims in a dream and said "I am the way," the station received thousands of letters from Muslims in North Africa and the Middle East, now understanding their visions and wanting to know more about this Jesus who is not ashamed to call them brothers and sisters.

This metamorphosis begins within, articulated in the heart, cracking open the shell, coming out into the air beneath God's sky, humbled by realizing how vulnerable we are, the way Emunah knew she was at risk, unable to protect herself.

God prepared her a way when darkness covered the face of the deep and God's spirit hovered over the waters. God produced a friction that caused the presence of light. "Let there be light," and there was light. And God saw that the light was good. And God separated the light from the darkness. God called the light Day, and the darkness he called Night. And there was evening and there was morning, the first day (Gen 1:1–5).

The earth spun in the light, bringing night to day. Land emerged, plants began to grow. Then, on day four, God created the sun, moon, and stars to be light bearers and time keepers. "Let there be lights in the firmament of the heaven" (v14) "to give light upon the earth" (v15). Light rays reflected off the moon and water mirroring light back to the sky.

Words from heaven had begun serving the new creation. Wisdom was there when he set the heavens in place, when he marked out the horizon on the face of the deep, when he established the clouds above and fixed securely the fountains of the deep (Prov 8:22). The turning of the earth and the winds give rise to the Gulf Stream warming under the southern sun.

---

5. Amightywind.com, "Accounts Multiply Of Muslims Who Have Encountered YAHUSHUA."

Traveling fast up the coast under a constantly blowing wind, the stream spreads its warmth as it leaves the Gulf of Mexico, creating space where new lives begin.

The water is God's signature. The act of immersion tells us we've been rescued from hopelessness. Presented in Genesis, water is our first introduction to God's plan and becomes an ongoing conversation until Revelation when time ends at the river of life. At the edges of all the earth's waters where the ceremony of baptism takes place to remember how God treasures us, someone is saying yes, I will follow. God is going to guide through uncharted places because we've never come this way before. We've never faced this global awareness of persecution, wars, threats, pollution, and policies flowing downstream onto the culture.

When the Israelites followed, the people had to step into the rushing river of Jordan for it to part and allow them to carry the ark of the covenant across to guide and guard their journey. The people built a memorial of stones to mark the place and time. The Lord had made a way to cross, the way he had when the people crossed the Red Sea to be delivered from Egyptian bondage, "so that all the peoples of the earth might know that the hand of the Lord is powerful and so that you might always fear the Lord your God" (Josh 4:24). The enemy was left behind.

No one but God could do this.

The first song Israel sang together as a people was the Song of the Sea (Exod 15:1–8). When springtime's Passover moon wanes over the seventh day of the celebration, the Hebrew people sing the Song of the Sea, remembering the day when Pharaoh's army was drowned in the Sea of Reeds and they were raised. The song rings with the poetic power of the stars singing at the birth of creation. "I will sing to the Lord for he has triumphed gloriously." "The enemy said, I will pursue, I will overtake. I will draw my sword; my hand shall destroy them. You blew with your wind; the sea covered them; they sank like lead in the mighty waters. They are as still as stone till your people, O Lord, pass by, till the people pass by whom you have purchased. The Lord will reign forever and ever."

Stepping into the waters marked the end of a past history and the beginning of a new spiritual freedom. Faith says to God, "You can make me clean."

The Jordan was where Naaman was instructed to bathe seven times to heal from leprosy (2Kgs 5:10). Gentiles were taken to the water for ritual cleansing as God's voice washed over the roaring floods of sin and emerged

Chapter 1

them to serve the God of Israel. John, known as Yochanan the Immerser among his people, baptized the Jews ushering them into the wedding of Christ. Confessing their sins, unworthy to even carry the sandals of Jesus, they were immersed at Enon near Salim "because there was much water there," and in Bethany beyond the Jordan, on the east bank near Jericho (Matt 3:6, John 1:28, 3:23).

Thirteen hundred years after the Hebrew people were freed from Egypt, John followed Biblical law by immersing people in a natural body of water when he stood in the River Jordan. A mikveh means a body of water not filled by human hands but created by the spirit of God gathering it in one place through his cycle of rains and springs. The concept originates in Leviticus (11:36) when the people were instructed to use only a spring or cistern to collect rainwater to become ritually clean from sin, never gathering water with human hands. Immersion in undefiled waters was performed everywhere in Jerusalem with an estimated 500 mikvehs filled with rains being used at the time Jesus walked there.

This is the river that witnessed the confluence between the Father who spoke, Jesus who came out of the water, and the Holy Spirit who rested on him. Jesus knew in Judaism there could be no change for the men, women, or children without the *tevilla* (immersion). To step into the promise sheds all of the cultural norms that were outside of God. Under water we are without breath, detached from old life, all of self submerged without compromise. The water of judgment is held back as the covenant people of God pass through.

Sun streams into the shallows that frame land where saltwater plants thrive. Life in water intermingles with life in the air. An entire parish of birds feed from the top layer of sunlit water, boats launch, and children splash, but most of the ocean is down below, far beyond the sun. The light that began shining from heaven 2,000 years ago greets those raised in baptism as they pass through the beleaguered and confusing twilight. The waters subdue iniquities and sin sinks in the depths of the resplendent sea (Mic 7:19). "You were buried with him in baptism, in which you were also raised with him through faith in the working of God, who raised him from the dead" (Col 2:12).

The margin of the ocean drops into a steep two mile descent into the abyssal plain. Descending through the deep blue twilight, bigscale fish swarm the waters equipped with long sharp teeth and expandable jaws. Night falls and the creatures who hide in the depths during the day rise to the surface to feed on clouds of plankton hanging on the surface. Shoals of fish find the plants, dolphins feed on the fish, feeding at night and spending their days playing.

Farther down into the ocean the light dims into a black midnight and time seems to slow. Deep drifters pulsate blue-green bioluminescent lights penetrating the dark as they feed on what trickles down from above or eat other food they can capture. The ctenophore, related to the jellyfish, has iridescent cilia to wave around to scare away predators. It captures other fish with long tentacles. Firefly squids have a glowing photophore on their heads, one around their eyes, one on their body and one on the tips of tentacles to use as a flashlight to see in the dark, communicate, lure prey, and deter predators. Dragonfish with their big eyes and enormous mouths lay low here during the day and surface to feed at night. Long strings of snipe eels with flat little heads have jaws that curve out to catch shrimp. Sperm whales dive this deep, greeting each other in their underwater world as they search for giant squid.

Most of the midnight population are mollusks able to turn inside out to use spiky tentacles to chase predators or capture prey, and crustaceans, octopus, and jellyfish colored black or red to disguise them in the darkness. Only blue light from the bioluminescence is seen in this depth. Other colors in light do not travel this far into water. The few fish that dwell down this deep have transparent skin. Starfish and sponges live here, with slow metabolism to survive the scarcity of food. There are no plants. At the sea floor basket stars raise their arms to catch floating particles and seapigs plow through and eat mud like earthworms. The light show of floating, swirling, and zooming flashes can be seen by the over-sized eyes of blacksmelt, but not seen by tripodfishes that are blind and rely on smell and touch. From this deep nearly freezing crushing pressures, churning nutrients are constantly being brought up to the surface.

"How many are your works, Lord! In wisdom you made them all; There the ships go to and fro,and Leviathan, which you formed to frolic there" (Ps 104:24–26). High and lifted up, exalted over all, who is like our God. He looks far down and sees. He condescends to come to us, binding himself to us in love. Knowing this takes away fear. The depths can be crossed.

> For I know that the Lord is great, and that our Lord is above all gods. Whatever the Lord pleases, he does, in heaven and on earth, in the seas and all deeps (Ps 135:5–6).

Chapter 1

The oldest sea turtle fossils are thought to have navigated the world's oceans since creation began, thriving in large groups. From heaven God declared "all the earth is mine" and directed ocean currents to continue their circuit over earth. His nesting ridley females in 1947 were an abundant 89,000 keeping their species present in his ocean. Then people began hunting them for their eggs. Human populations demanded them for meat, their skin, and their shells. Over-fishing killed the juveniles. Nesting sites were destroyed for beach resorts and their home in ocean water was poisoned with oil spills. Sunlight gleamed on the shrimp trawlers that snared them on their way through the sea. By the 1980s only a few hundred turtles were seen nesting.[6]

Many populations of life in the water went extinct. Those who survived continued with the mandate to follow the call God put on them even in their shrinking territories. On land the young became vulnerable to systematic attacks being waged on schools. Children are used as suicide bombers. Forced to recruit as child soldiers, thousands have had to endure and inflict death and violence in more than twenty war-torn countries. Killed, maimed, orphaned, kidnapped, deprived of a vision for the future or health care to grow strong, disintegrating governance and loss of family and community has left them wounded and caught in confusion they often cannot yet speak about.

God's son came as a child refugee, fleeing the genocide of King Herod with no safe place to lay his head during his childhood. His family survived because Joseph left his job in Bethlehem to escape the death. They had to travel quickly and would not have brought much with them as they fled into another land.

High above, heaven knows the depths the young must cross. So precious are they, God instructs, "See that you do not despise one of these little ones. For I tell you that in heaven their angels always see the face of my Father who is in heaven" (Matt 18:10). "If you come across a bird's nest beside the road, either in a tree or on the ground, and the mother is sitting on the young or on the eggs, do not take the mother with the young" (Deut 22:6). The attention of the angels is always turned toward God's omniscient glory. They wait on his command. Present at creation, when the law was given to the Israelites, when Christ was born, in his agony in the garden, at his ascension, and caring for those at the time of death, the angels, countless in numbers, surround God's mercy seat.

---

6. Encyclopedia of Life, "Kemp's Ridley Sea Turtle."

The Sand of the Sea

> And when they went, I heard the sound of their wings like the sound of many waters, like the sound of the Almighty, a sound of tumult like the sound of an army (Ezek 1:24).

Jesus, the Lord of armies of angels, wants us aware of heaven. Scripture refers to heaven more than 200 times in the New Covenant. Beyond the stars where God dwells is a place so profoundly unimaginable that the apostle Paul was forbidden to reveal what he experienced of it (2Cor 12:1–9). John was told not to write everything he saw (Rev 10:4).

We are told there is a river, "the streams of which make glad the city of God." The river flows with mercy, in gentle drops and powerfully lifting currents, triumphing over judgment. Yet here below the feeling of being tossed and overflowed, sinking and crashing onto unwanted shores, unanchored as oppressions sweep the land, we cry out for heaven to guide. "Why have you made men like the fish of the sea, like creeping things without a ruler over them?" (Hab 1:14).

Emunah derives from the Hebrew root *aman*, meaning secure and supported in a firm action toward God's will. Like so many members of God's creation, the ridley turtle may be the last of her kind. She was born in Tamaulipas, a sixteen mile stretch of beach on the northeast coast of Mexico, the preferred nesting site for the sea turtle mothers. The nearness of a continental shelf provides a safe current for the babies out to the ocean's foraging grounds in coastal waters.

The ocean's companion, the moon, hung high in the sky reflecting a path of light in the water to guide the baby turtles. The water sings a soft cappella as the babies emerge en masse to increase the chance of more surviving the run to the sanctification of the sea. Car headlights, street lights, lit up buildings on the beach confuse some of the hatchlings. Wandering in the wrong direction toward artificial light, they can be picked off by crabs and sea birds in the morning sun. Tire tracks leave ditches that some fall into and can't overcome.

The emerald walls of the water are the only refuge. Weighing just half an ounce, Emunah raced across the sand. A wave caught her and the ocean welcomed her. She plunged through the green curtain and swam under a school of mackerel swarming there to feed. Into the hidden depths, her front flippers, fused with long digits to glide her through the water beat like wings, her rear flippers steering her course.

Her world of the Atlantic Ocean spans one-fifth of the earth's surface. The Atlantic stretches her waves into the Hudson and Baffin bays, the Gulf

Chapter 1

of Mexico, the Caribbean Sea in the west, the Baltic in the north, Mediterranean and Black seas in the east and the Weddell Sea in the south. To the north the Atlantic flows with the Pacific Ocean through the Bering Strait into the Arctic Ocean. The Atlantic's southern waters join the Pacific through the Strait of Magellan in South America and meet to combine in the Southern Ocean in Antarctica. Four times as much land drains into the Atlantic than drains into the Pacific or Indian oceans, with more rivers including the Mississippi, Congo, and Amazon adding to the ocean's volume of 85.1 million cubic miles.

Emunah feels the rhythm surge through her, the waves cover her, hide her, and carry her into the heart of the sea. Her past is behind her. Safe now, protected by the rocking blue cold housing of God's creation, she surfaced to take a breath. In total trust and reliance, like a baptism she was unified with all the members of the ocean. God designed this. The Spirit sanctifies by showing us the way, sensitive to the currents. "When the Spirit of truth comes, he will guide you into all the truth, for he will not speak on his own authority, but whatever he hears he will speak, and he will declare to you the things that are to come" (John 16:13). After explaining this to his disciples Jesus asked his Father to sanctify them in the truth; your word is truth (John 17:17).

Jesus said to watch for the seasons. The Israelites had been told to watch for spring's full moon, when the ocean lifts its high tide, to hold the Passover in every generation to remember they are a people who once were in bondage. Moses, in a basket lifted from the water, would be told that the Lord hears the cries of the people and remembers his covenant. He instructed Moses to tell the people he will lift them out from under the burdens of slavery with an outstretched arm and great acts of judgment. "I will take you to be my people, and I will be your God, and you shall know that I am the Lord your God, who has brought you out from under the burdens of the Egyptians" (Exod 6:5–7). As the moon shines its fullness into the night, the first cup of the Passover is lifted. It is the cup of sanctification. The people were instructed to celebrate the first Passover in readiness to leave quickly.

> In this manner you shall eat it: with your belt fastened, your sandals on your feet, and your staff in your hand. And you shall eat it in haste. It is the Lord's Passover (Exod 12:11).

Fleeing to the edge of the land, the number of people looking for safety through dangerous sea journeys is increasing. Taking to water is the hope of a beginning transformation. They see the truth of their helplessness in the face of the enemy. Sanctified by truth, we are separated from the world, the old things pass away, all things are becoming new. The journey begins.

Emunah swam now losing sight of the shore, driven to transform into a two-foot long hundred pound grey-green adult. On the seafloor under her, rivers flow as seawater seeps up, dissolving and collapsing layers of salt to form depressions. The saltier water settles into the depressions and flows inside its own shores, drawing fields of mussels around edges of under-ocean lakes, feeding on bacteria to convert methane and other ingredients of the deep into energy.

Paddling around the continental shelves formed when the ocean flowed over the land thousands of years ago, sea turtles prefer the shallows where light is present. The shelves provide a place for underwater plants and animals by holding an abundance of sunlight from the sky with nutrient sediment washing in from rivers and waves. For people it is a place of fishing and became a place for petroleum that formed in ancient days as plants and animals fell to the rock in the ocean floor. A wealth of cold methane, hydrogen sulfide, and oil seep out of the sediments around the margins framing the ocean. Benthic zones, zones where the sunlight reaches, host creatures living closely with both ocean and land, some burrowed into the bottom, others swimming just above the sands.

Five species of sea turtles swim the northeast continental shelf—the green, hawksbill, Kemps ridley, leatherback, and loggerhead. Emunah's species is the smallest member of the sea turtle family. She dives in search of fish, crabs, jellyfish and snails, her heart-shaped shell streamlined for the water. The deeper she dives, the colder it becomes. But she never feels frightened. She belongs here.

Chapter 2

When you pass through the waters, I will be with you (Isa 43:2)

IN ITS LAST AGONY yearning and groaning for the births that God has designed, all creation waits in eager expectation for the children of God to be revealed (Rom 8:19). The painful moaning mingles with hope as the spirit of truth prays with us to transform. Omnipresent and searching, the spirit causes thirst for the knowledge, even the depths of God (1Cor 2:10) and the mystery of our own creation. As Father, God provided all that is needed, every plant yielding seed for food. God made earth and out of the dust of earth he made man, breathed life into him and he became a living being. Moved by man's loneliness he created woman to complete his companionship.

    This begins the story of heaven and mankind. The Lord walked with Adam and Eve and taught them how the moon, the sun, and stars kept time and they taught it to the children who would grow to populate the world. God designed land to cover only 29 percent of earth's surface, with homelands for each people group bounded by the ocean and its rivers. Human nature now walked with a sense of being strangers on earth, finding ways to feel at home by interacting with the rivers, the animals, the birds and sunrises. Every generation called for an answer. The groaning began filling earth, sky, and ocean. "We were pregnant, we writhed, but we have given birth to wind. We have accomplished no deliverance in the earth, and the inhabitants of the world have not fallen" (Isa 26:18). But God had not abandoned Adam and Eve. He promised a redeemer that would come through their children.

    God continued to shepherd the generations. His sound was like the whirlwind he spoke out of to Job (Job 38:1). The psalmist declared "The voice of the Lord is over the waters; the God of glory thunders, the Lord, over many waters" (Ps 29:3). Humanity sensed his presence as they tried to extract his secrets from nature, longing for heaven to be present again.

God's words stayed near. "It is not in heaven, that you should say, 'Who will ascend to heaven for us and bring it to us, that we may hear it and do it?' Neither is it beyond the sea, that you should say, 'Who will go over the sea for us and bring it to us, that we may hear it and do it?'" (Deut 30:12–13).

The Torah is embedded with stories of prophetic dreams, visions, and visits of angels. The Talmud considers God as a concept without end, having no boundaries in time or space. Dreams and visions are an accepted communication from God to pass to generations in oral tradition.

Even in the surroundings of a dark time, God reached Habakkuk with the message that he was going to do something new, something the people would find hard to believe even though they had been told in advance. Times would become even darker but the glimpse of the glory to come sustained Habakkuk.

On Jesus' last night, he's washed the feet of his disciples, just eleven committed men. It's his last chance to talk with them before the crucifixion. Preparing them to transform the world, he knows they will be rejected, martyred, imprisoned, and persecuted in a world denying God's authority. He looks at them and says, "Let not your heart be troubled. I go and prepare a place for you. I will come back and take you to be with me that you also may be where I am," knowing this would sustain them through the most difficult battle in all of history (John 14:1–4).

The Lord, the Creator of the very ground he walked on, was forced to wander from place to place in a world of accusations hostile to the truth of God. After his arrest, Jesus faced Pilate who asked him if he was a king. Jesus answered, "For this purpose I was born and for this purpose I have come into the world to bear witness to the truth." (John 18:37). Jesus gave us the truth about heaven.

Our Father is there. Our names are recorded there. Our inheritance and citizenship are there. The throne and elders are there. Nothing in this world can compare to heaven. Deeply thirsting to be cleansed and restored, prayers rise searching to commune with God again and be known by God. Aspiring to see God, Moses was put in the cleft of a rock as God manifested his presence, filled with loving kindness as he passed by. David, who had so much material wealth, wrote Psalm 27 still aching to know God. "One thing I desire, that I might behold the beauty of the Lord, that I might see you, worship you, be in your presence." The prophet Hosea thirsted. "So let us know, let us press on to know the Lord" (6:3).

Knowledge of heaven brings a faith wild and free as the ocean, answering only to God and the winds that cradle life. Hope shimmers on the jeweled waves pushing onward through day and night, in swells of love that drench the shadows in the valleys. This is no contrived liturgy or formalities that follow a prescribed pattern. "I had heard of you by the hearing of the ear, but now my eye sees you" (42:5).

Seeking the tidal pools left behind when the waves recede, the tide returns for the lives stranded in shallows. Residents such as anemones, sea urchins, barnacles, whelks, and sculpins create new interactions in these isolations, continuing to still belong to the sea. But they are apart from the body. Bringing words onto shore like unfurling tides to gather and bind each heartbeat to the heart of God, believers come crossing the waters to redeem until the end of time.

"Jesus appeared saying, 'It's me. Follow me.'" "I had a dream that Jesus came to my window and said, 'come follow me.'" ""They had a Jesus dream, and some of them had many Jesus dreams." He was told to "leave this place and come follow me." Jesus appeared to him and said, "Son, I am the way, the truth and the life. Give your life to me and follow me." "That night I saw Jesus in a dream." "You have been saved, follow me."

The call is a rush of current circling earth, lifting onto mountains, seeking out the valleys, falling on Muslim communities, bringing about an immersion in dreams, a baptism rising in the morning as a new person. As the rest of culture heaps unrestrained degradation upon God's son, Jesus continues to walk among us.

Follow me. The words gather, not to reform, but to restore those who belong in the glorious body clothed in heaven's majesty, more brilliantly sunlit and unconquerable than the ocean. For out of Zion shall go the law, and the word of the Lord from Jerusalem (Isa 2:3). In the face of intensifying anti-semitism, the Jews sent their evangelists, Paul, Peter, Barnabas, Timothy, and others bringing *HaDerech* (the Way) in accordance with prophets, justice, and grafting others in through the baptism. The word *derek* is from the root *darak*, meaning to tread; thresh; by implication to walk; also to string a bow by treading on it in bending.

Solomon said, "And though a man might prevail against one who is alone, two will withstand him—a threefold cord is not quickly broken"

(Ecc 4:12). When God gives a vision, he brings together people to pray in encouragement for the purpose. The disciples in Scripture are never seen on their own. They went out and came in with other believers. They prayed "make us bold, make us brave." We are "joint heirs with God and Jesus" because even when stranded alone in the shallows or down in the dark when the pressure was so great and the pain did not stop, we kept believing him.

Gathering energy from the warm waters of the Caribbean moving constantly north with the Gulf Stream, storms come mixing the warm surface with the cold saltier deep. The deeper water becomes warm and surface water cools. The rain adds more fresh coolness. Storm waves rise blending with the air, gusting formidable spray in the winds. The larger marine animals such as sharks or whales sense the coming change in pressure as waves on the surface approach and they dive deeper or swim away from the area. Fish dive into the calm, people head into a safe place and anchor to the end of the story that tells of heaven's victory. Others suffer from the quick change in salt and are found dead and washed ashore when the storm passes and the skies calm. Floods come and immerse the world in another deluge, like in the days when Noah was the righteous man as others remained unconcerned, to give way to the voice of the Messiah. Stories of harm are quieted, immersed under his promises, days past are remembered and tomorrow seen through the sight of faith. Many are called into safeness but we are told that, like the storm of Noah that saw only eight people safely on the ark, it will be one family out of all of humanity, born in faith who enter during cataclysmic floods (Luke 17:26).

Hundreds of feet beneath the surface, the turbulence of the storm stirs the currents into a commotion, remembering for weeks afterward as shipwrecks resettle after being swayed and lifted, oil pipelines need repair after being broken, seabeds are exposed needing sand to be replaced. Coral beds rustled by the muddied turbulence are clogged, still struggling, like our lives on land, to recover long after a storm.

The magnificent angel standing with one foot on the ocean and one on land is a presence of God's authority to fulfill the plan of restoration. As earth plunges into gloom, the angel stands straddling the land and sea, bestowed with a rainbow around his head, a sign of the heart of God toward his creation even as the great storms pass.

> Alas, the uproar of many peoples who roar like the roaring of the seas, and the rumbling of nations who rush on like the rumbling of mighty waters! (Isa 17:12).

Chapter 2

The Atlantic, Pacific, Southern, Arctic, and Indian oceans merge with each other through waterways flowing over earth with sea turtles, fish, and unimagined creations apportioned in all the waters. Having been heated, the Gulf Stream's sixty-mile width meanders out of the Gulf of Mexico carrying warm water north along the coast of the United States where it combines with the North Atlantic Drift. Passerines fly thousands of feet overhead, shadows across the sky moving with prevailing winds as below the stream continues up to Canada. Slowing to one mile per hour, the water moves past the shores where 10,000 Syrian refugees arrived in 2016 with hope of rebuilding their storm-shaken lives in safe and secure harbors.[1]

Canada agreed to receive 25,000 refugees as part of its humanitarian program. Countries surrounding Syria were stretched caring for the influx of more than 4.3 million people fleeing the gun-fire and death in Syria. Being uprooted from their long-time traditions centered on family, the children arrive cloaking the memories in a private heart, yet escaping the wrath that God is preparing for this region. It is here, Damascus, Syria's capital city, that the prophet Isaiah said destruction would be so great that the city will be nothing but a "ruinous heap" (Isa 17:1). Man will look to his Maker, his eyes will not look to the altars or what hands can make, but fasten on the Holy One of Israel (v7).

The Hallel, meaning Praise, is expressed in Psalms 113 to 118. When Jesus finished his last Passover meal, he and his disciples sang the Hallel, a tradition that continues today. They sang of their journey out of a land of strange language, when Judah became God's sanctuary and Israel his dominion. All of earth and ocean trembled at the power of God's hand to deliver.

> The sea looked and fled; Jordan turned back.
> The mountains skipped like rams, the hills like lambs.
> What ails you, O sea, that you flee? O Jordan, that you turn back?
> O mountains, that you skip like rams? O hills, like lambs?
> Tremble, O earth, at the presence of the Lord, at the presence of
> the God of Jacob, who turns the rock into a pool of water, the
> flint into a spring of water (Ps 114:1–8).

"We know that the church is built on the blood of the martyrs and persecution generally strengthens the believer rather than destroying the church," Hank Blok said. Board member of the Mars Hill Christian Radio Network, he sees adversity drawing souls to the savior. "People walking on

---

1. UNHCR, "10,000th Syrian refugee arrives in Canada to rebuild life."

the ground do not need a life jacket even though they know that one is a very worthy safety tool. It is those who are on the water that know that they need them. Today, too many people do not think they need a savior. And so they do not feel that they need an 'Eternal Life jacket' and do not put one on. I believe that the Lord, who is 'not willing that any should perish, but that all should come to repentance' (2Pet 3:9) is allowing so many to go through the hardships, I cannot even grasp how difficult this must be, to come to an understanding that they have a greater need, not of present life and comfort from their present conditions, although that is desired and helpful, but of eternal life as found only in the Son of God through his work on the cross for their redemption, and ours."

Striking the water to part the sea is making a way for salvation, even as the waves rise and the threats chase us. It causes thought to pull inward, searching for reasons in inner sanctums. The Lord invites us, "Come, my people, enter your chambers, and shut your doors behind you; hide yourselves for a little while until the fury has passed by" (Isa 26:20). The bounds of waters rising over us cannot inhibit prayer from reaching heaven. That is why Paul delighted in the difficulties. When his world was most threatening and he was most alone was when Jesus was realized as the strength (2Cor 12:10). Refugees who find faith in the living God are unique, already knowing sanctuary is not a building. God once connected to his people through the temple where mediation took place between heaven and earth. The destruction of the temple is commemorated on *Tisha B'Av*, knowing that the resting place of God's presence in the world cannot be destroyed. The Lord who dwelt among his people now dwells in them.

> The hour is coming, and now is, when the true worshipers will worship the Father in spirit and truth, for such the Father seeks to worship him. God is spirit and those who worship him must worship in spirit and truth (John 4:23–24).

More than 50 million people are living forcibly displaced from their homes because of conflicts and persecution, most from Palestine, Afghanistan, Iraq, Somalia, Congolese, Myanmarese, Columbia, and the Sudan. Several more million remain displaced because of natural disasters,[2] suffering loss of familiar landscape and community as well as loss of what they thought to be their future.

---

2. UN Resources for Speakers, "Refugees: The Numbers."

Chapter 2

"It is generally the church, through teams of churches and individuals as well as the so-called 'Christian' countries that are reaching out to the unfortunate," Mr. Blok said. "Is there any humanitarian assistance coming from the Islamic countries who seek to preach their faith through the destruction that they are causing rather than through the compassions of a loving God? Apparently not. But that's the difference between our God and Satan, between Love and Hate, between a loving God who gave his only son rather than a demanding Allah with nothing to give. Our God gave and provided assurance of salvation in the Lord Jesus who paid the price for our sins. The Islamic god provides no assurance because he can't. I believe that many refugees, as often noted in the broadcasts from Mission Network News, are finding peace within their circumstances through the Lord Jesus Christ. In the shadow of a verse like Matthew 6:26—For what is a man profited, if he shall gain the whole world, and lose his own soul? or what shall a man give in exchange for his soul?—what is more important, a peaceful life back in Syria or any of the other parts of the world being affected by this human travesty, or eternal life for all who will come by faith to him. That turns a travesty into the happy means of bringing souls to their needs and then donning the 'Eternal Life jacket' so desperately needed."

Most, an estimated 99 percent, have been in exile in cities or camps for years with no end in sight. Nearly all are from developing nations that cannot afford to care for the young, the elderly, or the infirm. In 2014 only 126,800 refugees were able to return to their home countries, the lowest number in thirty-one years.[3]

> The alien living with you must be treated as one of your native-born. Love the alien as yourself, for you were aliens in Egypt (Lev 19:34).

Coming together from many denominations, dozens of churches have signed on to help Canada protect these now stateless people inside their borders. There is a place at God's table for them. The sky of heaven over them has not changed the words of Jesus that bind their comfort to God. He defends the cause of the fatherless and widow and loves the foreigner residing among us (Deut 10:18–19). Desperate for protection and surrounded by strange, sometimes unwelcoming faces, refugees are among the world's most vulnerable people.

---

3. UNHCR, "Worldwide displacement."

"Hopefully, we see the love of Christ coming through and not just knee-jerk, emotionally charged reactions," Mr. Blok said. "The bottom line is to find out if there is continued prayer and interest in the ones to whom support is given, whether it be funds or Bibles or both. Is there a deeper interest and possible contact with the refugees that are being assisted or not."

There is a difference in meeting a need and reaching out to a person, he said. "It appears that personal contact with people who are the hands and feet of the Lord Jesus is as important, or more important than just sending help. It can be well understood that most Canadian churches cannot send personnel and so, constant prayer and possibly notes sent with gifts to the receiving NGOs and ministries on the ground in these places explaining the caring of the church family back home could possibly be passed on to those helped to provide a tie between the churches and the people helped."

The bloody senseless wars and executions of humanity are bringing unreached groups to new cities. Churches receiving their cry for help are celebrating because they are becoming more aware of the needs of others and of each other, even as they are lamenting because not enough has been done for relationship with different cultures. North America has been a refuge for a diversity of people, for Mennonites, Jews, Irish, and others building houses of worship that fit each need. Those who were hunted down for their beliefs with lives shattered in pieces left behind stepped off ships seeking the light of grace. Taken from all that is known, friends and family gatherings, the scent of native wildflowers and the view of the sun setting on the horizon at home, they come torn in trauma, preoccupied with thoughts of the hills and gardens now forlorn with the absence of their laughter. Suspended without roots, their need to be watered as a new life is formed is bringing a unity among believers learning from each other how to offer services to newcomers. They are organizing a shared vision in the gaps where churches can fill roles of friendship, housing, and advocate for resources.

Reflecting the voice of many, Mr. Blok said, "Oh that there may be Christians even within this crowd of the displaced who are yet at peace with God through the love of Christ in these circumstances, and an example of calmness in the midst of the storm. Peace is not the absence of distress but a serenity in the midst of these horrible circumstances. May such Christians be a blessing to those around them."

As prayer covers those adrift on strange currents, some Syrians are choosing to bide where the sweet scent of white petaled jasmine pervade

Chapter 2

the countryside and summers are hot and dry on the coastal homeland, rather than risk the unknown. Only three out of every ten households contacted for resettlement in Canada relocate.[4] "Some families are still hoping to return home, others are concerned about their ability to integrate into another country, including learn the language," said Aoife McDonnell, an external relations officer at the UNHCR refugee agency in Jordan where every government-issued ID lists a person's religion.

For those who already lost family, leaving behind more members can be unthinkable. They continue on, raising children in their own language where ancestors are spoken of and their own culture takes pre-eminence. Those who are physically unable to make a dangerous journey wait with hearts pleading for resolution.

Witnessing this happen to his own people, Jeremiah wrote the book of Lamentations. Waves of grief washed over his soul as he was told of his people being driven into darkness without any light, children who go hungry in the street, walled in and crying for help, the waves roused in dark roiling bitterness rolling over and over in deepening anguish. He has made me desolate, Jeremiah said, cowering in gravel, bereft, beyond all endurance. Remembering their former beauty, Jeremiah said it's just a memory now.

But this I call to mind, and therefore I have hope:

> The steadfast love of the Lord never ceases; his mercies never come to an end; they are new every morning (Jer 3:21–23).

Jeremiah remembered all that God has done. "Therefore I will hope in him" (v24), though others don't comprehend how God's chosen love him so much they are willing to put their yesterday, today, and all of eternity in his hand.

As the warm Gulf Stream moves northward, the North Atlantic Drift sends a branch to flow across to Ireland and Great Britain bringing fish populations and climate to northern Europe, turning south to join the Canary Current. A complexity of tides reach the eight-mile wide strait of Gibraltar that flows into the Mediterranean Sea, separating Gibraltar and Spain in Europe from Morocco in Africa. The Mediterranean, meaning "middle of the earth," is at the center of the ancient world. Its waves wash up on the borders of Europe, North Africa, Asia Minor, and Palestine, a place ships of timber sailed the coast for Solomon's projects. This is where Jonah fled to and boarded a ship at the port of Joppa. Later Paul sailed this sea traveling to Cyprus

---

4. Williams, "Why some Syrian refugees decline Canada's resettlement offer."

and from Greece to Palestine (Acts 9:36–43). Harbors on the Mediterranean, east of Jerusalem, brought goods to peddle in markets of Jerusalem. Fish, fruit, oil, grapes, syrup, merchants for wool, ironware, clothes, wood, bread, vegetables, were brought from the sea across the Jordan where wine shops and sweetmeats are found along narrow streets.

Here Jesus walked among the covenant people and said, "Do not think that I have come to abolish the Law or the Prophets; I have not come to abolish them but to fulfill them" (Matt 5:17). As the current brings the salty water from the Mediterranean Sea into the north Atlantic deep water, words carried from beaches on the Mediterranean cross the Atlantic telling of the time Paul crossed the northern arm of the Adriatic Sea, the northern part of the Mediterranean Sea. He was bringing the words of Jesus to Rome after being held prisoner in the city of Caesarea for about two years. A tempestuous wind called Euroclydon rose from the northeast, blowing cyclonic gusts, catching the ship in the Mediterranean Sea as the sailors valiantly tried to steer the rudders.

The mistral that blows on the northern Mediterranean sustains cold northwesterly winds reaching sixty-two miles per hour that can continue for days. The current of cold is drawn from the north by the flow between high and low pressures, picking up speed as it funnels through the foothills of the Alps.

"When the fourteenth night came, as we were being driven about in the Adriatic Sea, about midnight the sailors began to surmise that they were approaching some land" (Acts 27:27). The water was 120 feet deep, then ninety. Fearing they would be dashed against rocks, they dropped four anchors and prayed for daylight (v29). The sea was so furious, the sailors let down a lifeboat.

Then Paul said to the centurion and the soldiers, "Unless these men stay with the ship, you cannot be saved." So the soldiers cut the ropes that held the lifeboat and let it drift away (v 31–32). Paul urged the sailors to eat. They hadn't eaten for days and he encouraged them, saying "You need it to survive. Not one of you will lose a single hair from his head" (v35). He broke bread and handed it around. Afterward, they threw bags of grain overboard to lighten the ship. Daylight broke and they cut loose the anchors, untied the ropes that held the rudders, hoisted the sail to the wind, and ran the ship aground in a sandy beach of Malta. The ship's stern was broken to pieces by the pounding surf (v 39–41). Those who could swim jumped into the water and made it to land. Others rafted in on planks from the ship. Everyone reached land safely. Paul recorded the islanders as friendly, building a fire to warm them because it was raining and cold. They were welcomed to a nearby estate where they stayed for three days. There they met a father sick in bed with fever. Paul went in to see him, prayed, and healed him. Others who were sick on the island came and were cured and learned of Christ.

"They honored us in many ways; and when we were ready to sail, they furnished us with the supplies we needed," Paul said (v 10).

Storms may come to fulfill a purpose, as it did for the people on Malta when Paul stepped into a boat that sent ripples into the world. A calm sunny day and God sends a wind from his storehouse. A breeze comes in off the ocean, strengthens as it flutters the leaves of the trees, lifting paper from the ground, hats off heads, until the trees are blowing sideways, bending to stay rooted. The gentle waves become higher, intensifying under the wind's command, lifting up and lapping the shore, cresting, rising, coming further. Whipping into a surge over the land, pushing everything in its path as it spreads wings to drench, rearrange, knock down, and scatter.

These storms polish our faith as we realize how he leads us. We are reassured the waves combining to slam beaches, take out boats, penetrate inland to break against our hearts are temporary, but our joy will be forever (2Cor 3:17–18). A fresh wind follows. The mistral clears the clouds bringing a sky of abundant sunlight, blows away dust and brings clear air. The disciples could see mountains miles away. Bringing new ethnically centered ministries to understand the roots of the faith of Abraham, disciples didn't hesitate to believe they should cross.

When Claudius commanded that all Jews leave Rome, Aquila and his wife Priscilla resettled in Corinth to become a blessing to others. They were tent makers, like Paul. When Paul arrived in Corinth, he went to stay with them and found work with them to sustain himself. From there he spoke in the synagogue to persuade the people that Jesus was Messiah (Acts 18:1–4).

Follow me. The disciples followed Jesus right into a storm. Obeying only heaven, storms can come to protect us. After Jesus fed the 5,000, the people wanted to crown him as an earthly king like David. So that they would not get caught up in this sense of earthly power, Jesus took his disciples into a boat. A great storm arose, swamping the boat with waves and tossing it around. Jesus was asleep below. Their first response was to go to him and cry out, "Save us Lord. We are perishing" (Matt 14).

Jesus rose and rebuked the storm. Instead of a sense of earthly power, the disciples marveled at how even the winds and sea obey Jesus.

> When he calls to me, I will answer him; I will be with him in
> trouble; I will rescue him and honor him (Ps 91:15).

A storm can reveal the path to take. Unbelief is rooted in wanting the wrong things. The crowd wanted Jesus to be crowned a worldly king. Wanting darkness more than light, they turned away from him when he didn't fulfill this. Jesus brought his disciples out of those shadows and into a boat where their thoughts were inclined to be changed. To be born again, cleansed, is to be moved in a new direction displacing the old thinking. Believers crossing unpredictable waters have set a course toward heaven, knowing they will arrive safely just as Jesus had assured Paul he would go to Rome and Jesus said let's cross over to the other side to the disciples (Mark 4:35). He had proclaimed the plan. They would cross.

In Ezekiel 16's disturbing chapters from 2,600 years ago, Ezekiel is commissioned to bring the Lord's word of judgment. The people were faithless to the covenant and the devastation that Babylon would bring to Jerusalem in 587 BC would be overwhelming.

Sixty-six times Ezekiel's prophetic words say, "Then you will know that I am the Lord." Intent on the people awakening and seeing their abominable behavior despite the privilege they had been given as a covenant people, he wanted them to know they were acting so badly that Sodom appears righteous in comparison. Sacrificing children to their idolatry and spiritual prostitution, in depths of unbearable separation from God, still God did not abandon them. Poised in their final days, about to fall, the Lord said, "yet I will remember my covenant with you. I will establish for you an everlasting covenant."

Ezekiel 37, 38, 39 speak of Israel coming back to their land. They will build it up and be surrounded by a league of nations in the north, south, east, and west who want the land. Today military bases surround the land. An enormous oil well has been found in the Golan Heights. The US is far from diplomatic relations with Israel. Ezekiel said there would be no countries to help Israel. The individuals called to be the church would rise, being grafted into the faith, but the nations would not. Some say the stage is set for Russia, Iran, and four north African nations to invade Israel in the war of Gog and Magog (Ezek 38–39).[5]

Magog, a grandson of Noah (Gen 10:2), had descendants who settled to the north of Israel, possibly in Europe and northern Asia. We are told

---

5. Bible Prophecy Tracker, "Turkish Leader: Hitler's Presidential System Is Worth Emulating."

they are skilled warriors (Ezek 39:9,15). In Ezekiel's vision, the battle appears to occur during the first three and a half years of the tribulation, after Israel has become a place of peace for her people. In the latter years Gog will go against the land where people are gathered on the mountains of Israel, brought out from other countries to dwell securely. Gog will advance coming like a storm, a cloud covering the land with armies (Ezek 38: 8–9) Gog will "come from your place out of the uttermost parts of the north, you and many peoples with you" (Ezek 38:15). Gog will be defeated by God himself on the mountains of Israel in a slaughter so horrible that it will take seven months to bury all the dead (Ezek 39:11–12).

The events exploding violence around the map have left even Christians in the shadow of fear for their children's safety. How can we tell our children that they are safe when the enemy stalks our world? Peter said have no fear of them. Don't be surprised at the fiery trials. Do not be troubled but in your hearts honor Christ. (1Pet3:14–15). The calm comes in honoring the glory of Jesus as Lord. Peter advised to be always prepared to give a reason for your hope, even in the face of lies or death. On the brink of eternity, we face cancers, bombs, gunfire, financial loss, accidents, and false hopes. The enemy of Jesus has us locked in his sights. The Lord plotted the course as he did for Noah when the waters rose and he was not overcome by the waters of judgment. The battle proves God's love.

> I will bring you against my land, that the nations may know me, when through you, O Gog, I vindicate my holiness before their eyes (Ezek 38:16). Then they will know that I am the Lord (v23).

Sparkling blue, the sea of the Mediterranean fills deep basins in the earth marked by a history of violent upheavals, long golden beaches, and rocky cliffs. What happens here carries to the world. The sea is in constant communication with the Black Sea to its east through the Dardanelles and Bosphorous straits and out its west in and out of the Atlantic through the strait of Gibraltar. The Atlantic feeds the sea continually, coming alongside Africa and joining the water as the Mediterranean evaporates tons of water every year, leaving salt that the Atlantic carries out to assure its circulation.

Emunah followed the current of the Gulf Stream, a swiftly flowing river in the ocean running northward along the east coast. The Atlantic continues further, into the Arctic Ocean's 5 million square miles. Arctic air greets the Gulf current as it arrives in the north, making it colder and heavier. It plunges into the bottom, becoming saltier, then turns back on itself to become the north Atlantic deep current. Descending into the pitch

The Sand of the Sea

dark where no light at all reaches, the deep north current flows over jellies on the bottom, traveling south through a channel between Greenland and Iceland's black sands. Climbing over rocks, cascading over the edge, the conveyor drops into a two-mile long waterfall under the ocean that tumbles millions of gallons down to the Atlantic abyssal plain. The plain of the ocean's floor covers more than half the earth. The largest living world on the planet is under water in perpetual night. Some creatures scientists recognize from the twilight layers. Others never have been seen before.

The deep north current comes down past Canada with its cold water passing the highest tidal range anywhere on earth splashing on the coast. Reaching up fifty-three feet, the Atlantic breakers hurl against jagged boulders, creating massive cliffs, and releasing nutrients into the water to support its marine life as it steadily scoops out Canada's bays on its way around the world.

Twelve hundred years later the current will complete its circuit and return to the Arctic.

Chapter 3

Who calls for the waters of the sea and pours them out on the surface of the earth, the Lord is his name (Amos 5:8)

CONFINED BY THE SHORES, the ocean reaches to touch all the lands by being lifted by the sun, gathered in the clouds and carried across the sky to wear down the high mountains, fill lakes, and assure the course for rivers. Helped by gales of winds and rising volcanoes, the ocean has been everywhere, powering the rain, carving horizons, dropping dew on lilies, and snowflakes on tree tops. Evidence of its presence is found in sea fossils where flowers now grow on sunny inland places.

Genesis 7 tells how the ocean covered all the high hills and swept away life on land. Science shows us rock layers on every continent have fossilized remains of billions of dead animals and plants buried rapidly in sand, mud, and lime. Invertebrates of the sea are entombed in the rim of the Grand Canyon, swept up from the ocean floor to cover earth 8,000 feet above sea level. Fossils of brachiopods, a clam-like organism, are embedded in the Redwall Limestone. Horn coral remains are here, which grow in solitaire on the sea floor, rooted in soft sediment, opening its cup to feed, tucking its body into its skeleton and extending spiral tentacles into the water to sting its prey. The canyon's oldest trilobites were found curled into balls for protection, faceted with up to 15,000 lenses in one eye. Bryozoans, lace corals, crinoids, sea lilies, clams, ocean snails, sponges from the sea floor, and even fish teeth leave testimony of the ocean in the heights of mountain ranges.

God would point and the waves would go, like his church through deserts and forests, crossing rivers, filling valleys, baptized with drops of his power to pass over mountains. A stream of followers flow from his command into the world of the lost, quenching the crying, touching the dying, making their way across all lands. Jesus spoke: "Whoever serves me must follow me; and where I am, my servant also will be" (John 12:26). And the word of God kept on spreading (Acts 6:7).

Long before the Himalaya mountains pushed up to be the world's tallest range and bar-headed geese migrated over their tips at nearly 28,000 feet, the lands were flooded to leave behind fossil ammonites and coiled marine cephalopods in the limestone beds. The sea turtle fossils found in the Great Plains once swam in seawater where dust storms now blow across miles of flat lands in South Dakota. The largest, the Archelon fossil, a relative of the leatherback sea turtle, measured more than thirteen feet long and sixteen feet wide from flipper to flipper.

You covered it with the watery depths as with a garment; the waters stood above the mountains. At your rebuke the waters fled, at the sound of your thunder they took to flight (Ps 104:6–7).

Scripture tells that "on that day all the springs of the great deep burst forth, and the floodgates of the heavens were opened" (Gen 7:11). Water burst volumes from inside the earth for 150 days (Gen 7:24), adding water to the ocean to raise the sea level. Not until 2007 did scientists discover the deep interior of earth holds vast water reservoirs in the mantel. The ocean floors are covered by molten lava that also released, raising the ocean floor a few thousand feet higher, carrying sea creatures beyond the shores. As the molten rock cooled and the ocean floors sank, the sea began to drain off the continents into the deep ocean basins.

> The mountains rose, the valleys sank down to the place that you appointed for them. You set a boundary that they may not pass, so that they might not again cover the earth (Ps 104:8–9).

Nine thousand feet above the Mediterranean Sea a blue snow-capped mountain peak emerged stretching twenty-eight miles along the northern horizon that today borders Israel, Lebanon, and Syria. Called Mount Hermon or Mount Sinai, it can be seen from the Jordan valley, the heights of Gilead and the plain of Esdrelon.

The Lord and his disciples are thought to have climbed this mountain the day after a Sabbath to be away from the crowds. On the way they passed hills of mulberry, apricot and fig trees, walked past pears and oak. As they ascended to rockier ground they climbed among dwarf shrubs, rugged cliffs, and boulders with scant vegetation covering the ground. The evening was warm and the summer sky flushed the horizon with hues of purple. Jesus and his disciples could see the sun setting over the Sea of Galilee about forty miles away as the light disappeared into shadows, the bird song quieted, and the sun lowered beyond the Mediterranean.

They made camp on the summit all night, weary after the long climb. The moon appeared, still bright from the Passover evening, shining on the servant of God as he stood in the night speaking to his Father. The stars he had created shone brightly ordered in their constellations. Prayer flowed from the spot he stood alone, apart from everyone, words that continue blessing through generations of believers. It was here his disciples witnessed him transfigured to shine like the sun as he spoke with Moses and Elijah. Again, as it did at his baptism and as it once led the ark of the covenant, a bright cloud covered them. A voice from heaven said, "This is my Son, whom I love; with him I am well pleased. Listen to him!" (Matt 17:5).

Both the lawgiver, Moses, and the prophet, Elijah, had gone to high mountain places seeking God. Isaiah in the midst of his people's troubles said, "Come, let us go up to the mountain of the Lord, to the house of the God of Jacob; that he may teach us his ways and that we may walk in his paths" (Isa 2:3). Moses met with God on Mount Sinai. Paul says that the Israelites could not look at Moses because of his brightness (2Cor 3:7). Nine hundred years before Christ walked up the mountain, Elijah fled threats against his life, running hundreds of miles to Mount Horeb where he went into a cave (1Kg 19) and remained until God spoke to him.

> Send out your light and your truth; let them lead me; let them
> bring me to your holy hill and to your dwelling! (Ps 43:3).

The ocean uncovered mountains so we can seek God's countenance and lay our concerns before the Lord. We are lifted from the baptism. The waters drip away and we are able to stand where channels of his mercy flow to our hearts from his reservoir of holiness. We are baptized in water, then baptized with the Spirit.

After Noah the next immersion of creation was the Torah calling out the people to be the nation of faith. They had been physically lifted from slavery in Egypt. Now they were spiritually freed. Crowds went up to the temple, singing the songs of ascension as they climbed the hill to the place that God had chosen to meet with them. It was a turning to God, leaving behind life in the world as they steadily made their way up to the heights of Jerusalem. Psalms 120 to 134 are the songs of ascent that speak of our journey to the presence of Jesus. "I lift my eyes up to the hills," the travelers sing. "Too long have I lived among those who hate peace." Living in a world of conflict, many feel miles from the presence of God. "Woe to me that I dwell in Meshek," hundreds of miles to the north of Jerusalem between the Black and Caspian seas, or "among the tents of Kedar," hundreds of miles to the south in what became Saudi Arabia. Knowing they are one of God's people, but living among people who do not know the living God, feeling far from his presence for far too long, the songs are sung as they climbed toward the place of his presence. "I rejoiced with those who said to me, Let us go to the house of the Lord."

Just turning and beholding him gleans strength from his presence. In the time of the temple there were pagan people living in the hills and they had to be ignored as the people passed through. Shading them from the heat of the day, God promised he would not let their foot slip. He would not slumber or sleep, but remain awake like a father watching over them.

The joy as they start out on their journey soon turns into the difficulties of a long and arduous distance, driven into the wilderness as Jesus was where he was tempted not to continue. Even knowing the destiny will be glorious, the journey becomes tiring. The relief of the ending is still miles away. Psalm 126 sings about praying in hope, sowing in tears, being restored by the rains that plow a path through the deserts that only God brings. Turning their song they ask God to intervene with the refreshing spirit to help their limitations so that they may sow the work that is in their hands to do. When they arrive they sing, " Our feet are standing in your gates, Jerusalem. For the sake of my family and friends, I will say, "Peace be within you" (Ps 122).

God showed his wonders in the preview of the Messiah. Celebrating with the people their freedom from physical bondage where they began to think like slaves, to become spiritually free with the Torah, God gathered a people to inspire the world to influence compassion.

Jesus and his disciples descended Mount Sinai into the valley toward his death, the enemy he would conquer. As they walked they would have known scripture praising the dew of Hermon (Ps 133:3), its lions (Song 4:8), and its cypress trees (Ezek 27:5). Today its bottom slopes are inhabited by villages of minority groups such as the Druze and Alaouites that sought refuge centuries ago. Arab guerillas shelled Israel from the western slopes on Lebanese territory where they settled themselves in the late 1960s. Israel Defense Forces responded with air attacks on their hideouts.

Rains quickly absorb into the porous rock of the mountain to reappear in springs at the foot of the mountain and feed the river Jordan to begin its flow southward to Kinneret, the southern shore of the Sea of Galilee, passing the place of Jesus' baptism as it rushes down to the mineral-laden Dead Sea in Judea. Forming the boundaries between Jordan and the West Bank, the river provides water for Israel, now a resource bringing conflict between Israel, Jordan, and Somalia. Mankind struggles to bring solution.

"We are failing perhaps the most basic human commandment we were given," said Rabbi Yosef Kanefsky of B'nai David-Judea in Los Angeles.[1] He said climate change "is going to create serious hardship, whether for people who are living in areas that can no longer grow food, or living on islands overrun by seawater, or people who are subject to ferocious storms. We have the obligation to think about all of humanity as being part of our realm of responsibility, given that we are largely responsible for climate change."

The California drought was in its fourth year with road signs warning residents of water restrictions. Many rabbis are teaching restraint as it's taught in the Torah. The concept is explained in the principle of letting the earth lie fallow every seven years, requiring responsibility personally and collectively.

"We need to restrain ourselves with dealing with *adama* (soil)," added Rabbi Arthur Waskow, director of the Shalom Center in Philadelphia, Pennsylvania, and member of the Jewish Renewal movement, known for his work on Jewish environmental ethics. "In the story of the Garden of Eden, God says to the human race, 'There's an abundance here, eat it joyfully, just a little self restraint. Don't eat from that tree.' They don't restrain themselves, and the abundance vanishes."

The experience in the dry desert is a spiritual thirst intersecting with physical need. The Hebrew prayer for rain expresses the natural anxiety felt in Israel for the seasonal rainfall, without which there is famine, thirst, and disease. In supplication a melody is sung to God "who causes the wind to blow and the rain to fall," a prayer inextricably tied with their history. There are six parts in the prayer for rain, referring to water in the lives of Abraham, Isaac, Jacob, Moses, Aaron, and the Twelve Tribes. The prayer acknowledges the importance of water to God in planting Abraham, the wells Isaac dug, the Jordan that Jacob crossed, Moses drawn out of the Nile's water, water for the mikveh that purified Aaron, the water divided for the twelve tribes and the bitter water that was sweetened. The prayer seeks God's mercy to continue the cycle of water from the ocean to the clouds to

---

1. Leila, "Local rabbis speak up about the drought."

The Sand of the Sea

the land so there will be no lack. *Mayim L'Chayim* in Hebrew means Water is Life.

The ocean sustains life on earth, containing mysteries still being explored. As bacteria becomes resistant to remedies from plants and flowers on land, the ocean with its amazing unexplored diversity offers more for science to discover. An anti-tumor medication derived from sea squirts and a painkiller from a cone snail are on the market. Scientists collect sponges, corals, and ocean organisms, discovering a chemical that breaks down the shield that bacteria use to protect from antibiotics. Extractions fight some of the worst infectious bacteria. Instead of harvesting the marine ecosystems, scientists are able to copy these chemicals in a laboratory.[2]

The Lord designed the ocean to sustain life and its wonders to be discovered. When ocean water freezes, it does not contain its salt. Glaciers, icycles, and icebergs are made of fresh water. The ocean water cannot live without its salt. It would no longer be ocean. Seawater's salt is made of dissolved minerals that run into the ocean from rains, rivers, and melting snow. The salt mixes into the deep as the great ocean conveyor carries its cold water on its way down to the equator where salt condenses around the 25th parallel, rainfall is low, and evaporation is high. The current cools the ocean here where sperm whales sport below the surface of the equator's line. The water in the north Atlantic sinks into the ocean's conveyor belt because it's cold and salty. If too much ice melts into the north Atlantic, the water will be less salty, the conveyor current would be slowed and could stop spreading warmth through the climate.

Change in water can push conflict or meld cooperation, bring health or spur disease. It can bring food insecurity, especially to poorer communities that already face water scarcity. As if navigating through fogs settling from continued concern, we don't know where we're going. Prayer rises and we hear silver-winged birds calling out above letting us know home is near, but we haven't yet arrived. Unparalleled in human history, clashes between peoples are among the signs Jesus said to discern so we'd understand the season the angle of light shifts and rises on the horizon, now lengthening shadows of the end days. Therefore watch, he said.

As more people flee gang violence and torment, the US saw a 44 percent rise in asylum claims in 2013, up to 36,000. Nine thousand people of Central America fleeing the northern triangle of El Salvador, Honduras, and Guatemala found eligibility in the US Refugee Admissions Program

---

2. Ocean Today, "Medicines From the Sea."

that opened doors for vulnerable people who may otherwise be prey for human smugglers. This number expanded the 85,000 already coming into the US that year, 3,000 of who were from Latin America and the Caribbean, 10,000 from Syria. An unprecedented number of children fleeing Central America were seen at the US southern border in 2014 and 2015. In response the government set up the Central American Minors Refugee/Parole Program for children to apply. Only five children came through in 2015.[3]

The Assyrian homeland is centered on the Tigris River flowing into the Persian Gulf and encompasses parts of what are now northern Iraq, northwestern Iran, southeastern Turkey, and northeastern Syria. The US welcomed 2,290 Syrian refugees between 2011 and 2015 when the Syrian civil war began, according to the State Department's Refugee Processing Center. Between 2013 and 2015 the UN referred 22,427 Syrian refugees to the US for resettlement, an unknown number being Christian. Sixty-seven percent were children under twelve. The administration could admit no more than 10,000 in fiscal year 2016.

Tides of bloodshed are overflowing the boundaries of peace with injustice, snatching up the sons and daughters, smothering the truth of God's words. Youth are hopelessly floundering in depths where God's word is not being spoken. Jesus warns that false teachings will increase, but also gave the assurance that God will work powerfully on behalf of his elect.

> Yet through the scent of water it will bud, and bring forth boughs like a plant (Job 14 9).

We are sanctified by being washed of water (Eph 5:26). An atonement has been made to cleanse us (Lev 16:30). We are clean because of the word of God spoken to us (John 15:3). We are redeemed by the words of truth (John 17:17).

> And now why do you wait? Rise and be baptized and wash away your sins, calling on his name (Acts 22:16).

Emunah preferred waters fringed by sparkling quartz crystals and shell fragments, nearer shore where the deep part of the waves touch the bottom, slow and drag along the sand, pulling the crests to topple over each other. Here she is safer from the sharks and large fish that prey on young turtles. Sea turtles cannot pull their heads and limbs into their shells the

---

3 Lee, "US Agrees To Take In More Central American Refugees."

way a land turtle is able. Their escape is in swimming quickly away. She swam along following the margin of the ocean to southeast Florida where the boundary of the sea adds color to the nearly pure white sand spotted with dark fragments of coral and mollusk. Near the water's edge the grains are larger as waves wash up more shell fragments.

Further along the peninsula above Tampa Bay turtles find the sand becomes fine and soft again, the dry dunes white like sugar ideal for sculpting. Then the sand becomes nearly black with patches of dark fossil fragments mixed with white quartz, feldspar, and mica, painting colorful shades of browns and grays with shells polished by the ocean that mix with patches of orange from coquina shells that absorbed iron oxide.

The northern Gulf of Mexico habitat is the world's second largest dead zone, created when less oxygen is able to dissolve in the water.[4] Marine life die if they try to live here. It began with farmers using fertilizers to increase crops. Agricultural run-off combined with urban run-off and sewage carrying excessive amounts of nutrients into the Mississippi River draining from thirty-one states and two Canadian provinces carries 2,320 miles into the Gulf. Producing large algae blooms that sink, decompose, and deplete the water of oxygen, the water became hypoxic. Crabs, snails, and starfish, unable to leave the area, die. This effect of mankind has increased 25 percent between 2014 and 2015.

Critically endangered, facing extinction, Emunah swam around the Gulf of Mexico, an area of offshore oil with chronic spills. Equipped with strong jaws without teeth, the ridleys are designed to grind up a diet of crabs, clams, mussels, shrimp, sea urchins, and fish. Two of her main feeding grounds as a youth and as a returning adult is in the northern and southern Gulf, both near major oil exploration.

Oil permeates the waves from offshore drilling discharging during exploration. Tanker accidents and ships routinely being cleaned add more mixing with natural seep from the ocean floor. Cars and industries send oil pollution into the air where the wind carries and it falls into the ocean. More than all these, oil and oil products dumped down drains find the way into storm drains causing the most damage. Fur and feathers exposed to oil can no longer warm animals and birds. They freeze to death or ingest the oil and become blind or ill with damaged livers.

---

4. National Oceanic and Atmospheric Administration, "2015 Gulf of Mexico dead zone above average."

Chapter 3

For decades millions of gallons of oil have spilled into the ocean with rescue efforts recovering, cleaning, and nursing as many sea creatures as possible. After the 2010 Gulf spill, they brought them to the Audubon Aquarium of the Americas, in tandem with the New England Aquarium staff. But the oil is there, recurring like a besetting sin. Wind ripples across the stretch of liquid covering the 60,000 square miles of the Gulf. The wind pushes more and the ripples grow into higher and higher waves, speeding faster and further across the open ocean. Deep under the water swells round the surface moving beyond the wind, meeting other sea waves advancing from other directions causing the waves to confuse in a turmoil of speeds and heights. The oscillations harbor fields of petroleum and gas, aggregates of sand and gravel, polymetallic nodules, and precious stones.

On April 20, 2010, the Deepwater Horizon oil rig exploded and sank in the Gulf of Mexico.[5] BP oil began leaking 3.19 million barrels on the ocean floor forty miles off the coast of Louisiana before the Macondo well, 5,000 feet beneath the ocean's surface, was capped eighty-seven days later. Kemp's ridleys depend on this site for nesting. More than a thousand miles of the Gulf's shore from Texas to Florida was impacted by the oil spill swept in by a mix of different size tides.

Workers from BP, the Deepwater Horizon owners Transocean, government agencies, and scientists descended on the Gulf to contain the spread of oil slicks into coastal ecosystems. Every spill is different. Crude oil and many petroleum products are a combination of hundreds of chemicals, each with a distinct set of behaviors and potential effects in the marine environment. Some substances differ only in a single carbon atom on a long molecular chain involving dozens of atoms. Even chemicals with nearly the same molecular structure can behave differently in water, air, land, or an organism.

Dispersants were used to break it down underwater and the water column mixed it into a twenty-two mile long oil plume suspended beneath the surface. Some of the oil sank to the floor like stones of anger, shame, and lies that settle in the mind making the soul sick. It attached to phytoplankton, damaging deep sea coral and unseen lives. Out on Queen Bess Island brown pelicans congregated on their nesting area, black with oil in need of rescue. Fish floated belly-up in the sludge. Seabirds whose feathers had even a small bit of oil were impeded from flying or diving for food. Seabird deaths numbered in the hundreds of thousands.

5. Smithsonian Institute, "Gulf Oil Spill."

An oil spill in ocean water spreads differently than in freshwater. Tides and currents, winds and temperatures all converge to have workers questioning the best response. Surface oil was skimmed where it stuck together in large slicks. Dispersants break down the oil into smaller droplets that can be washed away or be more exposed to bacteria that breaks it down. But the dispersants enter the food chain or get buried in sediments. Clean-up of the Deepwater Horizon oil spill used more than 1.4 million gallons of chemical dispersants, sprayed over the open water from a plane and injected into the wellhead. Striped dolphins were seen swimming among the oil patches.

Years after the spill wildlife on the shoreline were found born afflicted. Fish had lesions and deformities. Shrimp were born without eyes. Heart defects were found in developing larvae of bluefin tuna and other fish. Invertebrates in the deep water and along the coast were harmed. Shrimp fisheries were closed. Corals found 4,000 feet below the surface near the explosion showed tissue damage and were covered with oil. Baby coral had lower survival rates and found it difficult to settle and grow.

Three hundred and thirty-five dolphin deaths were counted in the year following the oil spill. Ten days after the Deepwater Horizon accident, April 30, 2010, 156 sea turtles died, most of them Kemp's ridleys smothered by the oil. Many of the 456 oiled turtles rescued, cleaned and released in Grand Isle by the US Fish and Wildlife Service were Kemps ridleys. Scientists gathered sixty-seven eggs from a nest along the Florida Panhandle to incubate them at NASA's Kennedy Space Center. Fifty-six hatched. Twenty-two were released. The long term effects on their nesting sites are not yet known.

Maine's Marine & Environmental Research Institute collaborated in the investigation of the Gulf's life, from phytoplankton, fish, and birds to marine mammals and people. The Institute reported in July 2010 that the oil that sickened the Gulf was shrinking on the surface. Workers had little left they could clean. They warned that just because the oil wasn't seen, the oil was not disappearing.[6] It was being shifted by the volumes of dispersants that keep the crude beneath the waves, displacing it to another place in the water. The dispersants directed the oil away from the surface and shoreline into a water column and the seafloor. Surface and shallow water species were spared but the animals in the food chain were chemically toxic. Members of the body of the ocean would be lost. The oil hovers, churning in the water columns, difficult to track and measure its plumes.

---

6. Marine and Environmental Research Institute, "Oil Spill Response."

Chapter 3

> Therefore the land mourns, and everyone who lives in it languishes along with the beasts of the field and the birds of the sky, and also the fish of the sea disappear (Hos 4:3).

Yet the currents are still stirred to follow God's instruction. "We know that the whole creation has been groaning as in the pains of childbirth right up to the present time. Not only so, but we ourselves, who have the firstfruits of the spirit, groan inwardly as we wait eagerly for our adoption to sonship, the redemption of our bodies" (Rom 8:22–23).

Creation faints and the sighing at the approaching end comes louder and faster as any birth. Jesus warned of famines, earthquakes, wars, all the beginning of labor pains. Some will abandon the faith and follow false teachings, believing they have truth. Lawlessness will pervade society. The character of people will oppose the truth (2Tim 3:1–9).

Malevolent toxins may lay unseen beneath the surface, the water appear to offer its sparkling refreshment, but the grief that comes where the false words seep into our world reels heavy with anger, pulling hearts to the ground as we flounder and splash trying to stay afloat.

Sand blowing off the northwest African desert is lifted by the wind and carried to blanket hundreds of thousands of square miles of the eastern Atlantic Ocean. The cloud of Saharan sand came in February 2000 rising in warm air lifting dust 15,000 feet above the desert and out across the water, as far as the Caribbean where weather services issued air pollution alerts. The coral reefs are vanishing under the sand storms, no longer able to sustain the beautiful underwater gardens.[7] Uncommon that time of year, a plume of the Sahara dust again moved off the African coast in June 2005 to be carried more than 5,000 miles westward, a brown haze across the Atlantic bringing poor air quality over southern Texas. Sahara's dry dust moves in bursts of winds from the central Atlantic altitudes tracking as far west as the Gulf of Mexico each year and occasionally all the way to South America to fertilize the Amazon rainforest and settle in regions of conflict.

In Nigeria as many as 12,000 people, many of whom were children, have been killed since 1999 when Shari'a law was implemented by Muslims. In 2010 the US Commission on International Religious Freedom reported 500 people in a Christian village near Jos "were hacked to death with machetes and then dumped into wells."[8] Many of them were children.

---

7. The Weather Channel, "Saharan Dust."
8. United States Commission on International Religious Freedom, "Annual Report."

Eight-year-old Nankpaqk experienced an attack on his village in Plateau State by Muslim militants in 2002.[9]

"When the riots started it was a Friday and my dad was not at home," he said. "He rushed home that evening and told us to run away. When we were on our way out, we ran into the rioters. They told us to go ahead of them, and all of a sudden there were gun shots, and I was shot in my back." Nankpaqk lay on the ground. His mother told him to stay down as she tried to escape to find help. But one of the attackers struck Nankpaqk's shoulder with a machete. The pain was so bad, he passed out. When he regained consciousness he went to look for his family.

"I saw my younger brother shot dead," he said. "I saw my younger sister dead; she was shot too. A few meters away from that place I saw my mother's corpse on the ground, beheaded." He had no time to grieve for his murdered family. If he were to survive he had to keep moving and get to a neighboring village. There, he learned that his father who was a local pastor had been tortured before being killed by Muslims during the attack on his community.

The gentle green hills and steep rock cliffs of Nankpaqk's homeland were no longer safe. "I was just crying," he said. "I felt they had killed me too alongside my family members. Being alone kept bringing back the memories of those who were dead."

As Jesus calls, "Follow me," he eagerly awaits the day we will sit at the banquet with him, watching for us like a groom waiting for his wedding.

"Therefore if you have been raised up with Christ, keep seeking the things above, where Christ is, seated at the right hand of God. Set your mind on the things above, not on the things that are on earth. For you have died and your life is hidden with Christ in God" (Col 3:1–3). It is a place that has never forgotten the pristine Garden of Eden where the Lord walked with his people. When Jesus declared to the thief beside him on the cross, "Truly, I say to you, today you will be with me in paradise," he chose the Greek word *paradeisos,* which means "park" like Eden bountiful with life. The word, taken from the Hebrew word *pardes,* describes a land flourishing in forests or orchards, a glimpse of God's paradise being restored with us (Rev 2:7).

It is the Father's garden. Will this generation growing up very much fatherless both in family and in spirit in North America be able to stand, to look into someone's eyes and say yes, I believe Jesus, knowing it could mean

---

9. Voice of the Martyrs Canada Newsletter, "My Faith Was Never Shaken."

their death? Instead of being ruled by atheistic messages pushing Jesus to the edges, are they taught to take what is there and redeem it, whether television, music, Internet, or the signs on buses proclaiming there is no need of God. Because the Holy Spirit came, not to give us more approval or materialism in this life, but so Jesus would be glorified. Children not raised with the goal to influence society with the spirit of Jesus are left chasing only the fleeting success of careers, possessions, and money. With orphaned hearts prideful for accepting all beliefs, they will remain mute as Jesus is erased from the children's lives in a country turning away from its heavenly father.

In Hebrew, the word translated as serpent is *nahhash*, describing something that is serpent-like, insinuating its ways into situations like chemicals into water. The poise of women in the 1950s changed rapidly in just one generation from the way they held themselves in a certain way, disciplined in their modesty, to having no sense of guarding their sacred gifts. Neatly ironed shirts were worn by her family, her hair carefully done, and jewelry that her mother had worn was pinned to her blouse. She held her own counsel. They had less shopping available and were more careful with the income so that everything was cherished. Men comprehended how their weekday jobs served the Lord by caring for family. The immersion of sacrifice cared for wives, washing with the water of the word. Nudging the moral compass past true north, women are being devalued, the sacred bond of marriage is dismissed, and the bride of Christ is obscured.

As in the days of Sodom and Gomorrah, the people became trapped to gain approval by being what someone else wanted them to be. Attitudes value only what another person can do to gratify someone else, no longer a people of grace cherishing their gifts to be nurtured. The loneliness of not having someone to plan goodness into tomorrow, side by side, sharing the heart's prism of yearnings toward God. In schools children are being taught that bi-sexuality is normal, giving way to thought that multiple sex partners and sodomy are approved behavior. Churches falling down to this are failing to heed Paul's instruction to see to it that no one fails to obtain the grace of God. On June 26, 2015 the US Supreme Court assented to the human desire to sin and ruled that all state bans on same-sex marriage are unconstitutional. The ruling overrides any state that refuses to issue marriage licenses to same-sex couples, although the ruling was left in question when Alabama officials refused to issue the licenses.

Yet God has promised not to leave us as orphans. Immersing with his spirit, God wants us to hear him the way his son hears him. If we turn to our heavenly father, the hearts of fathers will turn to their children and the hearts of children to their fathers, or we are destroyed (Mal 4:6). Efforts to remove prayer and the Ten Commandments from public gatherings, the words "under God" from the Pledge of Allegiance, all try to forget the sacrifice of Jesus. He was humble and came in gentleness, but his words are a forceful shoreline where even demons fled and winds and sea obey.

"Do you not know that the wicked will not inherit the kingdom of God? Do not be deceived: Neither the sexually immoral nor idolaters nor adulterers nor male prostitutes nor homosexual offenders nor thieves nor the greedy nor drunkards nor slanderers nor swindlers will inherit the kingdom of God" (1Cor 6:9–10). The sin is in not believing Jesus. Such were some of you, Paul says.

The call raised up Amos to announce God's holy judgment on the northern kingdom of Israel and call the people from their self-righteousness. "The songs of the temple will become wailing" (Amos 8:3). "Behold, days are coming," declares the Lord GOD, "When I will send a famine on the land, not a famine for bread or a thirst for water, but rather for hearing the words of the LORD. People will stagger from sea to sea and from the north even to the east. They will go to and fro to seek the word of the LORD, but they will not find it. In that day the beautiful virgins and the young men will faint from thirst." (v11–13).

The dire consequence God gives his people is in verse 14: "They shall fall, and never rise again." In the West, we are the first generation facing a post-Christian culture since the dawn of the Christian faith. No other generation has lived in a culture that was once Christian but now is not. Having prospered, the young country decided there was no need to give thanks any longer. They had put aside their idols of wood and stone to become believers, but in its place they put man and their own higher power. The wonder at the bounty of beauty and well-being that God graced the land with became lost and instead a set of entitlements affirming whatever people wanted affirmed.

From coast to coast the young are seeing less of God's word. Children are left bewildered while they sit in pews where light should be found. For I was hungry and you did not feed me (Matt 25:42).

Revelation 9–11 tells us that during these days there will be an outpouring of deceptions conforming even believers to the world's ways. Making us think he doesn't exist, like the oil no longer visible but wreaking havoc under the surface, the enemy gives an appearance of light, like plastic particles appearing to be food to the turtles, fish, and birds, but results in death. Those still in the ark of safety can look at the other boats around them to see if they're in a slow drift away from anchor and bring no truth to those around us. Setting an example for the youth coming up behind us, Jesus warned that anyone causing young ones who belong to him to sin would be better off if a millstone was hung around their neck and they were drowned in the depth of the sea (Matt 18:6). It would be better if they had died before they added this sin to their eternity.

Deception agitates and churns like sea foam washed back on shore for the winds to blow its toxins everywhere. In the book of Revelation Jesus tells us the church of Pergamum is under warning because of teachings in the character of Balaam. Balaam had been unsuccessful in prophesying against the people of Israel (Num 22) so he advised the king of Moab, Israel's enemy, to create a campaign to seduce the Israelites away from their identity in God. Using foreign women to tempt the men into relationships and pagan rituals, the Israelites who opened this gate came under judgment (Num 25:1–9). Peter said Balaam's way is to promote false faith accepting thinking outside of God's truth (2Pet 2:15). Jude referred to those "who perverted the grace of our God into a license for immorality." They say they have light. God says they are blind. They say they are wealthy. God says they are poor.

Rather, speaking the truth in love, we are to grow up in every way into him who is the head, into Christ (Eph 4:15).

At a National Prayer Breakfast, President Ronald Reagan designated 1983 the national Year of the Bible by Proclamation 5018, saying, "Inside its pages lie all the answers to all the problems that man has ever known." Twenty-seven years passed. In 2009 Rep. Paul Broun (R-Ga) introduced resolution 121 to the 111th Congress, proposing 2010 the Year of the Bible, saying the Holy Scripture has unified, healed, and strengthened its people. The resolution died in referral to committee.

Christianity may be under attack but it will not collapse. The Pew Research Center confirms that America is becoming more secular, but the faithful are remaining strong in following Jesus, living among the tares that Jesus will separate. Divorce rates are at 25 percent for first marriages, according to the AFA Journal.[10] Among those of faith the National Survey of Families and Households reported divorces were 50 percent fewer between

---

10. Reed, "The real threat to marriage."

1987 and 1994 when couples come together with others in the mind of Jesus to share communion, in contrast to the world's thinking.

In a post-Christian country, some believers are feeling it unnecessary to evangelize. Efforts to share the truth of Jesus become tepid out of worry of offending, yet Elijah never worried about Baal being brought up among the people as he demonstrated there is only one living God. Daniel lived in a pluralistic society under bondage and demonstrated choices for God every day. The worry comes when God's people waver between the two, not speaking of the living God. The Pew study asked adults if they believe their religion is "the one, true faith leading to eternal life" or if "many religions can lead to eternal life." [11]Stunningly, two-thirds of Christians surveyed believe that many religions can lead to eternal life.

The survey of more than 35,000 US adults found that those who believe God pray every day and regularly attend church continue to decline in numbers among the growing population of youth now becoming adults. They most often check "none" as their religion, now accounting for 23 percent of the adult population, up from 16 percent in 2007.

> The night is almost gone, and the day is near. Therefore let us lay aside the deeds of darkness and put on the armor of light
> (Rom 13:12).

Jesus could do miracles and healings when open hearts asked, "Are you the one?" He tells us that there were many widows in Israel, but Elijah went to only one. There were many lepers in the time of Elisha, yet he healed only one (Luke 4:35–37).

Paul tells us, "For although they knew God, they did not honor him as God or give thanks to him, but they became futile in their thinking, and their foolish hearts were darkened" (Rom 1:21). They exchanged the truth about God for a lie and served the creature rather than the Creator. God gave them up to their passions. "For their women exchanged natural relations for those that are contrary to nature; and the men likewise gave up natural relations with women and were consumed with passion for one another, men committing shameless acts with men and receiving in themselves the due penalty for their error" (Rom 1:26–27).

Paul did not want the people ignorant of the ancestor's walk with God. They all passed through the sea. They all were under the cloud of grace. They were all baptized into Moses in that cloud and in that sea.

---

11. Pew Research Center, "US Public Becoming Less Religious."

Chapter 3

But God was displeased with many of them, whose bodies were left scattered in the wilderness (1Cor 10:1–5). He referred to Numbers 25 when Israel was in Shittim and the men began to indulge in sexual immorality with Moabite women. So serious is the sanctity of marriage between man and woman that when Israel yoked themselves to Baal, the Lord's anger burned and in one day 23,000 were killed by God's instruction and another 1,000 later.

Paul let the warning stand. Don't conform to the world. If we're trying to please the world's thinking, we won't be listening to the Holy Spirit's lead.

Ezekiel tells us the destruction of an entire nation came, not because an enemy was stronger, but when Israel weakened from within, failing to give attention to God's words. Church does not fail because it is abandoned by God or by those true to God. The death is in each individual member who forgets to put the word of God at the center of each decision.

Pauls's letter to the Romans warned the church not to become arrogant against the original branches. It is not the church that supports the root, but the root that supports the church. But parts of the church drifted and became the messengers God was concerned about being blind and deaf, a people trapped in holes and hidden in prisons, with none to rescue, and none to say "Restore!" (Isa 42:20–22).

Garry Ingraham might have spent his entire Christian walk believing if we say the sinner's prayer and attend church regularly everything must be fine. But it wasn't fine. Garry was profoundly broken, sexually and relationally, and thinking "if they knew who I really am they wouldn't have anything to do with me."

Garry says it is relationship that wounds us and relationship that will heal us. Founder of Love and Truth Network[12] in New York, he assures those he ministers to that, "God wants the best for us. He has already prepared our path toward wholeness within the healing framework of his community. He will see us through the journey as we cry out and depend upon him." Churches may organize support for addictions, alcoholism, drug abuse or overeating, but the root cause of these symptoms often remains overlooked. Christian leaders need to realize that sexual immorality is coming out of the shadows as a powerful counterfeit to meet deep and legitimate needs.

No longer fishers of souls, the tightly woven message of atonement and crucifixion gets discarded like nets. The mission becomes more about

---

12. Ingraham, "Who We Are."

changing the culture of the lake. There may be the assumption that becoming a Christian means there are no more emotional problems, causing believers to hold back the process God has designed. Yet our weakness is where our most fertile ground will bring about a new objective and create new relationships. It is here the depth of God's grace is experienced.

After twelve years of ministering to individuals and communities dealing with sexual struggles, Garry and his wife Melissa formed Love and Truth Network as a non-profit in 2013 as a standard bearer to the design of man and woman created to be God's image. Melissa is a National Certified Counselor and licensed as a Mental Health Counselor.

"Though I grew up in a Christian family, it was a home without much warmth or love," Garry said. "Our church was legalistic and unbalanced. As a child a realization began to set in. I was developing strong and growing attraction to other guys. After praying for years and begging God to take away what he clearly condemned in scripture, I worked up the nerve to approach several Christian leaders about the battle going on inside of me. They provided no answers and offered no help or support. After that I rebelled altogether. Looking for 'Mr. Right' while experiencing sexual 'freedom' took a huge toll on my life."

Because fathers come looking for us when we're lost, the Lord sent his spirit like a tide gathering Garry in on a current that led him to a church offering to walk alongside him even with all his sin and weakness.

"Over time the men treated me as if I belonged with them," he said. "That was a new experience. They cared and showed the real love of Jesus to me. Just by being in relationship with me they began to call out the good of the masculine established in me by God from the beginning. Honestly, they didn't really even know what they were doing. They were just good men who understood their own depravity and didn't view or treat me as uniquely screwed up. God began to use his sons and daughters in this healthy church to reveal and bring out the truest me, the man I was created to be."

Making the crooked ways straight takes healing through experience in community, requiring patience and trust in God to work it his way. When faced with Goliath, young David took off the armor that the soldiers had given him and stepped out with the weapon God had given him. Unsanctified weapons cannot win this battle.

"For most of us, our surrender to Christ in how we steward our sexuality will be a life-long journey of sanctification," Garry said.

PART 2

The Father of Light

STARS

By Grace Wu

Grade 6, Broadview Avenue Public School, Ottawa, ON 2015[1]

> each vulnerable but special
> delicately cupped in my hands
>
> 10 years ago my mom gave them to me
> each representing a desperate wish
> hoping that one day I can accomplish them all
>
> I spy a green one hiding
> "I am handicapped, jobless, and powerless
> I will never get a job – no one wants me
> I hope this can change"
>
> I see a black star
> "we're poor with no medical treatment when needed
> doctors don't take us seriously
> I hope this can change "

---

1. UNHCR Canada, "Refugees and Human Rights Poetry Contest."

In the corner there is a red one
"I am a girl, a prisoner
because I went shopping alone, because I'm a woman
I hope this can change"

Stars
each one vulnerable but special
delicately cupped in my hands

Wishes
treasured in the bottom of my heart
longing for a world full of peace, love and equality

Chapter 4

Every good gift and every perfect gift is from above, coming down from the Father of lights, with whom there is no variation or shadow of turning (Jas 1:17)

GOD BROUGHT CREATION OUT from darkness with the words, "Let there be light." The radiant energy illuminated his works, pouring beams through the darkness to awaken seeds and prepare the earth for man. A spectrum of colors blended violet in its shorter wavelength, to blues and greens, yellows and oranges, and stretching its longest wave in red. Light poured on the earth, breaking the paralysis of the dark. The seeds shed their shells and reached toward the light, covering the earth with trees offering fruit, bushes with berries, and plants and flowers to give strength. Earth eagerly took in the light to sustain the cycle of foods for all creation's members.

The ocean pulled back to make the boundaries of countries. Volcanoes reshaped landscapes. Earthquakes were set in motion to make mountains and clear vast acres for forest. Lightning cleared fields for flowers and all the animals that would make it home. The fastest of energy, light needed no solid, liquid, or air to move through as it sped through space at 186,400 miles per second.

As oxygen built up in the ocean, graceful kelp grew forests where sun waded in the shallows. Single-celled phytoplankton by the microscopic billions burst on the water's surface, blooming when storms bring a surge of nutrients up from the bottom, coloring the ocean with spectacular colors.

The ocean contains parts from both sky and land in balances of sodium and chloride that keep marine life alive. Refracting infinite mysteries, seawater runs out ahead of the wind blowing overhead, carrying minerals weathered from rocks brought to sea by rivers or released into the ocean from the bottom's hydrothermal vents.

As the Gulf Stream off the east coast of North America flows out for thousands of miles to bring northwest Europe's temperate climate, El Niño (Little Boy) can come in from the Pacific and turn warm water toward South America. Prevailing trade winds can shift weather from the west coast of South America all the way to Australia and influence the Kuroshio Current that cares for the coral reefs off the east of Japan. Other currents flowing toward a beach travel up narrow channels into rip tides to pull large amounts of water back into the sea, moving as fast as eight feet per second.

Thousands of years ago the Bible spoke of wind, telling scientists, "The wind blows to the south and goes around to the north; around and around goes the wind, and on its circuits the wind returns" (Eccl 1:6). The trade winds run for generations to pick up again and blow the warm water back into the western Pacific for it to upwell the cool water into the surface of the eastern Pacific. This is La Niña's signature, displacing the jet stream northward, bringing drought to the south and heavy rains to the Pacific Northwest. Together El Niño and La Niña (Little Girl) influence food production and water supply around the globe.

All of it is powered by light.

Sun beams onto the ocean so silently it disturbs nothing in its path. Interacting with the water to evaporate, precipitate and determine salt levels, the sun's heat pushes the ocean's currents and together they decide weather.

From the deep Emunah looks up as the sparkling daylight opens the emerald curtains. She was learning the language of the light. Navigating the Atlantic's curving coastline, its long stretches indented in and out with many gulfs, bays, and inlets, she remained below the surface for hours. At midday she comes to bask above water when the jellyfish retreat into depths away from the bright of day. When the sky blushed with sunset she dove again as the sea jellies began resurfacing.

Ridley's sea turtles often stay a lifetime in the warmth along the coastal waters but some will venture with the current of the Gulf Stream along with countless other species, up along the sheltered estuaries and bays all the way to the Canadian Maritime Provinces and the Gulf of St. Lawrence, even across to explore the coast in Europe and into the Mediterranean Sea where the stream brings warmth to melt away the winter and bring lush fields. Some of Emunah's kind have drifted with the current all the way to Ireland's coast where powerful waves excavate great tons of rocks from the cliffs with sand and pebbles thrown against rocks, storms compressing air in the crevices, releasing it rapidly to widen a space. Scientists question if the Gulf Stream might stop because polar caps are melting more fresh water into the ocean off the coast of Greenland, making it less salty and lighter. The North Atlantic deep current would no longer be heavy enough to sink and push the conveyor around the earth. When the ocean is changed and winds change, the heartbeat that shapes harvests, weather, and all of life will alter.

Sweeping the world's concerns, massive floods triggered by the ocean flow onto some countries. Other regions are faint with drought. In January 2016 the UN Member States met to discuss the food insecurity left by the El Niño weather phenomenon.[1] Sounding the alarm, Stephen O'Brien, the UN Under-Secretary-General for the Coordination of Humanitarian Affairs, said, "If we act now, we will save lives and livelihoods and prevent an even more serious humanitarian emergency from taking hold."

El Niño and a La Niña event is expected to continue to effect the world with a mix of above or below average rainfall. The impacts on food resources will last years, Mr. O'Brien said, especially in Central America where more than 4.2 million people are affected by the most severe drought in their history. South America, the Pacific region and east and southern Africa will be left in hunger. Drought brought water restrictions as reservoir levels lowered. The cost of maize more than doubled in some places. There is no moisture in the soil as the people look ahead to another poor season. Inventories are depleting. Supplies are tightened. Floods, landslides, and droughts leaving forests vulnerable to fires are being anticipated in as many as thirteen countries. The UN foresees an estimated 22 million people will not have enough food in East Africa where drought effected the north while other regions received massive rainfall, leaving another 3 million people vulnerable to floods. The need for humanitarian efforts more than tripled in 2015 when 10.2 million people needed emergency food. The scale of the problem requires donor support which can take up to five months to reach the people. El Niño challenges global humanity to commit to working together in what Mr. O'Brien calls uncharted territory.

"The warning signs are there," Mr. O'Brien said. "Are we prepared to act on them?"

"We and our children face a growing crisis in the health of the creation in which we are embedded, and through which, by God's grace, we are sustained. Yet we continue to degrade that creation," the Declaration of the

---

1. United Nations News Center, "El Niño has put world in 'uncharted territory.'"

Evangelical Environmental Network[2] states. Founded in 1993 EEN and its Youth Evangelicals for Climate Action work to raise responsible choices because of the degradation of land, water, air, and culture. "Because we await the time when even the groaning creation will be restored to wholeness, we commit ourselves to work vigorously to protect and heal that creation for the honor and glory of the Creator—whom we know dimly through creation, but meet fully through Scripture and in Christ," they say. "Our responsibility is not only to bear and nurture children, but to nurture their home on earth."

The north Atlantic current pumps its cold water southward along the east coast of the Americas then crosses the equator rambling through canyons and mountain ranges. Reaching the deepwater currents circling Antarctica clockwise, the conveyor belt circulates around the continent in the longest continuous flow on the planet. Carrying water all the way from the Arctic's shore, the current rains down onto the abyssal plain to feed gardens of coral brightly colored by the hand of God. Other seabeds are barren, having been plowed by icebergs.

The current rounds northern Antarctica churning up nutrients for the phytoplankton ringing the continent with blooms. Rushing along its pathway it continues eastward then splits up the east coast of Africa into the Indian Ocean as another branch reaches around southern New Zealand into the Pacific Ocean. As the conveyor approaches New Zealand the deep current climbs a chain of underwater mountains covered with an astonishing number of brittle stars. Flowing up the slopes, the current delivers food to the brittle stars. The range rises an island peak above the surface where whales swim in the rich ocean surrounding the island. Elephant seals settle on the shores to breed and sleep. Thousands of royal penguins live here and breed nowhere else. Colonies of king penguins cover an entire beach. Every creature here is sustained by the rich current traveling the world.

The current sweeps past the thousands of reefs of coral secreting hard exoskeletons to support coral polyps in the northeastern coast of Australia. The Great Barrier Reef is the largest living creation on earth, visible from space. The reef grows 600 types of coral, home to countless species of colorful fish, starfish, turtles, dolphins, and mollusks. Research finds more than 6,000 species of coral in the ocean, some in vast forests 20,000 feet down in the dark cold waters growing 300 feet tall.

---

2 Evangelical Environmental Network, "Evangelical Declaration."

Chapter 4

Deep sea corals can live for thousands of years feeding on microscopic animals floating in the water. On the rocky floor, in the canyons, and on continental slopes they provide habitat for God's creations and commercial fish stocks such as crabs and halibut off the Alaskan coast and monkfish off the New England coast. Now at risk of harm from bottom trawls catching fish in deep water and concentrations of carbon dioxide increasing in ocean gyres, coral is weakening even before it's been discovered. Troubling changes beneath the surface bring stress on northern Australia's agriculture and a wide swathe of Central America and Brazil. East Africa outbreaks of Rift Valley fever in sheep, goats, cattle, camels, buffaloes, and antelopes, and sometimes lethal to humans is also alerted because of heavy rainfall bolstering mosquito habitats.

Hungry desperate families don't always have resources to bring sick children to be assessed. UNICEF estimates nearly 4 percent of children under five suffer severe malnutrition, a fatal condition, with flood areas having higher rates.[3] Although screening and treatment for malnutrition is available through UNICEF in more than 90 percent of the districts in Malawi, only 50 percent of the estimated children are being seen. A strengthening El Niño weather phenomenon is putting children at risk of hunger, lack of water, and disease. In Somalia about 855,000 people are in crisis and in need of food, with nearly 70 percent displaced by conflict inside the country's borders. In Zimbabwe the numbers tripled by spring 2016, peaking at 1.5 million.

"Follow me," Jesus said, "Come to me. All who labor and are heavy laden, and I will give you rest." (Matt 11:28). As he perfects praise amid the oppressions, he comes to restore the entire created world. "For in him all the fullness of God was pleased to dwell, and through him to reconcile to himself all things, whether on earth or in heaven, making peace by the blood of his cross" (Col 1:19–20).

I will give you rest, Jesus voice resonates from heaven. I will forgive you. I will cleanse you. Follow me. I have opened heaven for you to give you light. I will give you a counsellor. I will give you a purpose that influences mercy for others. I will never leave you. I will return. I will bring you to heaven to be with me.

But we are afraid. "Do not fear for I am with you."
We want peace. "My peace I give you."
We can't carry this. "Cast your anxiety on me."

---

3. UNICEF Status and Progress, "Undernutrition."

But we want happiness. "I have spoken to you so that your joy will be complete."

I will dwell with the contrite and humble, God said, telling Isaiah that he is a high and holy.

The broken and contrite, seeing their need for God, are in the highest and holiest of places. The man who limped painfully to come to Jesus, covered in the dreaded leprosy, fell on his knees and said, "If you are willing you can make me clean" (Luke 5:12). His faith opened empty hands to receive. His only question was, will you make me clean? "I am willing," Jesus said.

The humbled accept him and cling to him. Knowing the world will take back everything it has given, Jesus showed that this cannot be the source of our joy. Even spiritual gifts of tongues and prophecies will cease. To this Jesus said, "Rejoice rather that your name is written in heaven" (Luke 10:20). A name in heaven, in glory with him, a gift that can never be destroyed will never fail. Jeremiah lived a life surrounded by unimaginable brutality. Yet he said, "Your words were found, and I ate them, and your words became to me a joy and the delight of my heart, for I am called by your name, O Lord, God of hosts" (Jer 15:16).

He inhabits eternity (Isa 57:15) "in whom are hidden all the treasures of wisdom and knowledge" (Col 2:3) and requires "strength to comprehend with all the saints what is the breadth and length and height and depth" (Eph 3:18) He then justifies him who has faith in Jesus (Rom 3:26).

The justification is God's covenant with us, a promise declaring us righteous and upheld."Who shall bring any charge against God's elect? It is God who justifies, who is to condemn?" (Rom 8:33–34). Our guilt has washed away. "There is therefore now no condemnation for those who are in Christ Jesus" (Rom 8:1). We are forgiven. "Blessed are those whose iniquities are forgiven" (Rom 4:6–8), cast as far from east as west, entirely by God's grace. To reach that avowal, Jesus said "unless you're born again."

Stepping into the water of baptism brings us relationship with each other, wading into paths of righteousness, for we were all baptized in one spirit into one body, whether Jews or Greeks, slave or free. We who hunger for his truth in a world telling lies were given the one spirit (1Cor 12:13).

The ocean laps the land, inviting the listener to be touched by eternity, transformed by a glimpse of the hope creation stands on, seen in the sun blessing the rolling currents and the generations of waves capturing light to spill on shores. Where God restores worship, the people are restored.

Chapter 4

Paul, when he said we want to present everyone perfect, and James when he said to endure that we may be perfect and complete, were saying we are to live life in worship. Presenting the body as holy, the air we breathe, the water we drink, and our effect on the ocean merge to combine in respect for God's plan to restore. Worship is in acknowledging the foods God seeded for our health, thankful for the sun that returns each morning, the moon that guides the tides and times of festivals foretelling his coming. Worship discerns the pollution that was not there when God created us from the pristine first immersion. Worship seeks God's help, presenting hands that are a little cleaner the farther we follow. Worship guards our steps.

The savior tells us to seek him daily with worship, renewing our spirit with him on the way to heaven, because in heaven we will continue to serve God.

> His servants will serve him (Rev 22:3).

The ocean is continually renewed, not conformed to the world, but replenished by God arranging the rains, the rivers, deep springs, and the return of morning's sun to wash it clean again. The symbol of God's process was created by Solomon as a round bronze basin standing in the court of his temple. Its forty-five-foot circumference rested on the backs of twelve bronze oxen facing outward, grouped in threes facing the four directions of the compass. It could collect thousands of gallons of water. This sea was placed for the priests to wash themselves. Under its brim gourds completely surrounded the sea. Its brim was made like a lily blossom (1Kgs 7:23–26).

Immersion in water is an expression of a changed heart. In the ancient temple in Jerusalem the law required the mikveh, the immersion to purify before entering the temple grounds. It ritually restored purity because nothing unclean can enter. Turn from your sins, for the kingdom of God is near, John said (Matt 3:3). It was the first step in consecration, as Aaron and his sons were chosen to serve God as the people's representative and were brought to the entrance of the tent of meeting to be washed with water (Exod 29:4). The giving of the Torah was the next immersion after Noah's time. The people gathered on Mount Horeb to be set apart for God. Israel as a people were being transformed into a nation given a way to be restored to God. The Lord told Moses, "Go to the people and consecrate them today and tomorrow, and let them wash their garments," to be ready for the third day when God would come down on Mount Sinai before them (Exod

19:10–11). God gathered a people to himself, redeemed across the ages, for an unimagined purpose. He told Moses, "Gather the people to me, that I may let them hear my words so that they may learn to fear me all the days that they live upon the earth" (Deut 4:10). So important was this people to God that he put all things under his son's feet and made him the head over all things for the church, which is his body, the fullness of him who fills all in all (Eph 1:22–23).

Immersion in flowing water became the way to be purified and healed. All the washings the elders did before they could enter the temple that represented God's house (Lev 8), meant that we could not dwell with God unless first immersed in the sacrifice of our lives. God was showing us that he is holy and only then could he accept us. "God founded the earth upon the seas and established it upon the rivers" (Ps 24:2). Washing became an atonement. A day of new beginnings. We cannot approach God without the washing of Christ, returning again and again to what cleanses us. The old has passed. What has come is new and fresh (2Cor 5:17).

Total immersion in flowing water or a ritual bath were used to purify or consecrate. Lepers and unclean persons of Aaron's seed had to wash their entire bodies in water before they could eat holy flesh (Lev 22:4–6). Anyone in contact with a body or articles of an unclean person was required to wash their body and clothing and were considered unclean for an entire day (Lev 15:5–10). On the annual day of Atonement the high priest washed his entire body before entering the holy of holies. Levites were purified by water of the sin offering being sprinkled on them (Num 8:15). From this culture, John came and baptized his people in the rushing river of God's creation to prepare them to serve the kingdom.

God gathers his church like raindrops building a body of water to cleanse others as they turn from the world's ways. Turning from sin and toward God is known as *T'shuvah* in Hebrew. Stepping into the water we are separated from the past. We rise from the water identified as a new creation. We receive a new nature. Through the birth we inherit Christ's meekness, a submission that may take us where we do not want to go. In anguish and battling the choices as Jesus did in the dark night in the garden, we may have to bow under torturous suffering. This is the meekness that inherits the earth.

Immersion in water accompanies immersion in God's spirit. The second baptism John spoke of is the baptism of the spirit of God. "I baptize you with water for repentance, but he who is coming after me is mightier than I, whose sandals I am not worthy to carry. He will baptize you with the Holy Spirit and fire" (Matt 3:11). To all who received him he gave power to become children of God (John 1:12). Others, unbelieving are "children of wrath" and "sons of disobedience" (Eph 2:3, 5:6). "If God were your Father, you would love me" (John 8:42).

For what great nation is there that has a god so near to it as the Lord our God is to us, whenever we call upon him? And what great nation is there, that has statutes and rules so righteous as all this law that I set before you today? (Deut 4:6–8).

In their hearts believers determined not to let their young be taken by the enemy as the world frantically looks for answers in the tangle that sin has caused. Rationalizing and inventing solutions has created new problems including the remedies offered by humanism and counseling that says it's good to get angry, talk about "me" and "my" rights, drugs to numb feelings, all instead of returning to God and immersing in his wisdom to be cleansed of a corrupt world. The chasm widens.

The west winds and the easterlies sent by Jesus move flows of water in circular surface currents known as a gyre. There are five main gyres in the world's ocean: two in the Pacific, two in the Atlantic, and one in the Indian Ocean. Other smaller gyres are found in seas and the single gyre flows around Antarctica where bottom water touches down 13,123 feet. These gyres have followed the same routes for millennia, guided by the shape of the land, the wind direction, and the Coriolis effect that pushes debris to the right in the north and to the left in the south.

Winds strengthening in the Pacific Ocean are changing the ocean currents, exhaling on shores where children are singled out by teachers, bullied, and tormented for following Jesus. Most places where religious persecution occurs are under Article 30 of the UN's Convention on the Rights of the Children that recognizes a child's right to know their heritage and language among their own people. The convention also protects children already harmed. Article 39 states "Children who have been neglected, abused or exploited should receive special help to physically and psychologically recover and reintegrate into society" with health and dignity restored.

Violations of the Convention continue unaddressed in many countries. The tears of mothers and fathers, grandmothers and grandfathers multiply through time, helpless to save the children. The ocean's acidity increases, 30 percent more acidic in the past two centuries, the fastest rate scientists have found in generations of years.[4] The acidification of the ocean is a consequence of too much carbon dioxide in the atmosphere. About a quarter of CO_2 released from burning coal and oil dissolves into the ocean, absorbing 22 million tons every day, some 525 billion tons since the industrial age.

Rivers carry nearly 10 trillion gallons of fresh water and 20 billion tons of sediment into the ocean every year,[5] bringing dissolved minerals from rocks to buffer the water's pH. But so much carbon dioxide is dissolving so rapidly that nature is unable to keep pace with stabilizing it. Surface layers mix into deep water and currents carry into the entire ocean and all the waters it connects. Lives under water are unable to adapt fast enough. Dissolving shells are littering the Southern Ocean with dead sea snails. Carbonate ions bind up and make ions unavailable to corals, oysters, mussels, and other creatures needing it to build shells and skeletons. Biodiversity is being lost. Fisheries are vanishing. Other organisms that thrive in acidic water will proliferate as the pH gets lower.

Emunah and her relatives wear their fused ribs and backbone on their outside, in a protective shell called a carapace. Her two pairs of prefrontal scales on her head, five vertebratal back plates called scutes, five pairs of belly plates and twelve pairs of rimming plates called marginals decorate her carapace. Four scutes perforated by a pore are found on each bridge joining the plastron to the carapace. The pore is the opening of a gland that secretes a substance science hasn't come to understand yet. Each sea turtle species has its own design and number of scutes, except the leatherback turtle, the most ancient and the largest sea turtle. Leatherbacks have a thick, oil suffused insulating skin to allow it to dive more than 3,000 feet in search of jellyfish in cold deep water. Thousands of little dermal bones lie just below the skin which absorb nitrogen to allow the leatherback to decompress as it resurfaces.

Ocean acidification is occurring at an unprecedented rate up to 100 times faster than at any time during geological history. Predictions by the Intergovernmental Panel on Climate Change show CO_2 levels could reach 500 ppm by 2050 and 800 ppm or more by the end of the century, reducing the pH in the ocean by an estimated 150 percent by 2100.[6] This also effects

---

4   Smithsonian National Museum of Natural History, "Temperature and Chemistry."
5. Woods Hole Oceanographic Institute, "Know Your Ocean."
6. Woods Hole Oceanographic Institute, "Ocean Acidification."

earth's vital processes of photosynthesis. Phytoplankton on the surface ocean are responsible for half the photosynthesis on earth.

The change in water and weather puts the turtle's nests at risk from rising sea levels, heavier rains, shoreline erosion, loss of sea grasses, and the cues that tell them when to come home and nest. Loss of olfactory sense is already being experienced by sea life. If the world becomes a place the sea turtle can no longer survive, can it be a healthful place for any young to thrive?

Emunah follows the Gulf Stream current up to Texas. Southeast winds that began thousands of years before blow barrier sands inland converging with winds lifting waves along the coastline. Accumulating sand for generations, the wind and waves created the South Texas Eolian Sand Sheet, a unique sand plane that extends seventy-five miles inland with barren dunes and beach rock outcrops.In 1978, the U S Fish and Wildlife Service, National Park Service, Texas Parks and Wildlife Department, Florida Audubon Society, and the Mexican government joined forces to transplant eggs to Texas beaches in an effort to start a new nesting population. Thirty years later wildlife officials found 128 nests for sea turtles. They released 10,594 ridley hatchlings along the Texas coast in 2007.

Crossing a wilderness of water moving with fluid power, old cultures are shed through constant giving thanks, the new moons that renew the cycles washing the mind with each provision God sets before us. Family and homeland may be changing but the Lord appoints new relationship out of the ashes. The boundary of the Torah and the waxing and waning moons marking the seven annual festivals appointed in Exodus and Leviticus that reveal the plan of redemption moved to incorporate all peoples of the world. A higher glimpse of his intent is bringing every language to guard the kingdom's boundary, unafraid of saying "It is against God." God told Moses to instruct the people, "You shall not add to the word which I command you, nor take from it." Or the legacy we leave will lose the children to other gods and take them into captivity to other ways of living.

Because you have forgotten the law of your God, I also will forget your children (Hos 4:6).

> But to those who followed him Jesus said, "I am with you always, to the end of the age" (Matt 28:20).

Chapter 5

Awake, O sleeper, and arise from the dead, and Christ will shine on you (Eph 5:14)

To RESTORE MAN FOR his kingdom God again sent light.
"I will make darkness light before them, and crooked places straight. These things I will do for them, and not forsake them" (Isa 42:16). God's creation began with light and the breathing of life. Then death came. Spiritual forces settled on earth that do not want life to follow God's instructions. Man got caught in the darkness. He raged against the pain of death. God answered.

God looked upon the earth with a broken heart. He loved mankind, but love was not enough for them to respond to his warnings and his caring instructions. There was a plan in God's treasures "for the saving of many lives" (Gen 50:20). In heaven, in the twinkling of an eye, Jesus became an embryo cradled in the water of a womb. Birthed from the water, the incarnation is told to the world in Philippians as a sacred hymn, he who being in the form of God did not consider it robbery to be equal to God. He has existed forever, a holy being with God, before he came to Bethlehem far from the lofty position of his eternity.

"The people who sat in darkness have seen a great light, And upon those who sat in the region and shadow of death light has dawned" (Matt 4:16). As the people waited, as for a winter solstice that tilts earth back toward the faithful covenant of new growth, they could feel the entire tide shifting with news of Jesus birth spreading through towns. Paul tells us that to Jesus, Christmas meant surrendering (Phil 2:7). He made himself of no reputation, coming in the likeness of man because we needed him. He walked among people with all the power of his status, yet divested himself of his independence to follow a path of submission to his Father in heaven. Christmas to Christ meant serving as a bond servant giving his life as a ransom for many. John 13 shows him celebrating his birth into the world by donning himself with a servant's towel and washing the feet of his disciples. Jesus stood up to speak to those who will be the children of God, saying, "I am the light of the world. He who follows me shall not walk in darkness, but have the light of life" (John 8:12).

God asked the people to trust the light. The darkness did not comprehend. The planet became plagued by war and sorrow for thousands of years, yet never so dark that Jesus could not be found. If I say, "Surely the darkness shall cover me, and the light about me be night, even the darkness is not dark to you; the night is bright as the day, for darkness is as light with you" (Ps 139:11–12).

Knowing this is too wonderful to understand (v9).

Encountering the living God in a vision, Isaiah said, "I am undone." Habakkuk said, "my belly trembled." They had heard what God was like, but nothing could prepare for coming near him. The disciples were undone seeing the wind and sea were under Jesus command. When their nets were so filled that two boats began to sink and Peter realized in that moment he was standing in the presence of God, he bowed away saying, "depart from me, I'm a sinful man."

God's great grace is why we are able to stand in the presence of his holiness even when we fall to our knees exposed in our own limitations. In our weakness is our greatest strength, surging to go tell others about the king who saves.

The Lord's peacemakers come speaking about the star that shone the night Jesus was born as an infant, the light that dawned the morning he was raised from the dead, the streams of light that have persisted every day ever since. Each morning the light calls to people as the sun calls to earth, "Awake to righteousness, and do not sin; for some do not have the knowledge of God" (1Cor 15:34).

The light separated humanity to recognize one another by how they absorb the light. A chosen generation called out of darkness into his marvelous light, Peter, writing to Jewish believers dispersed around the Roman world, said they would be seen as a peculiar people (1Pet 2:9). "But if we walk in the light as he is in the light, we have fellowship with one another, and the blood of Jesus Christ His Son cleanses us from all sin" (1John 1:7).

"For you were once darkness, but now you are light in the Lord. Walk as children of light" (Eph 5:8). "You are the light of the world" (Matt 5:14).

Because light cannot be contaminated as the land, air, and water degrade, light continued to send its children. Jesus sparked lights of people, blazing in concern for victims of darkness. Churches in Jordan, Turkey, and Iraq respond to the critical need for temporary shelters for the traumatized. It's the opportunity to deliver from the hand of the oppressor. "Let the outcasts of Moab sojourn among you; be a shelter to them from the destroyer" (Isa 16:4).

The National Christian Evangelical Alliance of Sri Lanka, a member in the World Evangelical Alliance, is a multidenominational body seeking to transform the violence in Sri Lankan communities by advocating for human rights, seeking reconciliation, sharing the gospel, and supporting local pastors.[1] Voice of the Martyrs is a network of ministries responding to children who have lost one or both parents to persecution in several nations. VOM partnered with a children's residential school in Indore, India that became home for 125 children who fled their native state of Orissa because of brutal religious persecution.[2] Intercede International operates in Vietnam to strengthen the indigenous witness for our Lord by supporting spiritual strength to believers who are impoverished, few, or persecuted as well as widows of pastors.[3] Barnabas Aid supports a girls' rescue center in rural Kenya, a region where Christian girls and women live under the pressure to conform to traditional polygamy, female circumcision, and child marriage. Often these practices are forced on them and they are mistreated if they stand up for their beliefs. The rescue center provides a home, food, clothing, and hope.[4]

The savior calls on his people, his church, his bride. He is leading his people, commanding their words. Among the persecuted are those who carry the light, distributing particles everywhere, some very bright and seen across continents, others to light their home. The waves of light offered by the first small group of believers was sent across the ocean's waves to find God's people. But the warfare on light followed. The waters became polluted, the air became toxic, and gloom settled on the minds of people.

---

1. National Christian Evangelical Alliance of Sri Lanka, "About NCEASL."
2. Odden, "Facing Death."
3. Intercede International, "Vietnam for Christ."
4. Barnabas Aid, "Barnabas Helps Christian Girls Escape Abuse in Kenya."

Chapter 5

And it will growl over it in that day like the roaring of the sea. If one looks to the land, behold, there is darkness and distress; Even the light is darkened by its clouds (Isa 5:30). The day of the Lord , the great day of God Almighty will be terrifying, overwhelming, falling at the end of the seven year tribulation (Rev 9:11–21) and 1,000 years later at the end of the millennium. The void will be a dark emptiness, as dark as the days before the new creation. (2Pet 3:10).

All focus turns to where light appears. Two celestial bodies, the sun and moon, are the ocean's partners as earth rotates and the moon spins an elliptical circle around earth holding each other with centrifugal force. Every twenty-seven days the moon completes another spin pulling each particle in the ocean's liquid to follow its rotation around earth. About every eighteen months somewhere on earth the moon in its new phase ascends to cover the sun and an eclipse is seen on a narrow track of earth. For a few minutes the ocean will be pulled into the height of its tide. The phenomena occurs in the same place on earth only once every few hundred years, delighting mankind with its spectacle. Once each month the moon's first phase, the crescent new moon, passes between the sun and earth and the ocean brings the spring tide. During this dark night sky in the autumn, Rosh Hashanah is appointed as a time to reflect on the importance of our actions and the sovereignty of God. Also called the Feast of Trumpets, Rosh Hashanah is a prophetic memorial to the trumpet that will sound when the Messiah returns (Lev 23:24–25).

Not one part of these laws will pass from the law until all of them are accomplished (Matt 5:18). The ten days beginning with Trumpets and ending with Yom Kippur are called the Days of Awe, or the Days of Repentance. Custom is to symbolically cast off regrets and wrongs by walking to flowing water such as a stream or river on the afternoon of the first day and emptying pockets into the river. Often pieces of bread are used to toss in and be washed away by the river. A focus is on God's books that record our names. Referenced by Moses in Exodus, "if you will forgive their sin—but if not, please blot me out of your book that you have written" (32:32), the book is again told of in Revelation. "The one who conquers will be clothed thus in white garments, and I will never blot his name out of the book of life" (3:5).

Awakening to sudden bewilderment at the silence in heaven when Jesus opens the seventh seal (Rev 8:1), there will be half an hour of calm, the way a tide pulls out, gathering momentum, and the terrible promise is fulfilled. The second angel will sound. Something like a great mountain burning with fire will be thrown into the sea, turning a third of the sea to blood. A third of living creatures in the sea will die. A third of the ships will be destroyed, possibly by it bringing up a great tidal wave. The great star will fall through the sky burning like a torch as it falls into a third of the rivers and springs that nourish the earth become bitter.

You have not gone up into the breaches, or built up a wall for the house of Israel, that it might stand in battle in the day of the Lord (Ezek 1:5).

For the day is near, the day of the Lord is near; it will be a day of clouds, a time of doom for the nations (Ezek 30:3).

Then Jesus said to them, "A little while longer the light is with you. Walk while you have the light, lest darkness overtake you; he who walks in darkness does not know where he is going" (John 12:35).

The light could not be dissuaded. "The Lord wraps himself in light as with a garment; he stretches out the heavens like a tent and lays the beams of his upper chambers on their waters" (Ps 104:2–3). Light particles continue their way to the darkest corners, to be caught in the minds of some who carry it to others who cup the light in their hands in the face of winds of prejudice calling them bigoted, homophobic, intolerant, and politically incorrect.

God set bars of light to mark boundaries around our souls. God says, "Let my people go so that they may worship me in the desert" (Exod 7:16). Worship brings us to delight in God in our midst and to know how God delights in us, giving victory, rejoicing over us with gladness, renewing us in his love, singing over us (Zeph 3:17). Faith will ebb and flow like the ocean movements, the world fading into the background as heaven comes into focus in the foreground, then gone again, leaving us wondering can it, will it come. Follow me, Jesus said to Peter. Then the night came when Peter was asked if he was a disciple of Jesus. Standing beside a fire after Jesus was seized and taken into the presence of Pilate, Peter answers his own doubt and says, I am not.

The destroying angel reaches a vulnerable doubt and sets up a beachhead where it can advance to occupy. A thief stealing over the boundaries God has set, it moves like a shadow wanting the clamor of bitter sadness to grieve the Holy Spirit and break the heart of God. The incoming tides rise and fall, pulled by the moon and sun, ebbing out, and leaving pools of water in the sand. Trapped at the beachhead, disconnected from the currents like a pool left when the tide is out, recognizing that we have broken

Chapter 5

God's heart, we turn toward God to ask for more sunsets to renew our days. Peter was once again asked about his relationship with Jesus. "Peter do you love me?" Jesus asked. Forgiven, Peter's mind settled to bind up the broken hearted. The words come in drops of water that flow in rivulets from high places seeking out the low and humble. The drops accumulate into a river that streams for all who seek to find. Restoring the thirsting soul, the teachings convert a dry and desolate landscape into gardens of new life.

The greatest flow into the Atlantic comes from the ice melt carried by the East Greenland Current traveling to the Antarctic where increased solar radiation is reducing phytoplankton and damaging the DNA of some fish. Fishermen taking out fish illegally is also leading to the deaths of seabirds getting caught in the long lines. Seals, now that they are protected after being decimated in the eighteenth and nineteenth centuries, are renewing populations. Whaling is prohibited by international agreement south of the fortieth latitude. The troubled times are signaling the need for light in the collapse of a fallen world.

The Atlantic flows into the Indian Ocean pushing the water through an inlet to fill the Red Sea between Africa and Asia. It follows its path through the Gulf of Aden on the coast of Yemen where boats are drawn onto shore, left by those who survived crossing the Red Sea from Africa. On a Saturday in June 2014 sixty-two people died in the rough sea as their boat foundered trying to cross from the Horn of Africa. The deadly sinking brought the total of deaths in the sea to 121 that year. Aid workers stood ready to support Yemen with first aid and food as it documented the arrival of 16,500 refugees and migrants on Yemen's coast during the early months of 2015.[5] Since 2010 more than half a million people from Somalia, Ethiopia, and Eritrean boarded overcrowded small boats to cross the windy waters to reach Yemen. Smugglers have thrown passengers overboard to prevent capsizing or avoid being detected. One of many similar stories, a seventeen year old girl named Nurta Mohamed was shot to death in Somalia. Believing Jesus, Nurta fled her home to take refuge in the Galbadud Region after her parents were tortured with beatings, forced medications, and shackled to a tree for rejecting Islam. Her murder was considered an honor killing.[6] Solemn-faced teams of search and rescue report hundreds of casualties. The Red Sea has become a testimony to the prophets who warned of the coming days.

5. UNHCR, "Red Sea tragedy."
6 Voice of the Martyrs. "Muslims Kill Christian Women and Children."

Strife-torn and struggling, Yemen hosted 264,615 refugees by October 2015, most from Somalia.[7] In September a boat carrying sixty-eight passengers capsized on the Arabian Sea. Thirty-three survived, rescued by a passing boat. One swam to shore. More than 10,000 arrived in September and again in October 2015. Coming across the Red Sea hoping to find a reception of safety, refugees instead are finding facilities closed after being fatally attacked. About one of every ten Yemenis has had to find refuge in another part of the country, reaching more than 2 million displaced people. More than 120,000 have fled to neighboring countries.

Along the coast of the Red Sea, trees of myrrh lift knotty branches of small green leaves and throw their fragrance to passers-by. A balm of Gilead, the scent evokes God's remembrance of his people. Referred to more than any other perfume in the Bible, it drips fragrant drops of balsam first mentioned as an ingredient for the oil of holy ointment Moses was instructed to use in the tabernacle (Exod 30:23), crushed to release the scent and dissolved in olive oil.

Used for ceremonial cleansing, maidens were purified with myrrh for six months before being presented to the king (Esth 2:12). Myrrh was carried in sachets to scent the king's robes (Ps 45:8). The fragrance is a language testifying to the authority of God. Changing the atmosphere with the presence of grace flowing out from the Lord, the beloved in the Song of Solomon is compared to the spice garden where myrrh grows (Song 4:14). The bride eagerly seeks a meeting with him as he comes from the wilderness, perfumed with myrrh and frankincense (3:6).

Myrrh is the sweet scent of brokenness, pleasing to God, a medicine given in suffering and in preparation for death. The Hebrew for myrrh is *mor*, referring to the bitter taste, from *mar*, meaning bitter. Its resin is a dominant part of the small thorny tree's immune system. Harvesting involves wounding the tree to penetrate the bark into the sapwood. Though bitter, it brings sweet promise, comfort, and eases the pain. Mark, who would have known the medicinal uses of the local plants and trees, tells of myrrh being one of the three gifts the magi carried from the east to the Christ (Mark 15:23).

Myrrh was present at the cross when it was mingled with wine and offered to Jesus as he hung dying. The drink was the custom of Jews to give to those who were condemned to die by crucifixion, not to bring strength

---

7. UNHCR, "Refugees continue to reach Yemen."

Chapter 5

but to deaden the pain. Jesus refused the drink, remaining fully conscious as he changed the history of heaven and earth.

Myrrh was brought for his embalming when Joseph, a disciple, took the body of Jesus and wrapped it with the spices in linen. Nicodemus also came, bringing seventy-five pounds of a mixture of myrrh and aloes (John 19:39). Nicodemus had first come to Jesus under cover of night to ask about the meaning of being born again. After answering, Jesus told him that whoever lives by the truth comes into the light. Now he came, fully disclosed in his belief in the Christ, bringing myrrh to ease the preparation for burial.

In pharmaceuticals myrrh is an antiseptic and healing salve to apply to abrasions. Myrrh stimulates white blood cell production to increase resistance to infection and is one of the most effective antimicrobials among the plant kingdom. A compound isolated from myrrh battles successfully against drug-resistant cancers without damaging healthy cells. It is a tree whose gift rejuvenates.

Crushed by unavoidable wounding, believers release the anointing balm to overspread a hurt with the words that are the perfume of Christ's presence. For we are to God a sweet fragrance of Christ among those who are saved and among those who perish (2Cor 2:15). Jesus looking at his beloved scented with myrrh, burning for their redemption, is expressed: "Many waters cannot quench love, neither can floods drown it. If a man offered for love all the wealth of his house, it would be utterly condemned" (Song 8:6–7).

> Until the day breathes and the shadows flee, I will go away to the mountain of myrrh and the hill of frankincense (Song 4:6).

The 1951 UN Convention relating to the Status of Refugees defines a refugee as someone who fled their country "owing to well-founded fear of being persecuted for reasons of race, religion, nationality, membership of a particular social group or political opinion." Some 43 million victims of conflict live around the world.[8] Another 27 million remain displaced in their own homelands. Repatriating to their homeland is a challenge. Integrating into another country is a challenge as well. In 2016, twenty-five of these situations in twenty-one countries had no end in sight. A quarter of refugees, only 250,000, went home in 2009. It has become increasingly dangerous for humanitarian efforts because of armed groups that may include national and foreign armies, ethnic based militias, insurgents, and

---

8. UN Resources for Speakers, "Refugees: Overview."

bandits. The UN reports the system of asylum is eroding, especially in industrialized countries caught in mixed movements of migrants, refugees, and victims of trafficking, all coming with different motivations and status under international law.

Myanmar, on the coastline of the Bay of Bengal in the Indian Ocean, is a southeast Asian nation with more than a hundred ethnic groups, bordering India, Bangladesh, China, Laos, and Thailand. Both Christians and Muslims are persecuted here. During the past two decades more than 200,000 Muslims fled to Bangladesh after Islamophobia took root. Buddhism and Hinduism have been practiced here for centuries.

For years, the armed forces have bought children for bags of rice and cans of petrol, or pulled them off the streets and pushed them into the front lines of fighting. Parents have been hiding their children in Buddhist monasteries and begging Christian missionaries to take them away to one of the children's homes.[9]

The ocean rises and falls bringing tides to the coastlines that are the only gate to freedom for so many. The rising tide dashes over the sand and pebbles, satiates the shoreline with faith in its continuance. When a believer's faith is low, the tide has pulled out, leaving only isolated little pools very near each other, though the distance is insurmountable. The sound of the body coming in on cumulative tides is strong and clear, then fades again in its steady approach. Chords of melody entwine assurances with God's willingness to show the glory he has given his son. The promise is there though the waiting to know it seems far off. Jesus knows. In his agony on the cross he could no longer feel his Father's love, yet he still called him "my God." The tides carry over the abyss.

The truth in the light forbids the dark to come any further.

For it is God who commanded light to shine out of darkness, who has shone in our hearts to give the light of the knowledge of the glory of God in the face of Jesus Christ (2Cor 4:6). The light does not die. The creation begins with light, is redeemed with light, and ends with light. But to the world who follows its own ways, Jesus said, "If then the light within you is darkness, how great is that darkness!" (Matt 6:23).

> If only you had paid attention to My commandments! Then your well-being would have been like a river, And your righteousness like the waves of the sea (Isa 48:18).

---

9. Hearth, "Child soldier recruitment."

Chapter 5

Cresting into shapes, sculpting into ripples and tides, waves move water from one place to another. On the surface waves are pushed by wind moving swells that can travel long distances when the wind's speed and fetch enable it. Wind finds an expanse of open water and brings about the larges waves, including Hawaii's famously surfed shores. Rogue waves forming from storms can build to 112 feet out over the ocean as crests reinforce each other, unpredictable to sailors who hit these walls of water without warning. Waves can come from an earthquake or landslide that displaces huge amounts of water capable of destroying a seaside, reaching its waves up to sixty feet high, rushing in at 500 miles per hour. Consummated with the wind, filling our hearts, moving with the power of the sea upon shores, filled up from within, letting the spirit move in boundless ways, we are stirred by God's power to shine the light upon every shore.

With only 2.2 percent of the world's ocean protected, ocean leaders implemented more than twenty proposed new areas to raise the planet's ocean protection to 6 percent. Five hundred ocean leaders, conservationists, and stakeholders from more than fifty-six countries sat in a room together in Valparaiso, Chile in October 2015 and talked of fish populations that were battling for survival and the eight million tons of plastic finding its way into the ocean every day.[10] During the inaugural Our Ocean Conference they added more than 730,000 square miles to protected ocean areas. Chile increased Protections around Easter Island, San Ambrosio, San Felix and the Patagonia fjords where kelp forests sway, visited by an abundance of fish, including huge amberjacks and deep sea sharks, and enormous lobsters some nearly two-feet long. The deep sea bottom is still untainted. The US suggested creating national marine sanctuaries in Maryland and Lake Michigan. Panama, New Zealand, and Cuba announced adding areas of water. Secretary of State John Kerry drew attention to a direct line between black market fishing, black market drugs, smuggling, and human trafficking.[11]

"And between sea-level rise and increasingly frequent extreme weather—I woke up this morning, extreme weather in Asia, extreme weather in Europe, extreme weather in the United States, 500-year level floods—not a hundred-year," he said. "A hundred-year used to be the exception. Now it's 500 and beyond. Three months of rain dropping in three hours in several locations. And people now say that the ocean currents are threatened and

---

10. Graef, "Good news for our oceans."
11. US Department of State, "Remarks at the Opening."

we could lose what has been a staple of our existence in the Gulf streams and other streams as they shift because of the shift in the temperature of the water. And no one knows what the impact on climate will be as a consequence of that."

All agreed with Kerry's comment, "We can do more to safeguard important marine habitats like mangroves, wetlands, corals, sea grasses, which act as a natural shield from storm surges and flooding and which wind up often being the spawning grounds for the next generation of food."

Chapter 6

Deep calls to deep at the roar of your waterfalls;
all your breakers and your waves have gone over me (Ps 42:7)

DEEP CALLS TO DEEP, a magnificent storm of waves calling to each other, breaking with secrets of their unfathomable depths. Sounds from its yesterday plunge into tomorrow, leaping over human imagination full of expectancy in unseen gifts beyond the impassable light.

"Have you entered into the springs of the sea or walked in the recesses of the deep?" God asked Job at the time of his troubles (Job 38:16).

Most of our planet is beneath the water. Of this, three-fourths of the ocean is down below the twilight world, 35,000 feet in deep, bone-chillingly cold darkness. It's a place we feel the currents that pull us under when the world overwhelms and breaks against our landscape.

Just a few hundred feet down, darkness engulfs with a shock of cold that takes breath away. It's the anguish of loss when believers disappear in persecuted countries and we don't know what happened or how to help. The pressure in these depths can weigh down more than 16,000 pounds per square inch, utterly crushing the heart with the heaviness of a boulder.

Sinking through a world dimmed by tears, the light becomes far away as we fall toward the mire of irrecoverable death. The dulcet tones of the Lord's voice are melodious even here, pleasant to the ear as he calls us from the midnight. God's hand delivers even where we see someone drowning, choked by the thorns and weeds, but we cannot get to them. The fallen are jewels in God's kingdom, gold and silver that he sees covered in mire or the diamond that no longer reflects light.

The current in the deep ocean continues out onto the abyssal plain of the Pacific carrying north past spectacular dramas among predators and prey. The flow garnishes exquisite toroidal vortices produced by the dolphins and whales pulling water into donuts that spin in repeating rings when they dive. The water spirals its centers downward as Jesus opens his hand to bring plankton for fish and grace the corals with a banquet for tuna, hammerhead sharks, and others who gather at the mount. The deep cold reaches to Alaska and loops back as it warms and rises. This ends the journey of the cold and begins a return bringing warmer water. Spring winds blow from the north across the eastern Pacific, creating a cool current flow along America's west coast, pulling up deep water from below, drawing nutrients to the surface and swarms of krill for the blue whales.

The Pacific is the world's largest body of water, covering a third of the earth's surface, from the Bering Sea in the Arctic all the way to Antarctica's Ross Sea in the south. There are 25,000 islands in the Pacific Ocean—more than any other ocean.

In May 2009 scientists discovered the deepest eruption ever found. Nearly 4,000 feet beneath the Pacific's surface, the West Mata volcano rises underwater between Samoa, Fiji, and Tonga.[1] Explosions of red and orange flash in the dark water as molten lava oozes and flows across the sea floor. Spotted shrimp live near the volcano's rumbling where tectonic plates grate against each other. The volcanoes are studied to understand how ocean islands and undersea volcanoes are born and how heat from inside the earth makes its way to earth's surface.

At least 80 percent of volcanic eruptions occur thousands of feet deep under the ocean. The rim of the Pacific Basin is one of the most active of places. Called the Ring of Fire, the movement of tectonic plates has created a series of trenches and chains of volcanoes stretching 25,000 miles across the bottom. Unseen, underwater earthquakes, eruptions, and landslides generate tsunamis and storms.

Lava builds, cools, then adds layers a little higher until the top of the undersea mountain rises above the water and peaks in the sun. On the western fringe of the Ring of Fire, the Philippines is an archipelago of 7,107 volcanic islands covered in tropical rainforest. The people here experience frequent ground shaking as tectonic plates grind at the bottom of the mountains. A number of Muslim faithfuls live here. As the month of prayer and fasting for Ramadan pass with prayer asking God to reveal his truth, testimonies of dreams began being the talk of a village on the western coast. Member of the Tausugs, the largest Muslim tribe in the Philippines,

---

1 NOAA, "Scientists Discover and Image."

Chapter 6

a young man told of a dream seeing Jesus healing many people. He shared this dream with other Muslims to tell them that Isah (Jesus) can heal sickness. He prayed for those who wanted prayer and asked Jesus to heal them, saying "no one can save you but Jesus." He says he is still a Muslim, but now knowing that the power of healing comes from Jesus. Another confided to Mohaimin Datu, a Christian evangelist, the excitement of seeing Isah with a sword defeating a dragon in a dream.[2]

"And the dragon stood on the sand of the seashore. Then I saw a beast coming up out of the sea, having ten horns and seven heads, and on his horns were ten diadems, and on his heads were blasphemous names" (Rev 13:1). The dragon rises out of the sea which encompasses the entire world, and it draws from the multitude of people on the continents. He stands on the shore and summons his legions to war, empowering the world's sovereigns to oppose the people who belong to Jesus. Another beast rises from the earth to seduce the world into worship of the beast. The first beast has power like the ocean to influence the climate of the entire world's thinking.

Every life is vulnerable.

Christian evangelism has been diminishing in the southern Philippines, but church numbers fail to express the movement of Jesus behind closed doors, opening Bibles, and inside prisons of privacy asking who is this Jesus. No power can stop the church. It is Jesus who gathers the ekklesia. It is Jesus who proclaimed the gates of hell will not prevail against it. Songs of worship lift their notes unimpeded through the battles and tears to be translated into languages of every people.

In the Sulu Province the Muslim leaders set up their rebellion and persecution of Christ's believers in the early 1990s. The Philippine government is being fought against by three Muslim rebel groups, the Moro Islamic Liberation Front, Moro National Liberation Front, and the Abu Sayyaff Group who want a separate Islamic state. Warning they would behead more Christians if any missionaries threaten the Islam faith, the ASG demanded all visible crosses be removed in the 442 square miles of the Basilan Province or they would continue abducting and beheading Christians. More than 100 Christians have been killed by Muslim fundamentalists in the southern Philippines. Among them were radio evangelist Greg Hapalla and several missionaries in the early 1990s. The American couple Martin and Gracia Burnham, missionaries with the New Tribe Mission, were also abducted

---

2. CBN, "Islam Faithful See Jesus"

and held in captivity for more than a year. Martin was killed during a rescue operation in 2002. Gracia was rescued.

The Pacific reaches its currents into Korea Bay through the Yellow Sea between China and North Korea, splashing against the sands of North Korea where an estimated 40,000 believers are imprisoned, even children and grandchildren of anyone caught praying are taken into captivity. Reports of infanticide come out of the prison camps.[3]

Flowing into the Southern China Sea from the Pacific, the ocean frames Laos, north of Vietnam where in 2010 a twelve-year-old Som and about twenty of his Christian friends were singing songs of worship inside a village hut. A group of boys came along and jabbed them with taunts, "Your God is not a true God. If you come out we will beat you up!" Christ's youth inside locked the bamboo door and remained trapped for hours. Days later outside his school, Som was thrown to the ground by the same bullies. They hit his back and face until Som fainted, unconscious. He woke hours later and made his way home. His father reported the attack to authorities but nothing was done.

"Kids tell me not to be their friend," said Vannee, another twelve-year-old in Laos. "They don't want me to come to school because I'm a Christian. People threaten and curse us and tell us to stop being Christians. The police came and forced us to leave our home. I was scared. They threw my sister and me into a truck, then pointed a gun at my dad. My family has been kicked out of our home and village three times because we are Christians."[4]

The 9.0 magnitude earthquake eighty miles off the northeast coast of Japan on March 11, 2011 triggered tsunamis striking shorelines without warning. Leaving dozens of villages along 200 miles of coast damaged, the forty-foot waves struck the Fukushima Dai-ichi nuclear power plant 150 miles north of Tokyo. Emergency systems were disabled and crews had to use seawater to cool the damaged reactors. Much of the water washed into the Pacific, bringing the largest accidental release of radiation to ocean history[5]. Radioactive material from the explosions and fires at the plant lifted airborne to fall onto the ocean, mixing into the water. Fisheries off Fukushima closed because levels of cesium are above Japanese limits for seafood. Ken Buesseler, a senior scientist at the Woods Hole Oceanographic Institution in Massachusetts, assembled a research cruise of seventeen people

---

3. USCIRF Annual Report 2010.
4. Voice of the Martyrs, "Kids of Courage."
5. Woods Hole Oceanographic Institute, "Fukushima Radiation."

Chapter 6

from eight institutions to sample the waters surrounding the nuclear plant. They found levels of cesium had diminished quickly off shore, diluted into the Pacific Ocean currents.

Photosynthesis only penetrates so far as the ocean descends to its deepest trench dropping 36,000 feet into the Pacific's midnight zone. Creatures living in less than 650 feet where there is light are in the epipelagic zone. Below this is faint sun, the twilight called the mesopelagic zone down to about 3,000 feet. The bathypelagic lies between the mesopelagic above and the abyssopelagic below, taking the ocean to 13,000 feet down. Below this are the deepest trenches of the hadopelagic zone, named after hades. The abyss and hado have no light at all.

The floor in the deep is a mud of fine sediments and organic remains that sink after dying. Sandy places, unlike the shore that binds the ocean, are rare in the deep because sand is created by waves on coral and rocks on beach edges, too heavy to carry out into the currents to drop to the bottom. Here the lobsters, starfish, many kinds of worms, snails, and oysters move about on the floor.

The hope of the whole community depends on the tiny plants floating above in sunlight to produce food from the water. Animals consume the plants or scavenge for smaller animals all dependant on the seaweeds and billions of microscopic diatoms who begin life absorbing the sun's light. In a continuous cycle driven by blends of sun and water, zooplankton eat tiny plants and diatoms, the bivalves such as mussels, cockles, and clams eat the zooplankton, cod eat the bivalves and swimming deeper, orcas eat the cod. The food rains down and the ocean bottom community eats this rain.

Present everywhere, in oceans, rivers, lakes, ice caps, clouds, rain, under the ground, and in plants and animals, water is always moving and building life. "Truly, truly, I say to you, unless one is born of water and the spirit, he cannot enter the kingdom of God," Jesus told Nicodemus (John3:5). Born again in the Jewish culture means being made new. It can refer to marriage changing a person from an individual to a couple, or becoming a parent when a child is born. It marks a turning point such as the completion of a training that establishes a new position in a profession.

Gathering in every believer, teaching the science of God and connecting relationships, water expresses God's care flowing from scripture. All the way back to Genesis with the establishment of people with Abraham, God has called a people into community. Not only Israel, but outcasts and foreigners. Isaiah penned the thought of God, "My house shall be a house of prayer for all peoples (56:7). Because we need them. God gathers every member, no matter how deep the reach. He brings out the stars and calls them by name. Not one is missing.

Choreographed by the current continuing south along the east coast of Africa, framing the Sahara desert with low humidity under constantly blowing dusty winds, the branch of the deep conveyor loops back on itself and whirls eddies off into the South Atlantic Ocean. The eddies are islands of whirlpools in the ocean, lasting months, pulling in any debris floating nearby and swallowing it the way black holes in space swallow light when a dead star collapses. They warn of the anguish of those who vanish from the believers body as they slip into outer darkness, thinking the cost of changing their identity too much.

Whirlpools pull others into attacking this faith whenever those born of the spirit collide with those born only after the flesh. The language of lies the enemy speaks and the strategy to divide and separate battles its way from sky to sky. It sinks into our neighborhood, in our government and media methodically erasing the words of God from the lives of the children. In every place spiritual battles are fought in the space between heaven and earth. To be indifferent, to live as if the destroyer does not exist, is to fall into his trap and let the tide pull under.

Jesus came to bring us the truth to take up the defenses that heaven has made available to us. His way is more powerful than the enemy interfering in the home, busying our hours working, flooding with the noise rising off computers, television, traffic, and the sights filling mailboxes and magazines. The whirlpool can pull into a bondage of self-doubt. But life has begun in the deep of this baptism that Jesus opened for us to enter his heaven. We sink under the surface, unable to do what is before us, knowing we are inadequate. The spirit bouys belief, turning us to the full view of the light up above. The heaven touches us, raises us, and his billows of winds carry us up from the depths of blackness.

Only recently discovered by science, the Bible spoke of this outer darkness centuries ago. "And cast the worthless servant into the outer darkness. In that place there will be weeping and gnashing of teeth." (Matt 25:30). "Wild waves of the sea, casting up the foam of their own shame; wandering stars, for whom the gloom of utter darkness has been reserved forever" (Jude 1:13). No radiation has been measured beyond the expanding universe, meaning there is only outer darkness.

Chapter 6

Just as spheres of light circle the precipice of black holes in space, a broad belt of ocean spray circles the funnels in the ocean, never being swallowed by it yet never being free from the pull of the maelstrom's downdraft. The Saltstraumen (Salt Current), northeast of Norway, brings the world's strongest tidal maelstrom on earth to the shores of the city of Bodo. Together the waves push up the sea level ten feet four times a day through a narrow two-mile channel creating a colossal tide called the Saltstraumen into an inlet between the North Sea, Greenland Sea, and the Skjerstadfjord next to it. Sixteen feet deep at its strength, the Saltstraumen has been in motion for thousands of years, left by glaciers pulling back.

Sweeping views of the ocean surface are known by man, but less than one percent of the sea floor has been seen, requiring submersible vehicles to bring us information. It is the deepest of valleys, where wave after wave pierces with sadness. It is the hardest days of a life.

Ayman Nabil Labib was gathered into the body of salvation when he was seventeen. He was killed after a classroom altercation in the Minya province of Egypt on October 17, 2011. His parents said their son was murdered "in cold blood because he refused to take off his crucifix as ordered by his Muslim teacher." Ayman also had a cross tattooed on his wrist in the Coptic tradition. Another cross was worn under his clothes. Witnesses said he was told to cover up his cross tattoo. He refused and took out the cross he was wearing under his shirt. Officials reported Ayman was beaten in the school yard, but witnesses say he was severely beaten in the classroom with the teacher's participation. Ayman ran to the washroom where the attack continued. By the time an ambulance arrived, he was dead.[6]

Precious in the sight of the Lord is the death of his faithful servants (Ps 116:15).

Adrift in a valley shadowed by death, when a doctor walks in and says there's nothing more to be done, when a job is gone, the home is lost, when a hope dies, we're plunged into the depths, treading with no solution. Life capsizes, no longer in the sun-filled sky, but sinking as sorrow upon sorrow overwhelms. In the harrowing darkness, do we still love him? The depths do not impede prayer from reaching God. Darkness cannot stop communion from finding him.

Darkness is how creation begins. The day of the Lord that ends the tribulation is a day of darkness. "The sun shall be burned to darkness, and the moon to blood, before the great and awesome day of the Lord comes"

---

6. Voice of the Martyrs, "Coptic Student Murdered"

(Joel 2:31). Who can endure it? (v11). There is gloom with no brightness, darkness, and not light (Amos 5:20). Ezekiel 38 and 39 tell of the future judgment coming against his people. It will consume beast, fowl, fish, and man. Species are going extinct at unprecedented rates, worldwide devastation is reported daily as earth is sickened and Zephaniah's predictions of false religion, wrong beliefs, philosophy from the tree of knowledge with no fear of God alter morality, politics, family, health, harvest, and water.

Whirlpools are concentric circles, smaller the deeper it goes, shrinking our world into a limited focus of pain. Youth growing up in Christian families have the support of a church community when the world targets their faith. Faith is a protector that eases the effects of psychological trauma that other children who are harassed may not have because faith brings the living God who has a long term story to tell us.

"We forgive the Hindu radicals who attacked us," ten-year-old Namrata said. Namrata suffered injuries from a bomb blast in the Himalayan Mountains near the Indian Ocean in 2008. "They were out of their minds. They do not know the love of Jesus. For this reason, I now want to study so that when I am older, I can tell everyone how much Jesus loves us. I feel very loved by the people of India and by so many people who have prayed for me."[7]

Under the baptism the injuries are cleansed. To forgive gives respect back to ourselves, returns purity to our identity, and God's cherishing of ourselves when another had disparaged our worth. Light raining from heaven drops on each believer who follows into the water. A new identity is found, a clearer purpose of this life, a larger family, and another place to call home.

Immersing in water tells us we are forgiven. The cross tells of Jesus' trust in God's mercy. When sinking in the twilight world, realizing Christ is present everywhere, but is not given Lordship in every circumstance, there is darkness present pressing down against rising toward the light. Engulfing even the defenses and strengths we thought we had, the barren void softens hearts to hear the call of their name. It is from the deep that the waves part to make a way for rebirth. *Nabi*, meaning prophecy in Hebrew, to "bubble forth" like a fountain, comprehends God's will in the frenzied spray cast from angry storms.

> If there is a prophet among you, I the Lord make myself known
> to him in a vision; I speak with him in a dream (Num 12:6).

7. International Day of Prayer, "IDOP 2010: Hearing Their Cry: Children's Material."

Chapter 6

Jeremiah was only about seventeen when God shared with him the deep yearning for his people to return. Jeremiah wept often, knowing what would come upon his people because no matter how he implored them, they would not listen. A life alone with God, finding no human comfort, he was shown how children, babies, women and men would die grievous deaths, left unburied for the birds to devour (Jer 16:3-4). He preached for more than forty years never seeing a response to his words, his words sounding like foolishness to those who were lost (1Cor 1:18). The people didn't fully trust God. They took for granted they would be secure. Emotionally wrought, even believers like Jeremiah begin doubting God. Responding, God spoke in infinite faithfulness, telling Jeremiah that if he returns to trusting, he will be restored. "If you utter what is precious, and not what is worthless, you shall be as my mouth. They shall turn to you, but you shall not turn to them" (Jer 15:19).

> They have silenced me in the pit and have placed a stone on me (Lam 3:55).

> I called on Your name, O LORD, out of the lowest pit (Jer 38:10).

And thirty men were sent to bring Jeremiah up so he would not die. Scripture gives us multi-faceted images to help us understand our deliverance, God's heart, the earth's moan, the cry for healing, the tears for loss, the depth of our helplessness, the even deeper realm of God's mercy. Grieving is translated into jubilance even in a decaying world, combining in one song because Jesus made a way for recovering relationship.

Silken waves ascend the steps to the sky, pitch dark on a moonless night. Flaming with the sun rising and again clouded with pouring out rain, then giving forth thunder as arrows flash on every side. Skies change in constant expression. "The crash of your thunder was in the whirlwind; your lightnings lighted up the world; the earth trembled and shook" (Ps 77:17-18)."When he utters his voice, there is a tumult of waters in the heavens, and he makes the mist rise from the ends of the earth. He makes lightning for the rain, and he brings forth the wind from his storehouses" (Jer 10:13).

> These are the outskirts of God's ways, a small whisper of hearing him, and who can understand the thunder of his power (Job 26:14).

The plea for reconciliation in Jesus, the warrior of God, is answered. For all humanity, male and female, slave and free, every people group, rich and poor, healthy and ill, young and old, God's initiative is for his love to be known (Rom 5:8). His is a love able to move humanity to feel loved, understood, wanted, forgiven, and brave. The first believers knew this valor, for our sake. They told us to continue proclaiming the truth. They implore us to rescue those who respond from the terrible day of dark judgment we are moving toward (Rev 3;10).

For though we live in the world, we do not wage war as the world does. The weapons we fight with have divine power to demolish strongholds. We demolish arguments and every pretension that sets itself up against the knowledge of God. We take captive every fear of death to bring it into praise (1Cor10:3–5). The bottom drops out. The water rises over us. It is here we learn the secrets of the deep. Aware of what we would choose differently, it is here we find God is still the Creator of life out of darkness. The trial of our faith is precious, the suffering of this present age is not worthy to be compared to the glory that will be revealed (2Cor 14). Jesus purifies where no person can go with us. He cleanses when the accusations keep coming. He is our bedrock truth.

Imparting words to our minds and promises to our heart, he prepares us for the storms. Because the sky over us constantly changes, we are given to know that God remains the same, never changing, with us on the sunlit days and on the high and violent seas. He will be there in the deepest darkness of trouble, when we lay weighted on the ocean bottom, not to be lifted again until we soar on the wings of eagles safely to our home.

The sea floor is a perpetual place of birth and death shaping its geology and the history of the lands. Over millions of years of geological time the ocean basins grow mountains from the bottom plains, carving new habitats for organisms to live and sending others to live elsewhere. Shaping coastlines and determining if it will be muddy, sandy, or rocky, the ocean creates mysterious realms for beautiful creatures. Earth is a liquid planet, birthed from water, rotating just far enough from the sun so the water did not evaporate into the air and close enough to keep it from becoming ice.

The north Atlantic current that began off the Greenland coast returns over a vast mountain range 10,000 feet down called the Mid-Atlantic Ridge. Its peaks are more than a mile below the surface, rising from the flat plain. The conveyor belt washes over its corals, the sponges covering rock, sea lilies swaying in its current, and new species not yet discovered.

The Mid-Atlantic Ridge runs down the center of the Atlantic Ocean following curves of the coastlines and up the eastern edge of the Pacific

Chapter 6

Ocean. Underwater earthquakes and volcanoes are clustered around the ridges, formed by the sea floor moving, shifting its shape, carrying continents a long way from each other, and birthing new places for ocean water to fill.

Down in the deep life is sparse outside the hot springs of hydrothermal vents and cold seep communities around the mountains. Pillows of lava erupt where the earth is cracked opened. Spewing up from the sea floor, fluids carrying minerals shimmer in the water over rocks too young to have accumulated much mud. Life abounds in an unimagined assortment adapted to the dark of the deep ocean. Organisms living around the vents rely on chemosynthesis instead of photosynthesis as they convert minerals in the water into energy. Giant tubeworms with no digestive tracts churn in clusters existing on hydrogen sulfide in the vent water coming from inside brimstone in the earth's crust. In the volcanic cracks in the ocean floor about a hundred underwater vent systems leach minerals and nutrients to feed colonies of bright red tubeworms, mussels, and large clams. Feather duster worms, called serpulids, and tevnia tubeworms are fed on by the top predator of the vent community, the crabs. Chimaera, a fish found 4,200 feet deep, has no bones but is supported by cartilage and spots on its face that are sensory organs detecting electrical fields so it can find its prey and predator. Fresh lava flows as the seafloor continues its change.

The Mid-Atlantic Ridge is earth's longest mountain range.[8] The ridge begins under the long dark winters and summer's midnight sun of Iceland. The young land is born of volcanoes, rich in waterfalls, rock formations, steaming fields of lava, and percolating geysers. The ridges rise beneath the ocean down to the 58 south latitude which circles the globe crossing only ocean.

The ridge separates the ocean into two large rift valleys with many basins. Sediments contain terrigenous deposited from the land made of sand, mud and rock, weathered and washed by the sea, thickest near river mouths. Pelagic deposits, the remains of organisms sinking to the ocean floor, include red clays and siliceous oozes. The ocean floor shifts its plate tectonics, adding rock to the edges of the plates and the sea floor expands, widening the ocean between the continents. North and South America move farther away from Eurasia and Africa by about two inches each time the earth completes its annual spin. The youngest sea rocks are in the middle of the ocean, where the spread first began.

---

8. Woods Hole Oceanographic Institute, "Hydrothermal Vents."

The Father of Light

Near the Mid-Atlantic Ridge, eighteen-story piles of stone majestically tower, extending for 6,200 miles along the Atlantic's floor. Two dozen stone spirals in a region named Atlantis Massif look like a lost city.

The stone towers are unique, forming nine miles away from the volcanic cracks, extending a submerged mountain the size of Mount Ranier in Washington State. Towers gleam bright white, made of materials such as carbonate minerals and silica. Other ridges appear black. Steep sides of rock feather into ledges that sprawl out as wide as thirty feet. Spiraling upward 180 feet under the water, they are able to grow because the Mid-Atlantic Ridge buffers the rocks from eruptions that occur every five to ten years at the ridge's axis, and from the earthquake movements that are more frequent around the vents.

Called black-smoker formations, ocean water sloshes near hot magna and heats up. The hot water absorbs minerals from surrounding rocks and flows upward. As it rises, it cools and releases the minerals, which form towers of dark rock and nutrient-rich ecosystems.

Sections of glassy green rock known as olivine are exposed under small cracks in the ocean floor. The water seeps into the ancient mantel and reacts with the olivine to form a scaly green rock called serpentine. The interaction generates heat which triggers the same mineral deposits as black smokers but the deposits are made of different, paler rock. Fluids coming out of these cracks around the towers have not been found anywhere else. New and ancient life is here that has yet to be known, placed in the basin of the ocean to exist in scorching temperatures of 750 degrees Fahrenheit

Nearly 3,000 years ago, long before science discovered the ridge, Jonah wrote of the towering mountains and deep trenches in the ocean's depth.

> The waters closed in over me to take my life; the deep surrounded me; weeds were wrapped about my head at the roots of the mountains (Jonah 2:5–6).

It is a unique and terrifying deliverance from these depths where God prepared a great fish that would swallow Jonah, a prophet who lived in the late 700s BC. His is the story of storms correcting us when we are reluctant and begin to drift off course. We are disciplined because we are his children and also because he doesn't want us leading anyone else to the wrong pathway.

Jonah wanted to run from his enemies, the Ninevites in the capital city of Assyria. He was to bring an invitation of grace and forgiveness to the people who had harmed his people. Instead he ran away from the

Chapter 6

Lord, headed for Tarshish and boarded a boat on the Mediterranean Sea. Remaining with him, God caused a storm to surround Jonah, so severe that the sailors agreed to throw him overboard so God would calm the sea. Jonah wrung out every drop of his anguish as worship was birthed in the depths of the Lord's ocean. The great fish, sometimes translated as a huge creature of the sea, spit Jonah out on dry land. Carrying all that astonishment of the encounter with God's answer to his cry, Jonah journeyed 500 miles back to Ninevah and delivered God's message. Today Nineveh's oldest church commemorates Jonah's coming with the message of mercy for those who turn to God.

God used immersion once again to transform a man. Jonah failed to do as the Lord asked of him. But he rose from the water and again God came to him and spoke, telling him to go and 120,000 people were turned to God. He was not left to dwell in his failure but arose in the splendor of God's mercy washing over him, smoothing the fragments of shame and remorse. The Lord defines success differently than the world. The outward appearance of the rich man seemed successful but it was Lazarus, the beggar who sat at the gate, who was escorted to heaven. The widow who had only a mite to bring as a tithe won the heart of Jesus. The world looking at Jesus dying on the cross assumed his life to be a colossal failure.

Death in the abyss is the destiny of every life as the universe spins in a whirlpool taking back every breath. The act of baptism carries us down into it, believing Jesus, reaching for his hand to raise us from it. The storms will surround us, darkening the sky. Desolation filled even believers on the day that Jesus died, yet their spirit kept hope hearing that he had risen from the dead. With new life out of the death we carry a message. We are not to give up the Lord's territory.

> Your dead shall live; their bodies shall rise. You who dwell in the dust, awake and sing for joy! For your dew is a dew of light, and the earth will give birth to the dead (Isa 26:19).

When all in their graves, even from the ocean bottom, come out with those baptized into new birth, the new song will be joined that began when Jesus was victor over death and sin. In his glimpse of heaven, John said, "I heard every creature in heaven and on earth and under the earth and on the sea, and all that is in them, saying: To him who sits on the throne and to the Lamb be praise and honor and glory and power, forever and ever!" (Rev 5:13).

The Father of Light

Those in the old testament believed, waiting for the day God would send Messiah who could reunite the people and all of creation with heaven. Those in the new covenant wait for the day the savior will return. Always, the hope began with the truth of our inadequate selves and the realization that only entering the immersion into his body will transform us. The moment we act on this truth, God gives grace.

Shining from the east to the west, the sun bathes the ocean waves and every ripple as creation longs for the son. For by him all things were made, filling earth and heaven with his presence. Emunah swam through hundreds of miles of marine vegetation, letting herself rest from time to time. Offshore words were being spoken of prophecy, new Jerusalem, tribulations, world power, enemies of Israel. Nations take a stance against Israel from the east, north, west, and south. There will be no government to intervene on their behalf. Commentators predicting this would come to pass speak of Islamic terrorism and its worldview to conquer. Believers spoke of watching for the son to come out of the heaven to save us from the coming wrath (Thess 1:10). Nothing will be hidden.

> And though they conceal themselves from my sight on the floor
> of the sea, from there I will command the serpent and it will bite
> them (Amos 9:3).

In the dark times God's first response is to call his people "to prayer and the ministry of the word" (Acts 6:4). The covenant cannot be entered without being immersed through waters that cleanse from the deepest terrors. Our Lord Jesus came so that the world might be reborn in light (John 3:1).

It is not yet earth's darkest hour but it is darker in each generation. Good is called evil and evil is called good. Laws and policies trample on God's living words. Churches bearing the name Jesus give blessing to rejecting God's law. The suffering bleeding Christ who overcame death is reduced to being kind and accepting. We are in the age of grace and mercy, the age of Pentecost when the church is being birthed and heaven is open welcoming those emerging from baptism. In a moment, in a flash of light speeding down to us at 186,400 miles per second the grace will end. The judgment begins.

PART 3

A New Song

LOST IN TRANSLATION

By Amanda Marino

Grade 12, Langley Fundamental Middle Secondary School, Langley, BC 2015[1]

Crammed between these wooden planks
Like filthy cattle
Hearts beating fiercely
Through the putrid stench
Of disease and decay
Hearts beating fiercely
For freedom
Hunched over, starving, seasick
Sagging like dying trees
Stomachs aching for a home-cooked meal
But our home has been stolen
Children wailing
For mothers and fathers
Killed by the bombs
Brothers and sisters

---

1. UNHCR Canada, "Refugees and Human Rights Poetry Contest."

Caught in the crossfire
Hearts beating fiercely
But with each passing day
The heartbeats lessen
When we arrive
At our destination
Will the people there hear us?
Or will our existence
Become lost in translation

Chapter 7

Its measure is longer than the earth and broader than the sea (Job 11:9)

AFTER PREPARING EARTH FOR man with the light of the sun, moon and stars mingling with the water, the next thing God did was to fill his land and water with song.

God said, "Let the waters abound with an abundance of living creatures, and let birds fly above the earth across the face of the firmament of the heavens." And God blessed them, saying, "Be fruitful and multiply, and fill the waters in the seas, and let birds multiply on the earth" (Gen 1:20,22).

When God rested on the seventh day, all of earth and heaven were singing. Everywhere across all lands, the birds were each given a song to fill the winds and cross the waters. God told man, "But ask the beasts, and they will teach you; the birds of the heavens, and they will tell you" (Job 12:7) Man saw how God cared for all he had created. God said, "Are not two sparrows sold for a penny? Yet not one of them will fall to the ground outside your Father's care" (Matt 10:29–31). So don't be afraid.

The flood in Noah's time was the first baptism of water that God sent to separate out a human family. After 150 days Noah's ark came to rest on the majestic mountains of Ararat in what today is known as eastern Turkey between the Aras and Murat Rivers, a place of legends of the Garden of Eden where streams join with the Euphrates and Tigris rivers. Later the Israelites would import honey from its ports. As Noah's family waited in the ark, God sent a wind to blow over the earth and the waters covering creation abated. The fountains of the deep and the windows of the heavens closed. The sun came out and the waters receded from the earth (Gen 8:2–3). After forty-seven days Noah sent out a dove and the dove returned with a fresh twig from an olive tree. The sky had answered, the clouds parted and the land was habitable and began filling with song once again.

Then God established a covenant with Noah and his offspring and with every living creature. "I establish my covenant with you, that never again shall all flesh be cut off by the waters of the flood, and never again shall there be a flood to destroy the earth" (Gen 9:11).

It's the first time the word "covenant" is used in Scripture (Gen 6:18). Peter spoke of the earth being formed out of water and by water, through which the world had perished in the flood. The word for "perish" is the same as the word used for "lost" when Jesus told of the woman who finds her lost coin and rejoices. The coin could be useful again. Life on earth perished in the immersion of the flood but it was still there. Until the waters abated and the covenant was entered, man could not fulfill the life God created him to live. For a soul to be lost means the soul is still there, its purpose destroyed, but in baptism restored to follow God's light.

Noah was to trust God, laying in silence below deck as the sea lapped against the ark. When he built the ark and let God take the helm through the waters, he did everything as God commanded him. Through him nations would multiply and scatter throughout the earth carrying the covenant, establishing protocols, systems of justice, and times of coming together with the moon's phases, the sun, equinox, and solstice taught from the beginning of time, all dependant on the fire of light shining with the liquid water, the immersions that bring life.

As God looks on a rainbow from heaven, his chosen look from earth and understand our grieving is not without hope. He will redeem a people from the judgment. God's participation in the human story is a love so intense he jealously came to rescue us back to him, grieving when we are taken into captivity, celebrating with us when we march victoriously with him. The new covenant extended from the law of the Torah given to Moses. Jesus said whoever relaxes one of these commandments and teaches others to do the same will be the least in heaven. The law is impossible. No one can fulfill it all on their own. The laws show us a standard of righteousness that is not within us. It shows us how dependant we are on God. Jesus said he came to fulfill the law and prophets. "If you love me, keep my commandments." In Romans Paul exhorts us not to sin. We've died with Jesus. We've risen with him. He goes on to describe how conflicted he is in his own struggle. The things that he doesn't want to do, he finds himself doing. Oh wretched man. The answer, Paul tells us, is in the law of the Spirit of life

Chapter 7

in Jesus. There is no condemnation because the Spirit has done in us what the law could not do. It is not in the power of the mind to do. Jesus warns that unless righteousness exceeds that of the scribes and Pharisees we'll never enter heaven. Never. The kind of righteousness required is that of a heart thirsting toward him, a person recognizing their need for cleansing, a grateful heart graced with giving thanks in all situations, during all attacks from the enemy and temptations. It is a covenant of mercy.

Water and light have continued the cycle sustaining all creation with God's unchanging promise. Emunah swam with the currents God had designed after the floods abated and the first rainbow appeared. Sea turtles avoid the shadows, disliking dark places where predators may lurk. Entirely dependent on God's plan, she made her way up the coast, preferring water less than 150 feet deep all the way to Long Island where the ocean welcomes young Kemp ridleys by offering critical habitat.

The acres of ocean absorb carbon dioxide wherever it meets with air. Wind lifts the waves bringing more opportunity. The ocean's plants take in the carbon dioxide and give back oxygen. Fish and marine life breathe oxygen and give off carbon dioxide, just like land animals. About a quarter of the carbon dioxide created by humans burning oil, coal, and natural gas is taken in by sea water. As it absorbs more and more, it's becoming more acidic and less alkaline. Creations like mollusks and coral that depend on the balance of the alkalinity to make protective shells are at great risk.

North Americans consume much more energy per capita than any other region of the earth, twice that of Europeans, depleting resources and increasing greenhouse emissions.[1] Only about half of the globe surveyed by Pew consider climate change a serious problem, with the US and China among the least concerned. Yet God had declared each part of his creation to be good. Acid rain, endangered species, extinct species of flowers, birds, and fish that children will never know, deforestation, genetic engineering, and polluting water disintegrate the systems of the world as we move toward the final battle. When the afternoon sun lowers over the horizon, the fish are no longer slipping through the silken waters. Instead, islands of plastic and stains of toxins reign in the sunshine. When the bigger fish come looking for their sustenance, they leave unfed and hungry.

The water in tidal cycles pushes seawater up streams to places shorebirds depend upon. Seabirds sky dance, their wings gleaming with light over feeding grounds once filled with larger fish. Swooping and singing

---

1. Sustainable Measures, "Ecological Footprint."

in a dizzying array, they now find only small fish, unprecedented in past centuries. The history of the ocean is changing. Demand for commercial fishing leaving less food has pushed the birds to make their way down the food chain.

Mid-May at the Delaware Bay hundreds of thousands of seabirds stop over to regain strength gorging on the eggs of horseshoe crabs on their way to the Arctic tundra to breed. They share the eggs with eels and whelk, but also with fishermen who have taken truckloads of female horseshoe crabs to use as bait. Equipped with drag nets across the sea floor, they hoist thousands of these in one day. The horseshoe crab struggles to continue its population. There are no longer enough eggs to sustain the shorebirds and enable them to complete their migration. The colorful long-legged Red Knots especially are dropping toward extinction. Most of their population, an estimated 80 percent, pass through the Delaware Bay each spring as they make the epic 9,300 mile migration from South America to the Arctic breeding grounds, and back again in autumn. They arrive at the Bay as thousands of horseshoe crabs should emerge from the water's depths to spawn billions of eggs along the shoreline. For the Red Knots, it's the last critical feeding rest along the way. Migratory shorebird populations declined by nearly 70 percent between 1973 and 2016. Their habitats have been destroyed under construction. The State of North America's Birds 2016 reported 37 percent of the continent's birds are in urgent need of protection in every habitat. Threats to the coastline are taking an especially large toll. Further threatening the seabirds, cues in the weather signaling the time for flight to coincide with the spawning is changing with climate.

The Atlantic carried the first winter storm in decades strong enough to be called a hurricane in the middle of January 2016. At 1 p.m. on Thursday, January 14, Hurricane Alex sustained 85 mph winds as it spun more than 400 miles south of Portugal's Azores island volcanic peaks. The storm moved northeast raining down five inches, turning north over the Azores with storm force winds about 900 miles from Europe and 2,300 miles from the United States as it continued north toward Greenland. Its strength surprised the National Hurricane Center. Tropical storms are fed by warm waters between summer and fall, not in the Atlantic's mid-winter cold.

The sea churns and moves in a resplendent covenant with God. Responding to the sun's fiery corona moving the air, waves move toward the shores, water particles going up and down on the surface, bobbing a seagull

Chapter 7

in place, as they pulse from one particle of water to the next pushing the water before it.

Emunah floated up into high noon's sun and took a breath. She blinks at the panorama around her. A man stands on the promontory of sand at the water's edge. The waves leapt toward him, full of grace, cresting, sinking down so the next can come, their motion a unified effort to reach the shore like God's messengers in a never-ending plea. Each splash of the sea air brought him invisible healing, stimulating his senses, alertness, his immune system, and oxidizing his blood stream, as the splashes release 2,000 negative ions in balance to every 1,000 positive ions. Away from the polluted air of a large city where less than 100 ions are offered, the man prayed. The weight of the sun was on his shoulders as his words carried concern for the hundreds of believers being killed that hour across the ocean in a land of troubles.

> They seize bow and spear; They are cruel and have no mercy;
> Their voice roars like the sea, And they ride on horses, arrayed as
> a man for the battle against you, O daughter of Zion! (Jer 6:23).

As the splashing water splits particles of air, freeing electrons that attach to other air molecules creating a charge, the man of prayer looked up. Let us draw near with a true heart in full assurance of faith (Heb 10:22). Let us consider how to stir up one another to love and good works (v24). His spirit's thirst awakened a memory that has not yet happened, waiting for the morning that will dawn a new kingdom.

Christ's youth are especially targeted, girls kidnapped and forcibly married to Muslim men and boys are murdered. In Pakistan where the Indian Ocean reaches north to fill the Arabian Sea, Parveen, a thirteen-year-old girl, attends a Christian boarding school. One day while she was walking to her grandmother's house, girls in a car stopped to ask her for directions. The girls offered her two apples. Parveen ate the apples and moments later passed out in the car. When she woke she was in a strange house and told by the mother of the girls that she was now a Muslim and would marry her thirty-five year-old son. Parveen's relatives were able to rescue her.[2]

In the Punjab province of Pakistan, twelve-year-old Huma was abducted and forced to marry a thirty-seven year old Muslim. Her mother, Sajida Masih, took her daughter's plight to court but the courts have refused

---

2. Voice of the Martyrs Canada: Bold Believers Magazine.

to intervene, stating that they have no power now that Huma is a Muslim. Huma has since disappeared with her kidnappers.[3] Born into a Christian Pakistan family, two-and-a-half-year-old Neha was found bleeding and bruised, brutally raped. Her parents sought medical help at local hospitals but were turned away because they are a Christian family. The attack came after Neha's father was pressured by his boss to convert to Islam. Refusing, his daughter was injured so severely, she required complicated surgeries to repair what was inflicted on her.

These children wonder, why do people hate us? Why did neighbors attack their home, beat up their father and mother, murder their brothers. Why didn't God protect us if he loves us. The shattering psychological trauma crosses cultures and every background. To a child the afflictions make no sense. Carrying the heavy weight of pain, grief, depression, and anxiety all shroud their natural days as they wait for time that will start the clock ticking again. Obsessive-compulsive behaviors may express a need for a sense of control and order. Nightmares need an assurance no psychology can bring, loss of interest in the activities that once occupied them, fears sensitive to nightfall bring withdrawal, diminishing thought of the future is frozen in witness to violent death or torture of a family member.[4]

The sea has come up over Babylon; She has been engulfed with its tumultuous waves (Jer 51:42).

For your ruin is as vast as the sea; Who can heal you? (Lam 2:13).

But the wicked are like the tossing sea, For it cannot be quiet, and its waters toss up refuse and mud (Isa 57:20).

The pressure of the deep pushes against every side. When it engulfed his people, Daniel and his friends purposed in their heart to keep believing the God of heaven and earth not knowing whether it would bring them harm, just knowing he was to be believed above all else. Refusing the appetites of the dominant world around them, continuing their thanks to God, the enemy who prowls like a lion to devour did not come near them in the lion's den. Jonah when the storm stirred the sea also said, "I fear the LORD God of heaven who made the sea and the dry land" (Jon 1:9). Paul spoke, "Men, why are you doing these things? We also are men, of like nature with you, and we bring you good news, that you should turn from these vain things to a living God, who made the heaven and the earth and the sea and all that is in them" (Act 14:15).

3. Compass Direct News, "Pakistani Muslim Forces."
4. Ehntholt and Yule, "Assessment and Treatment."

Chapter 7

In grief, but not despair, they continued the words that were a battlement against the world changing them. They spoke waves of faith against the current of the times, rested like sand absorbing the shocks of a mighty ocean, the weight and power of which is immeasurable, and remaining a boundary when currents returned on them. "Resist him, firm in your faith, knowing that the same kinds of suffering are being experienced by your brotherhood throughout the world" (1 Pet 5:8–9).

When mankind decided to build the tower of Babel to represent their own power, God came down and disrupted them by dividing their communities into different languages (Gen 11). After the Passover lamb was fulfilled, the disciples were again in the upper room under a waxing moon seven weeks later. The holiday was Shavuot, the spring harvest festival marking the Torah being given to the people. It was the feast of Pentecost that entered the summer solstice, growing the first fruits through the time of harvest. The 120 Jews in that room suddenly heard the sound of the breath of heaven filling the house. In Genesis when Adam was formed, he was a body, but had no life in him until God breathed life into him. In Acts 2 the body of the church was lifeless, not yet ready to influence the world. Jesus breathed his spirit into this body, filling them from heaven. They heard the wind, then they saw a pillar of fire that separated into tongues of flames coming to rest on each of them. It was a visible fire that does not burn, like the burning bush Moses saw in Exodus 3 when God revealed his presence.

Then they spoke in other languages they had never learned as the Spirit enabled them. A crowd gathered when they heard their own language. Everything that divided them from the time of Babel faded away. In their varied gifts and cultural knowledge, every soul broken and flawed, they were unified in gratitude for the one salvation. The immersion of the Torah declared that God would dwell with the Jews. The next immersion, the Holy Spirit, reunited humanity and now said that God will dwell in them. Even if the temple is destroyed, God had a place to dwell, a people who are seen in a glimpse in heaven as the vast multitude from every nation who Jesus had prayed would become one (Rev 7:9). The fire of God touched every believer, purposeful to use every one who comes to his son.

The trickle that began with twelve disciples, deepened and spread to the 120, then 3,000 and another 5,000 were added in chapter five. The river Ezekiel was shown began as a trickle from the temple grounds. There is no source for a river in the dry land, only God. The river is running, flowing, living water alive with the Spirit of God. He has given a new birth into a living hope (1Pet 1:3). There is an endless supply, never drying up, as it flows through all seasons of summer and winter, deepening and widening, unstoppable. From Jerusalem the trickle of Pentecost strengthened through Galilee and Judea, through the Roman Empire and out into the world, flowing, expanding, deepening.

> For the earth shall be filled with the knowledge of the glory of the LORD, as the waters cover the sea (Hab 2:14).

Tirelessly the ocean mounts up with wings and carries currents around the earth, splashing its jeweled salted drops, quenching the thirsting lands, carrying the travelers bringing the words of *Sha'ar Adonai* (The Gate of the Lord). "This is the gate of the Lord; the righteous shall enter through it" (Ps 118:20).

"Follow me," Jesus said to the two brothers, Peter and Andrew, while walking by the Sea of Galilee. Going on from there he saw two other brothers, James and John in the boat with Zebedee their father, mending their nets, and he called them. Immediately they left the boat and their father and followed him (Matt 4:18–22). "Follow me," Jesus said to Levi, sitting at his tax booth (Luke 5:27). "Follow me," Jesus said to Philip on his way to Galilee (John 1:43). He gathered his people. He gave them light so they could lift others out of the waters of judgment into his promise.

The call from heaven is merciful, falling upon God's people to walk in a way that lets the mercy bathe all of earth. Jesus said he would not leave anyone an orphan. His own disciples, who he called his children, would experience this sense of abandonment when Jesus was crucified and their world fell apart. Life without the one who cared and could lead was suddenly dark and forlorn. None could replace Jesus until the gift of his presence in the Holy Spirit returned to empower them. I will come to you, he had said. He asked the Father to give them a counselor, the Spirit of Truth, that would be all that Jesus had been to them.

As creation eagerly waits for the children of God to be consummated in the wedding of God's son, the oceans struggle to do their part in balancing nature to support life. Pollution has poisoned the dwelling place of marine life. Their food becomes toxic. When turtles come ashore they find their breeding grounds destroyed. Their offspring are poached to use the eggs for food. Arctic sea ice is shrinking by four percent each decade since the 1970s. The Antarctic ice has increased by 1 percent as the cumulative effects of an expanding human population raises carbon dioxide in

Chapter 7

the atmosphere. Needing more electricity, factories, cars, planes, and technologies, in their thirst for energy gases are trapping heat and raising the temperature on earth. Thousands more of plant and animal species will go extinct if there is not time to adapt.

All eight species of earth's sea turtles are threatened or endangered. The green turtle, loggerhead, hawksbill, olive ridley, Kemp's ridley, and leatherback live in waters under the US Endangered Species Act. The flatback inhabits the continental shelf of Australia's king tides. The black sea turtle, often considered a Pacific green turtle, hatches in beaches of Mexico and swims the southern Pacific Ocean from Chile up to California, west to the Galapagos Island and New Guinea, crawling from the shallows to bask on the rocks on the sunny islands of Hawaii.

God designed one ocean to move as a single interconnecting body of water encompassing the planet. Bordered by twenty-one countries of differing cultures and 150 million people living on the stretch of its coast, the Mediterranean Sea experiences intense fishing and millions of visitors. The Mediterranean is an enclosed basin frequented by three sea turtle species, loggerheads, leatherbacks, and green turtles.

Large numbers of Atlantic loggerheads enter this sea and share foraging with the leatherbacks and green turtles, but only the loggerhead and green breed here. Severely exploited in the fifty years between 1920 and 1970, fisheries off the coast of Israel, Pakistan, and Turkey have decimated their numbers. Several thousand clutches are nested every year, most in Turkey, Syria, and Cypress, but few young reach their maturity. Intentional killing especially after being captured at sea is still high in some places. They are being struck by boats, afflicted by pollution, ingesting plastic, and tangled in nets. All year the sea turtles are seen in abundance along Israel's coast then wounded and dead wash onto shore during nesting season. Several international conventions protect sea turtles in the Mediterranean and the Israel National Nature and Parks Authority established a conservation project in the Sea Turtle Rescue Center.

Jesus and his disciples saw turtle nestings numbering in the thousands. Today they number only several dozen. Breeding female loggerheads are estimated today at about a hundred, severely declined. Currents arriving on Israel's north shores move sand southward. Coming in at the south, waves cause sand to push north. Sand is trapped, beaches erode in the north, losing nesting sites. Only tiny particles of sand get through where the currents meet at the beach of Tel Aviv, changing the temperature regulating the sex ratio of the sea turtles. Construction of a dam, massive sand mining in the beaches, and construction along the coast and marinas displaces more sand and narrows the beaches for nesting. Turtles nest furthest up on a beach where the sand is driest.

The port city of Tyre on the southern coast of Lebanon is a sea turtle refuge in the Coast Nature Reserve, just south of the city. A place of nesting for the sea turtles since ancient times, the effort is changing their fate. Operation Litani in the 1970s and the Lebanon War in 1982 between Israel and the Palestine Liberation Organization badly damaged Tyre. Bombs continued in 1983, destroying buildings. Rocket launching sites were set up around the city during the 2006 Israel-Lebanon conflict. Established in 1998, the reserve now covers 940 acres of a public beach of yellow sand, the ancient port and archaeological zone, and the conservation area. Among the cattails, sea daffodils and sand lilies, the reserve hosts nests for migratory birds, the endangered loggerhead, green sea turtle, Arabian spiny mouse, lizards, pipistrelle and European badger. The reserve borders the Rachidive refugee camp, a Palestinian refuge south of Tyre. In 2006 there were 18,000 residents in the camps, hoping to return to their homes.

More than 2,000 years ago, before the Christian faith rooted in this region, Jesus visited Tyre and healed a Canaanite child (Mark 7:24). Crowds came out to hear him speak. Paul lingered here talking with the disciples.

The twenty-two Arab nations in the middle east now face more than a hundred natural disasters because of rapidly changing climate. The Arab Sustainable Development Report 2015 forecasts earthquakes, floods, and storms impacting more than 210 million people by 2019. The UN Environment Programme, UN Economic and Social Commission for Western Asia, and regional experts report an increasing trend in natural disasters, with corresponding increases in human and economic losses. The droughts already effecting tens of millions of people are expected to continue. Floods, storms, and rising sea levels come with concerns for fresh water shortage. High population growth rates and the rapidity of urban development drawing on water resources are exacerbating an unsustainable consumption depleting the region's natural resources. The nations also face housing shortages and high unemployment among young people. UN resident coordinator and United Nations Development Programme resident representative Peter Grohmann said one of the challenges is changing the attitudes of the people.[5]

---

5. Arab Forum for Environment and Development, "Natural disaster warning."

Chapter 7

Drilling cores from the ice in the Arctic reveals the layers that have recorded changes in the atmosphere, oxygen isotopes, methane, dust, and volcanic eruptions found in microorganisms such as foraminifera. Microscopic foraminifera, called forams for short, have lived in the ocean for millions of years. The skeletons from ages past are buried in layers as they settle on the seafloor, telling a story of how the ocean and climate have changed over the ages. Core drilling is showing the connection between climate and the shifting ocean circulation.

Through these long-term temperature and nesting data, the Kemp's ridley serve as sentinels. Understanding the temperature effect on the embryos in their eggs beneath the sand, determining if there will be a ratio of females and males to procreate the species, to the currents and toxins in the ocean, other species facing drastic change may be helped and human dependency on the ocean better understood. The turtle will face more troubles if water and air increasingly warms. A small warming increases the numbers of female hatchlings, but larger rises in temperature shift the timing and rhythm of their cycle, when they migrate and nest. Extreme temperatures can kill the hatchlings in their nests. Needing the help of people to place eggs in shade or in other sites, sprinkled with water to cool the sand, the sea turtle is no longer separate from human choices.

The UN is supporting the contribution youth make through the coordinated efforts of the UN Framework Convention on Climate Change (UNFCCC) Secretariat. Youth now have a voice in international climate change negotiations. The young are raising educational programs, planting trees, promoting renewable energy, and talking together about their beliefs in a tomorrow.

Existing only in conflict and intensifying awareness of the distress of a fallen world, a child's individual strengths must be sought and built on, specific to the needs of a girl or boy. With a far-off look in her eyes, in a backwash of what no one could share, Grace Akallo[6] testified to the UN of her experience as a child soldier in Uganda that began at the age of fifteen. She said it is "the worst thing that could happen to any young person. Not only does it destroy childhood, but what's worse, it destroys the future. Abducted when they are supposed to be in school, instead of learning math, they are forced to learn how to shoot an AK-47. They are forced to become killers or rapists. When, and if, they eventually return, they are left to deal with their guilt in a society that does not accept them. Personally, I was

---

6. Pruthi, "Grace Akallo."

one of the lucky ones. While I escaped after seven cruel months, many of my friends did not. Some were killed, others suffered from sexual abuse that resulted in unwanted pregnancies and HIV/AIDS. Their experience is beyond suffering."

Grace's generation faces threats of regional turmoil and climate change that impact their health and economic stability. Social and environmental awareness is uniting them. Crisis brings people together, a dynamic God uses to bring strength into relations. "Therefore we ourselves boast about you in the churches of God for your steadfastness and faith in all your persecutions and in the afflictions that you are enduring" (1 Thes 1:4). Rejoicing for each other, Paul could see faith enduring as the burden of tomorrow becomes shared.

Every morning Li Liang wakes up on his parents' farm near the Gobi Desert in China and wonders if the entire cotton crop was destroyed by a sandstorm the night before. "Every year there are sandstorms, and every time there is a sandstorm our cotton is destroyed and we have to replant it, which costs a lot," he said.

Youth are facing poverty and a lack of energy, food, and water as a consequence of how we are in relationship with each other around the globe and how we respect God's sustenance for the final generation. Emphasizing individual and collective responsibility, youth are looking at how changing human activities can help their future health. Corals and fisheries are being damaged by illegal over-exploitation. Invasive species and marine pollution from sources on land, increasing sea temperatures, rising sea levels, and ocean acidification pose more threats to life, coastal communities, and national economies. Criminal activities such as piracy and armed robbery of ships threaten lives of seafarers and international shipping that transports 90 percent of the world's goods. Smuggling of drugs and trafficking persons by sea further threaten the ocean's security.

China's desert lays across 25 percent of the country, expected to expand to 40 percent. In the high peaks of western China's Qinghai-Tibet plateau the glaciers are vanishing. Rivers are drying. Li, at nineteen years old, has seen changes where he lives.

"When I was a kid, the desert was five kilometers (3.1 miles) away, but now it's right here," he said.

Failing crops and scarcity of water are causing hundreds of thousands of people to be displaced from their homes. Li's family will have to change the crop they grow to one that needs less water. China is transforming with

Chapter 7

a rapidly growing economy causing it to be the world's second largest producer of greenhouse gases. The country is committed to new technology and planting grasses and shrubs across the desert's edge.

The generations pass understanding the truths in deeper ways. Churches can no longer be separate from the environmental issues threatening the future well-being of all young. Countries can no longer remain separate from the actions of other nations. The tsunami has passed, leaving a demolished mess of a once familiar landscape their elders knew. Facing visual and tactile realities, youth are seeing the global church progressing in steps toward the tabernacle's holy of holies, expressed on earth toward God and heaven.

The 1.2 billion youth on earth represent 18 percent of the world's population. Sixty-two percent live in Asia. Seventeen percent of youth are in Africa. About 64 percent of these African youth and 84 percent of Asian youth live among people surviving on less than $2 a day.

Every night an estimated 1 billion people go to sleep hungry. That means one in every seven people who need the harvest of earth the most are the ones who cannot access it. Left chronically undernourished, children find it hard to focus on studying, are weak in energy, and grow up unable to bear healthy children. Ethiopian mothers hold children in their arms who weakly cry for food but there is no breast milk to feed the baby because the mother has not been eating.

In Ghana youth have taken on a bamboo bicycle project. They are planting trees in Ethiopia, promoting use of vegetable oil for biodiesel in Barbados, supporting bicycle use by partnering with restaurants to give discounts to those arriving on bikes in Costa Rica. In the United Kingdom they are learning investigative journalism, reducing local carbon dioxide emissions in India, and establishing swimming lessons for emergencies in Bangladesh. In the Philippines youth prepare for natural disasters. In Madagascar they are cyclone proofing schools and nurturing leadership YouthXchange in the Mediterranean. Programs on sustainable development and skills based learning materials are being taught in Nigeria. Youth are being trained on climate change in Columbia.[7]

"A new commandment I give to you, that you love one another, just as I have loved you, you also are to love one another" (John 13:34) is finding new pathways as the ocean's plight brings youth of different nations to work together in shared concern.

7. UN Joint Framework Initiative on Children, Youth, and Climate Change.

Chapter 8

God created the great sea creatures and every living creature that moves, with which the waters swarm, according to their kinds, and every winged bird according to its kind. And God saw that it was good (Gen 1:21)

AM I THE SEA, or the sea monster, that you set a guard over me? (Job 7:12).
To whom then will you compare me, that I should be like him? says the Holy One. (Isa 40:26). The fish of the sea, the birds of the heavens, the beasts of the field, all the creeping things that creep on the earth, and all the men who are on the face of the earth will shake at my presence; the mountains also will be thrown down, the steep pathways will collapse and every wall will fall to the ground (Ezek 38:20).

Framed by high cliffs, the Sea of Tiberias is Israel's largest lake and earth's lowest freshwater lake at 700 feet below sea level. Also called the Sea of Galilee or Lake Kinneret, the lake is north of the Jordan River's flow. Furious squalls break over boats in the sea, coming in with unexpected surges of wind funneling through the hills, colliding the cool air with the warm descending to whip up the shallows. It was on the shores of the Sea of Tiberias that Jesus revealed himself to his disciples after he was resurrected.

After the crucifixion, Peter, dejected and deciding to return to the sea he knew, said to the others, "I am going fishing." They went with him and got into the boat. But they caught nothing that night. At daybreak Jesus was standing on the shore. This was the third time he appeared after being raised. The water that once flooded the entire earth now carried the voice of Jesus to those off shore. "Children, do you have any fish?" The breeze was blowing on the disciples as they looked up. They did not recognize him. "No," they answered. Jesus told them to cast the net on the right side of the boat. Probably sighing because they thought they'd already done everything

Chapter 8

they could, they cast the net. They were unable to haul it in because of the quantity of fish brought up. Then they recognized him. Peter exploded into this sea, rushing through the water to get to Jesus on shore.

Jesus instructed them to baptize others as they go about living their lives, immersing them into the community of God. Jesus would not bring about change my himself alone or all at once like in the days of Moses. The reach of salvation is a result of millions of souls each baptized into their part through thousands of years. "Whoever believes in me, as the scripture has said, 'Out of his heart will flow rivers of living water'" (John 7:38).

With refugees facing water and food scarcity wherever they go, prayer in the waiting moments ask God why have you forsaken me. Even Job wondered. The children of Israel groaned and prayed, and yet forty more years passed before God sent Moses. Then God's children were held in the wilderness as many generations died asking, God where are you? We know God is present because we have these stories.

In New Testament accounts, wherever Jesus showed up and said "Follow me," great crowds came to him, so many that he had to go out into a boat to speak to them and an invalid had to be lowered through the roof because there was no getting to Jesus through the doorway. Some were curious to know who he was, others in the mistaken belief he would lead the people into an earthly government, and some wished for healing.

Yet only a few followed.

When Jesus spoke of this, he said, "I tell you the truth, you want to be with me because I fed you, not because you understood the miraculous signs" (John 6:26). Jesus, feeding the 4,000 with loaves of bread, told the people, "The true bread of God is the one who comes down from heaven and gives life to the world." The people asked that he give them that bread every day. Jesus replied, "I am the bread of life. Whoever comes to me will never be hungry again" (John 6:33–35).

The growing need for food banks and monthly dinners churches are offering are bringing in an increasing number of people. Yet when Sunday morning comes, many pews are empty, heralding a downward spiral into discouragement. According to a 2007 survey by Dr. R. J. Krejcir at the Francis A. Schaeffer Institute of Church Leadership Development, 90 percent of pastors frequently feel worn out.[1] Eighty-one percent of 1,050 Evangelical and Reformed pastors said there is no regular discipleship deepening at

---

1. Krejcir, "What is Going on with Pastors."

their church. Only 25 percent of their churchmembership attended a small group Bible study.

Jeremiah preached for decades without seeing any result to pleading with his people to return to God. The issue is not whether we adequately bring a result. Dispersion of instructions is about obedience. Jeremiah knew what God called his people to be, but they didn't see it and would not be called back to God. They were left to judgment under the reign of Zedekiah. All God asked was that Jeremiah yield and do his will and now, thousands of years later, we are edified and blessed because of the prophet's words. Jeremiah said, "I only have a little strength." God says, "I know that you can't do this, but I can." The Father whittled the army of 32,000 who answered Gideon's call to a mere 300 to defeat the warriors of the Midionites so that God would be glorified for the deliverance (Judg 7:7).

The enemy is multiplying, as Jesus said it would. Around us we see the dependable few who are always there. But above, if we look up, we have an inestimable audience of angels who watch from the grandstand of heaven. Paul spoke of this to Timothy commanding, "in the presence of God and Christ Jesus and the highest angels" (1Tim 5:21). The angels who assisted Elijah in his weariness, carried a message from God to Daniel, escorted Lazarus to heaven, and ministered to Jesus in Gethsemane, are invested in God's relationship with us.

He asks that our prayers persist. From heaven God sent an angel to Daniel, but for three weeks that angel was resisted by fallen angels preventing him from getting the message to Daniel (Dan 21). But Daniel continued to persevere in prayer through those twenty-one days, seeking God's answer although unaware of the warfare of the archangel Michael, the guardian of Israel.

Angels provide strength when we are weak. Elijah, exhausted and oppressed, sat beneath a tree and begs God to let it end. He falls asleep (1Kgs 19). All at once an angel touched Elijah saying eat and rest.

Again an angel is sent when Jesus was in the desert in the time of temptation to attend him. At his life's end Jesus pours out his soul in the garden of Gethsemane, staggering at the cross he faces. He prays, nevertheless not my will but thine. An angel from heaven appeared and strengthened him. After the angel came, still in anguish Jesus prayed even more earnestly and rose decisively to face his betrayer.

Chapter 8

We are never alone. Those very same angels attend to us (Heb 1:14). When Jesus says, "Follow me," the angels watch a spectacular race as the day is won.

The great ocean conveyor loops back across the Pacific Ocean, passes by northern Australia, and rejoins the other branch in the Indian Ocean. The currents blend as they tunnel through the south Atlantic heading north where some of the current shifts west to join with the Gulf Stream in the Caribbean. North in the Indian Ocean, the island of Java rises out of the water as part of a spine of thirty-eight ocean volcanoes sending the ocean current around them. Living here with her family, twelve-year-old Dini was growing up Muslim.[2] The month of Ramadan arrived and she began her fast and prayed the *tahajud* prayer that asks God for signs. She wept, seeking God to show her the way to live and promised she would follow him if he would reveal himself to her.

Her father had died suddenly and she had learned he had an affair with his sister-in-law Sundari, who was pregnant. Her mother was also pregnant. Her aunt, who was helping the family, left town. When the baby was born, her mother placed three of her children up for adoption and moved Dini and the other children to the town of Semarang. Dini became involved with the wrong friends at school and began getting into fights. She began to question her life.

As she prayed, a bright light appeared in front of Dini. A man wearing a white robe moved toward her. She knew it was Jesus. He held out his hand. "Follow me," he said. Her heart melted and, although her family harassed her for the choice and she was forced to leave home at sixteen, she followed, each step reverberating into her eternity. The family eventually reconciled.

As the north Atlantic deep current approaches Africa's Cape of Good Hope a young Islamic man attended an Islamic school in Africa, training to become an imam.[3]

"In school, I only learned about Islam," he said. "Parts of our teaching were about destroying Christianity. So we did what we learned, by attacking Christians once we finished our training." The students were encouraged to steal from and kill non-Muslims. Every new church in town was a target of attack, to be destroyed and the Bibles burned. The young man was further trained in Saudi Arabia. He returned home and imposed a rule that no village leaders or visitors could preach Christianity in his town.

2. More Than Dreams.
3. P Janelle, "After Dreams of Jesus."

Then one early morning before dawn he encountered Jesus. It was 2002. "I saw Jesus very clearly telling me to follow him," he said. He woke startled and told his wife. They were frightened because believing Jesus meant they would be infidels. He returned to sleep and immediately, "Jesus appeared saying, 'It's me, follow me. When you follow me you will pay a price, there will be persecution in your life, but in the end you will be victorious. I am with you.'"

He visited a church, asking to meet with the leaders. They were suspicious, knowing his reputation as one of the most inflamed Islamic leaders in the region. But he told them about the dreams and they accepted him and prayed for him. The news was carried quickly back to his town. He and his family were considered as good as dead. In his culture, when someone is dead their property is shared. The town people set his house on fire and took his cattle and property. He was jailed on false accusations and taken to court but the witnesses were proved to be liars.

The young man, once like Paul who tyrannized Christians before his encounter with Jesus, helped bring hundreds of people to faith. "The Bible became my weapon," he said. "I traveled many places to preach and teach about the Christian faith. I planted a church right in the compound where I live and many people decided to follow Christ. As a result, local villagers were upset. So again, they attacked me physically and burned my house. The voice of Jesus himself spoke to me in my dreams about persecution, so I knew it was going to come and was ready."

The north current spins in enormous eddies for more than eighteen years around Cape Hope, carrying warmth from the Indian Ocean into the Atlantic. The eddies are undersea storms whirling more strongly than hurricanes. Phytoplankton thrives around the eddies as the storms bring up nutrients from the deep to feed microscopic animals which in turn sustain other lives for hundreds of miles. Turtles search for these floating storms, following the eddies as they pump heat and salt around the planet.

As the ocean spins around Africa, a young boy in Nigeria named Mohammed diligently studied the Qur'an and how to rear cattle, which is the main livelihood of Fulani men.[4] But frightening dreams began to terrify him. After each one, a man in white would appear, deliver him from harm and guide him safely home. Then a dream came where he found himself under a tree reading many books. The man in white appeared and asked Mohammed if he wanted help. He picked up one of the books and said,

4. More Than Dreams, "The Story of Mohammed"

Chapter 8

"This book is from God. It contains the very Word of God." He explained to Mohammed that he was the savior of the world of whom the book spoke. Jesus asked him if he wished to accept him as savior. Mohammed, remembering how he had delivered him from his nightmares and calmed his fears, said yes. When his father learned he had become a Christian, he ordered him to leave home. Several months passed and Mohammed did not renounce Christianity. His father ordered men in the village to surround his son and force him to drink poison. He survived but was banished from the village, ambushed with poisoned arrows, arrested, and spent time in prison. Mohammed's father then tried to persuade him to abandon Christian faith by offering cattle to pay for a bride. Mohammed thanked his father for his generosity but continued to stand firm, saying nothing else can give him eternity.

A few years later Mohammed got word that his father was ailing. When he visited, his father apologized for the many times he tried to harm him and all that that was said against him. He assured his father he was forgiven. They spoke of Jesus as his savior. Three hours later, reconciled and knowing Jesus, his father died.

At our death angels will escort us to heaven. Jesus told the story of Lazarus who lay begging at a gate of rich man. When he died that poor man who the world deemed a failure was accompanied into the holy presence of God. Jesus reaches through the battle between light and dark when the swells are so strong carrying out to sea to places only angels can reach.

When Khalil was a child he began memorizing the Qur'an. As he matured he hardened into an Islamic fighter and received military training in a desert of Yemen. Khalil joined a group committing terrorist acts trying to overthrow the Egyptian government. Having decided that military practices were not practical in defeating Christian missionaries, the group's leaders assigned Khalil the task of writing a book to discredit the Bible and find passages that foretell the prophet Mohammed. Having an interest in searching God's words, Khalil completed the assignments, cross-referencing with the Qur'an. He discovered there was no mention of Mohammed in the Bible. Miserable with doubt, he wrote his conclusions. The leader threatened to kill him if he shared his findings with other Muslims. Khalil had become a *kafir* (infidel).

Praying for truth, Khalil went into a deep sleep. A man came to his dream and told Khalil he was the one Khalil was seeking. He told Khalil to read the Bible and that it could never be lost. Khalil's life changed course

A New Song

as the sun rose on a new day and he sought out nearby Christians. Washed in the water of baptism, Khalil's past fighting was swept away as he transformed into an instrument of righteousness.

> For God so loved the world, that he gave his only Son, that whoever believes in him should not perish but have eternal life (John 3:16).

Having our bodies washed with pure water, we can be confident in the great high priest who resides over the house of God (Heb 10:21–22). He is always near when we call for him to bring mercy, asking to "listen in heaven your dwelling place, and when you hear, forgive" (Kgs 8:30).

The threats encompassing the life of a child bereft with the disappearance of a parent brings a strange maelstrom of darkness. There is nothing familiar any longer. A child knows no way to mourn or make sense of their world. The millions of young refugees separated from family are torn with incredible stress, interacting with the world around them through a veil of uncertainty. The tangle of weeds in the bottom's darkness float up threatening to drag them under. People can be violent. Loved ones can disappear.

Families fleeing together and rebuilding a life fare much better than the lone child. But family members are shaken and suffering too. Memories of being tortured rage through their entire being. The world of the voyagers has been swept away leaving a chasm of emptiness at their feet. Life will never be made right in the way they knew it. Belonging to the collective that is the struggle of all believers promotes the well-being of God's promises. Reaching to touch a Bible, anguish is swept with new vision. Only then do they hear their own story.

Thoughts will wander to those already waiting on the dock of heaven's shores, knowing, with David's faith, that they will not come back, but we will go to them (Sam 12:23). Jesus told his Father that he wants us with him in heaven. He wants us to be transformed fully by the glory we now only glimpse by reminding each other that we are bordered within God's desire for us to make it all the way home. We are tabernacled by him in the shelter of a boat helmed by a skillful savior.

"Keep your voice from weeping, and your eyes from tears, for there is a reward for your work, declares the Lord, and they shall come back from the land of the enemy" (Jer 31:16). Though in pain we bring forth children, his promise will restore these children, transposing the wild winds into soft fluttering, waffling the waters with song when the light of truth comes. He is our bright Morning Star. Jesus has chosen his bride.

Chapter 8

Jesus told the story of an owner of a vineyard who hired laborers in the early morning, and more laborers came in the late afternoon. They both got paid the same. It wasn't fair, some complained. "Do you begrudge my generosity?" the owner asked. It is not fair, the children say. Losing homes and family while others prosper in safety. It is not fair, the adults say. Persecutors who harmed God's believers are now accepted and blessed. In the parable Jesus was telling us that God is not about fairness or none would survive. God is about mercy. Our life here on earth is about mercy.

Therefore I hate every false way (Ps 119:104).

For a thousand years the Israelites sang of the Messianic images written in Psalms 22, 23, and 24. Not yet knowing Jesus, but knowing God would deliver, David's inspiration echoed the longed-for promise. Growing up as a child among the people, Jesus knew these Psalms. Jesus sang of his own coming unbearable pain. "Why are you so far from saving me, from the words of my groaning?" (Ps 22:1).

> As his voice lifted in song, he would be thinking of us.
> The afflicted shall eat and be satisfied;
> those who seek him shall praise the LORD!
> May your hearts live forever (v26).

Parading down the streets of Tel Aviv, Christians were singing songs of praise to the Lord and giving out lapel pins that read "Israel You're Not Alone" to the Israelites who came out of their shops to greet them.[5] Traditional Jews, Moishe and Esther Cohen, came out of their jewelry store when they heard the singing. They had survived the Holocaust and arrived in Israel in May 1948. "I can't believe the songs you are singing," Moishe said. "These are the same songs, I hear every night in my dreams." For three months he had a recurring dream that he is awakened by the sound of shofars and trumpets. In the dream he runs to the front door to see what is happening. Thousands of people from the nation of Israel, wearing white robes, are ascending up through the clouds as the heavens are parting.

"That is when I see the heavens opening and the Archangel Gabriel and a mighty army in the sky dressed for battle. Their commander is riding upon a white horse and his eyes are a flame of fire. Riding behind their Commander are the Jewish patriarchs, Abraham, Isaac, and Jacob. Behind them are the Godly Jewish women, Miriam, Ruth, Sarah, and Queen Esther. Then I see King David and King Solomon and with them the prophet

---

5. Schwartz, "Orthodox Jew in Tel Aviv"

Elijah and his servant Elisha. They are all alive. Light is shining from them. They are riding horses."

Moishe sees the army of the Lord numbers into the tens of thousands descending from heaven to the Mount of Olives in Jerusalem. The Commander wears a Hebrew tallit which says "King of Kings."

"He has fire in his eyes. I suddenly realize I am seeing our Jewish Messiah," Moishe said.

He asked the Lord, "Who are you?" Jesus replied, "Moishe, I am the one the prophets spoke about." Moishe asked if he had a name. Jesus said, "They call me the Champion." Then he said, "Moishe, I died for you. I love you. Tell your Jewish family and your friends about me. Tell them I am coming soon. For there will be worship and praise in all Israel just as it was in the days of King David." Moishe woke up with the words ringing in his ears, "Moishe, I love you. I am coming soon."

The pastor of the visiting worship team read him Revelations 19, when John saw the heaven opened and beheld a white horse. The rider's eyes were as a flame of fire. He was wearing many crowns.

"Yes, it is him," Moishe said.

Chapter 9

He made the storm be still, and the waves of the sea were hushed (Ps 107:29)

BENEATH THE SURFACE a combination of movements bring the ocean a pulse in a rhapsody conducted by God to regulate weather, support rivers and fields, and absorb the sun's radiation. The waters brought people together and with them, non-native species. In one century people, plants, animals, and sea creatures alike mixed together across the ocean. Europe's green crab hitches rides in the ballast water of ships to both coasts of North America, to southern South America, Australia, South Africa, and Japan where it is a predator of mollusks and worms on the shores. The sea walnut, a stingless kind of jellyfish, is native to the east coast of North and South America. It was found in the Black Sea in the 1980s, washing into the brackish waters of the Caspian, the Mediterranean, Baltic, and North seas. Multiplying into enormous populations, the sea walnut collapsed local fisheries by feeding on the fish's zooplankton. The large veined rapa whelk was created to live in the Pacific, from Russia to Hong Kong. It made its way on ships to the Black Sea in the 1940s, spreading into the lagoons where it colonized and preyed on mollusks. In 1998 it was found in the Atlantic's Chesapeake Bay. Zebra mussels spread up canals, reaching the Baltic Sea passing into Denmark, Germany, Poland, Finland, and up the St. Lawrence River into the Great Lakes, fouling power plants, littering beaches with decaying mussels, devouring plankton, and reducing food available to the native species.

He has divided the sea by his power (Ps 74:13).

The ocean has no sympathy. It cradles the newborn, buries the old, powers the earth, remembers no one, hides mountains, explodes into tsunamis, moving with eternal grace following only God's instructions. In softest hues, then a fury of rioting, golden sunrises and silver with the moon, it births earth and carries sailors to its depth. A kaleidoscope of relationship come from its unity with the sun, the wind, and clouds. Pushing huge quantities of water, an underwater landslide, an erupting volcano or an asteroid falling into the ocean rushes tidal waves to spread in all directions. Rising up to forty-five feet crossing the ocean at speeds of 65 mph, the waves carry an entire column of water from the surface to its deep where the floor is moving and displacing the water. Successive waves converging toward shore scale the beach in a tumult pulling water ahead of it back into itself. Pulling away from the shore, building higher to break again with enormous force, the ocean magnifies its power in a wave that can last hours engulfing entire shorelines and dragging its spoils out into its body.

It is both God's expression of the promise of strength and a dirge of mourning playing for the dead. Then swiftly it pitches into a new repertoire with the meter of a *klezmer* dancing at a wedding. Its harbors open doors that only the Lord can open and no one close. In Smyrna on the Aegean coast a port joins Greece and Turkey, leading out to the Mediterranean Sea. Revelation speaks to the church in Philadelphia, a city by the harbor of Smyrna, a gateway in and out to the entire world connecting too to the Marmara and Black seas. The message from Jesus tells them he has placed before them an open door that no one can shut (Rev 3:8). They have a unique opening to testify to the world, but little strength. Living through hardship, entirely dependent on the Lord, they took his word and boarded ships that sailed under a wind moving at his perfect timing to reach another person. The enemies and hypocrites would be washed away. "I will make them come and fall down at your feet and acknowledge that I have loved you" (v9).

The exiled will soon be set free, and will not die in the dungeon, nor will his bread be lacking. For I am the LORD your God, who stirs up the sea and its waves roar (Isa 51:14).

In spring 2015 an ISIS fighter was zealous in slaughtering Christians until a man in white appeared to him in his dreams and said, "You are killing my people."[1] He confided in a worker with the international evangelical group Youth With a Mission that he began feeling sick about what he was doing. One day he stood in front of a believer, about to kill him, when the man said, "I know you will kill me, but I give you my Bible." The ISIS fighter

---

1. World Net Daily, "Isis Fighter."

Chapter 9

took his life and took the Bible. He began to read it. He had another dream and Jesus asked the fighter to follow him. He became a disciple.

The unprecedented number of visions and dreams speak of a hunger in these fighters who stood against the Christian faith. They meet secretly like the early church once had to do, in grief for believers being slaughtered, in prayer that brought the leadership skills of men like Paul into the fold. ISIS targets and kills anyone not allegiant with them, taking the women and children to sell into slavery. But they are not beyond the reach of Christ. Scripture says the waters will bring forth abundantly and the people will swarm against each other, breaking to pieces as they are vexed with adversities (2Chro 15:6).

> The nations roar like the roaring of many waters, but he will rebuke them, and they will flee far away, chased like chaff on the mountains before the wind and whirling dust before the storm. (Isa 17:13–14).

But as for you, be strong and do not give up, for your work will be rewarded (2Chro 15:7).

The sea washes away every trace of wrong footsteps taken across the sand. The power that raised Jesus from the dead is the power that raises from the immersions, leaving the wrongs to sink out of sight. Put off the old, scripture instructs. Leave it at the bottom of the ocean. Grace clasps us, holding us up the way Jesus held Peter's hand to walk on wind-roughened water. In the full light, as if standing above the expanse of water that separates heaven from the earth, we rise from baptism to be under his wings. Tabernacled by his heaven arching over us, led by the covenant that carries his instructions, his bread of life, the rod of the shepherd to part the pathways before us, we walk through enemy territory, guided to springs of living water.

Sea turtles hold relationship to the beaches and the ocean. The wondrous life in the intertidal zone is revealed when the tide pulls out. Coming in again the ocean gives itself to the plants, splashing over the lichen and algae on the rocks, and barnacles that hold on as the force of the waves bless snails and shore crabs, bringing in seastars and anemones to graze on the algae.

If Emunah's kind become extinct, both systems will weaken. Kemp's ridley is the rarest of sea turtles, with specially adapted flipper-like front limbs and a beak to complete its underwater work, especially balancing the crab populations. Sea turtles are one of only a few animals who eat sea grass that constantly needs cutting to help it grow across the sea floor. Sea turtles and manatees graze on these grasses, gardening the bed for others who depend on the fields for breeding and juvenile protection. Without the sea grass, many species will be lost and with them, the lives who depend on them for food. Beaches of sand retain few nutrients. Grasses and flowers don't grow well here. Sea turtles climb onto shores and lower the dunes as they create a nest, collectively laying more than 150,000 pounds of eggs in the sands. Eggs that do not hatch become nutrients for the dunes and plants are able to grow stronger. The coast becomes healthier. Without the turtles the coast would be unstable, erode without the deep rooted plants, and become unable to host wildlife.

The ocean divides the continents yet joins them together. The Lord set the bounds to restore borders to nations. "As for the western border, you shall have the Great Sea, that is, its coastline; this shall be your west border. And this shall be your north border: you shall draw your border line from the Great Sea to Mount Hor" (Num 34:6–7). Willing to cross the water, some saw the vast liquid as a bridge that carries God's words, shares stories from other parts of Christ's body of people, weaving together a tapestry of faith.

The Norse, Portuguese, and Spaniards explored beyond their coasts. Erik the Red discovered Greenland in the 980s. In year 1000 Leif Ericson left Europe to set foot on North America, which later became the province of Newfoundland in Canada. The ocean became man's history. It documented his crossings, the navigators sailing along the western African coast in 1415, Magellan crossing from Spain to the South Atlantic in 1519, sailing the straits named after him to enter the Pacific Ocean. By the seventeenth century entire families facing European persecution for their convictions about Jesus were boarding ships and crossing winter's rough Atlantic, cramped and crowded below decks, coming to form new colonies of religious freedom. The people wanted heaven to be vital in their new life as the ocean carried their hope. The seas became our map, marking ports established for people to meet. It marked the war when the RMS Lusitania was torpedoed on its way to Queenstown, Ireland, suffering the loss of 1,198 passengers. It measured our achievements. In 1927 Charles Lindbergh made the first solo non-stop flight across the Atlantic, flying from New York City to Paris. Adventurous spirits continued the ocean's legacy. In 2003 four people made a record 103 hour crossing in a RIB from Newfoundland's north Atlantic to Scotland through Greenland and Iceland.

Chapter 9

The water provided a corridor for trade routes and communication was established. Voyagers were forged by the fire of storms and learned not to be lulled by the calm of the sea. The ocean became the highway between Europe and America developing economy into the twenty-first century. Science began to make discoveries through the Challenger expedition, German Meteor expedition, and the US Navy Hydrographic Office.

The waters were harvested for their bounty. Nearly 100 tons of marine fish are caught each year, not including fish discarded as bycatch.[2] Coral reefs provide food and other resources that support 500 million people. Fisheries in the salt waters became severely emptied, once abundant with cod, haddock, hake, herring, and mackerel. The banks of Newfoundland, the Nova Scotia shelf, Cape Cod, the Bahamas, water around Iceland, the Irish Sea, the Dogger Bank of the North Sea, and the Falkland Banks provided eel, lobster, and whales in great quantities. Toxic waste, overfishing, oil spills, and trash brought death. Industrial fish farms brought worries about nature's health.

In the North Sea 184 rigs drilled offshore in 2015, some able to penetrate wells 40,000 feet. With the Arctic ice melting, oil companies are poised to bring in more drills.[3] The industry has pierced more than 100,000 wells exploring for oil since 1988, threatening coral reefs in thirty-eight countries. Streams of pollution from offshore rigs have harmed the ability of marine life to reproduce and inhibits kelp beds and coastal wetlands. Drilling fluids and metal cuttings were dumped into the ocean, each drill dumping 25,000 pounds of toxic metals like lead, chromium, mercury, and carcinogens like benzene into the underwater world. Pollution blows into the air.

In the UK and Norwegion sections of the North Sea, an estimated 1.3 million cubic meters of drill cuttings and wastes have built up the seabed in 102 piles of a massive 2 to 2.5 million tons. The ecological effects extend for miles smothering seabed life and turning the water noxious. To remove cuttings that have settled on the sea floor could release concentrations of pollutants into the water's currents. It is hoped they will be buried by the silt and mud.

All along the rim of the Atlantic's communities concerns are turning toward use of the ocean. Ship pilots speak of navigating safely among new wind farms. Fishermen and lobstermen want to protect fishing grounds as

2. Woods Hole Oceanographic Institute, "Know Your Ocean."
3. Culture Change, "No Offshore Oil Drilling."

industries speak of the need to tap the ocean resources. Listening to each other, they try to find a balanced answer.

Science's ARGO floats are bobbing under the ocean all around the world in more than 3,000 places. As a float moves through a water column, sensors record pressure, temperature, and salinity. After nine days, it drops down another 1,000 yards and records that depth. As it climbs up to the surface it continues recording and transmits the information to research centers by a satellite. The scientists use the data to map changes and reveal the warming trend. As the climate changes, warmer water expands and the ocean begins taking back its islands. Even a small rise alters coasts across earth effecting both land and marine communities.

The Arctic is especially vulnerable to temperature because as snow and ice melt, land and ocean surfaces absorb more solar energy. Traditional views of the Arctic as a non-navigable region are beginning a shift as earth's rising warmth melts glaciers and diminishes Arctic sea ice. Most models predict the Arctic will experience ice-free conditions for a portion of the summer by 2030.

Because ice cover cools air and water, plays a significant role in ocean circulation, and reflects solar radiation back into space, weaker and thinner sea ice has the potential to change currents in the entire ocean. Indigenous Arctic people are facing relocation and loss of community as ice melt erodes shoreline and melts permafrost. Populations like the polar bear are starving into extinction. Flora and fauna are experiencing extended growing seasons and the Arctic is hosting new species migrating northward with shifting weather.

The Arctic contains 10 percent of the world's known petroleum reserves and about 25 percent of its undiscovered reserves. The US exclusive economic zone has a potential of thirty billion barrels of oil reserves and 221 billion cubic feet in natural gas reserves. Minerals in the Arctic include manganese, copper, cobalt, zinc, and gold. Coupled with a rise in global demand for natural oil, gas resources, and improved accessibility, the Arctic has become a new focus for oil companies looking for untapped resources.

The warming in the Arctic region may improve the availability of certain resources, but it will redistribute others. A change of fish stocks will cause changes for indigenous Alaskans who depend upon the sea for subsistence. Resource planners and policymakers will need to examine new ways to manage open areas of the Arctic, balancing multiple uses.

Chapter 9

Shipping and transportation will benefit. The Northwest Passage and Northern Sea Route will both be navigable for longer periods of time during the summer, and may be used more often for commercial shipping. The Northern Sea Route would reshape into shorter distances between Northern Europe and the Far East in comparison to the Suez or Panama canals. Surface-vessel access to open water areas within the Arctic will gradually increase from the current few weeks a year to a few months a year.

Despite present good relations among Arctic nations, the area is a source of potential international conflict as countries seek to identify regions to which they can lay claim. The new Arctic will host multiple competing uses by many countries, now governed by the United Nations Convention on the Law of the Sea. The convention protects the national security, environmental, and economic interests of all nations, codifying the navigational rights and freedoms that are critical to American military and commercial vessels. In 2016 there were still overlapping, unresolved maritime boundary claims between the United States and Canada, Canada and Denmark, Denmark and Norway, and Norway and Russia.

The change in the ocean presents unique opportunities for the US Navy to develop partnerships with other nations, such as Russia and China, on research like hydrographic surveys. The long term potential in a changing Arctic is being assessed for the lack of supporting infrastructure, environmental hazards such as drifting sea ice, communications difficulties, antiquated nautical charts, low visibility, all hindering safe navigation. More search and rescue operations would be needed. The only American-owned deepwater port near the Arctic basin is Dutch Harbor in the Aleutian Islands.

The changing climate opening waters of the Arctic is bringing more human activity and altering policies on homeland security. The Arctic Region Policy that directs the departments of State, Homeland Security, and Defense to develop protections for US borders also projects a sovereign American maritime presence with other Arctic nations. The key to its success is cooperative partnerships with interagency and international stakeholders that will improve the Navy's capability to assess how the ocean is changing the Arctic.

The ocean is tasked with absorbing excess heat from the atmosphere and stores heat equal to the earth's entire atmosphere in its top layer. As the planet warms, the ocean takes in the extra heat. If the ocean gets too warm, its plants and animals will try to adapt or they will die.

A New Song

At the beginning of the food chain, the tiny animals, plants, and bacteria called algae and plankton float and drift through the ocean. Small animals like krill are sustained by the plankton. Fish, whales, and seals feed on the krill. Some places in the ocean krill populations have dropped more than 80 percent because the ocean warmed. Krill like to breed in really cold water. If the krill are harmed, the entire food chain unravels.

Coral is a fragile animal that builds a shell around itself and lives with colorful algae. The algae make food from sunlight and share the food with the coral. In turn the coral harbors the algae in a safe and sometimes sunny place. Fish come and swim here to find safe hiding places. But when the water becomes too warm, the algae cannot carry out photosynthesis. The algae dies or the coral spits it out. The corals lose their colorful sustenance and become weak. Known as coral bleaching, this is happening on a grand scale around the earth.

As the great ocean conveyor belt is driven by the balances of water density, too much fresh water melting into it on either side of Greenland where the Gulf Stream waters cool and sink would lower the ocean's salinity. The waters would no longer sink and the Atlantic north current and Gulf Stream could shut down in a few years time. Science does not know how much fresh water it would take to shut down the conveyor. The last two abrupt coolings in the Greenland ice core, the "Younger Dryas" event and the "8200 years before present" event, both happened when Lake Agassiz, a huge glacial lake in central Canada, melted and flooded down the St. Lawrence River into the North Atlantic as ice dams broke. The overturning circulation slowed as the fresh water puddled on top of the ocean. After about 1,100 years, during the Younger Dryas event, the current suddenly restored, for reasons scientists don't yet understand.

The currents moving on the ocean surface distribute heat around the planet. The North Atlantic Current and the Gulf Stream ferry volumes of warm salty tropical water northward to Greenland's coast and the Nordic Seas as the heat radiates off the water to keep countries of northwest Europe comfortably livable. The cooling of the North Atlantic, perhaps by the turn of the century, could trigger a disruption to the ocean's entire circulation pattern.[4] The impact on climate would be profound. Scientists are observing the overturning circulation current, mapping and charting its course, and creating models of possible scenarios. Data suggests that as less warm water flows north across the equator, the southern oceans will warm and

---

4. Schiele, "Ocean Conveyor Belt."

Chapter 9

the ocean around the equator would shift south. Belts of rain would follow. Decreased downwelling would leave the deep ocean with less oxygen. Decreased upwelling would carry fewer nutrients up from the bottom.

Israel's arid landscape set between two seas will see sea levels and rain patterns change with climate shifts. The Israel Ministry of Environmental Protection's 2009 report, "Adaption to Climate Change in Israel—Recommendations and Knowledge Gaps," developed a plan to begin the Israel Climate Change Information center in 2011. Climate will effect health and the spread of disease. Conserving God's natural spaces, coordinating plans to control invasive species and vectors with neighbors, and green architecture to increase sustainable living are listed as ways to mitigate impacts on the ocean's currents. The Sea of Galilee is experiencing colder water inflows from lake tributaries that are changing the stratification of cold and warm waters as demand for fresh water increases.[5] Water-saving devices and collecting rainwater top the list.

While most of earth's surface is covered by water, 97.5 percent of it is saltwater. Israel has a long experience contending with water scarcity. Desalinating the saltwater became important. On the forefront of technology, Israel scientists began exporting desalinating technologies in the 1960s, including vacuum freezing vapor compression. The scientists became the core of the government-owned Israel Desalination Engineering Co. which now is held privately as IDE Technologies. IDE deployed 400 plants in forty countries that together bring two million cubic meters of potable water every day. In Israel IDE launched the world's largest sea water reverse osmosis plant opened in 2005 on the coast of the Mediterranean Sea.

Water is the world's most rapidly vanishing resource.

The Sea of Galilee's large stocks of fish are a thing of the past. Jesus and his disciples frequented the Galilee village and Jesus produced huge catches for his disciples. It was a thriving fishing village with many of his followers, including Mary of Magdala. In 2010 Israel's Ministry of Agriculture banned fishing in the sea because of dramatic declines in stocks. Remembering the abundance of tilapia and the now vanished cichlid fish, the Ministry made plans to restore stocks to the country's fresh water lake.

Archaeologists from Israel's Antiquities Authority digging on the shores of the Sea of Galilee in 2009, a precautionary measure before a building project began, uncovered an ancient synagogue. It holds a large stone altar with intricate carvings on the outskirts of the city called Magdala in

5. Research Gate, "Long term stratification."

the New Covenant, today known as Migdal.⁶ It would have accommodated about 120 people. The synagogue would have belonged to a small sect of a spiritual community, speculatively a place Jesus came and taught. He traveled from place to place with his disciples (Luke 8:1–3) often meeting in small groups (Luke 10:38–42). Rabbis would regularly visit local synagogues and discuss scripture in community meeting places (Matt. 4:23).

He may have spoken about our tendency to postpone our transformation and remind that God will not contend with man forever (Gen 6:3). Faith became sight here, bringing the thirst of remorse to people seeing the barrenness of their own spirit. They would have bowed to his holiness, knowing well that Isaiah had said to seek the Lord while he may be found. They would have gone out to the villages with him as he preached, healed, and recognized others who belonged to his flock. "And wherever they do not receive you, when you leave that town shake off the dust from your feet as a testimony against them" (Luke 9:5), warning not to become dust that God shakes off.

For you are a people holy to the Lord your God. The Lord your God has chosen you to be a people for his treasured possession, out of all the peoples who are on the face of the earth (Deut 7:6). I will bless those who bless you, and him who dishonors you I will curse (Gen 12:3).

The Jewish people descended from Abraham and Sarah's son, Isaac. The Arabs are descendants of Ishmael, Abraham's son with a slave woman, Hagar (Gen 16:1–16). An angel spoke to Hagar, telling her that Ishmael would be the father of a great nation (Gen 21:18) but his hand would be against his brothers (Gen 16:12). Ishmael grew thinking he was the heir to Abraham. Suddenly he was displaced as an outcast in the desert when Isaac was born. Muhammad descended from the tents of Abraham through Ishmael and gave rise to the Muslim beliefs that haven't received the blessing of God's authority placed in Jesus. The destiny of the Arabs and Jews are irrevocably tied together.

Reconciling at the confluence of Jesus, a new generation of Arabs and Jews meet speaking a new language of thankfulness for redemption. In November 2016 at a three-day council to pray about how to bring the word of God to their peoples, 260 pastors, youth leaders, evangelists, and ministry leaders came together embodying decades of their labors proclaiming the Christ to Arabs and Jews. Despised, shunned by family and friends, they have lost jobs and homes, but their joy is complete. Cold-blooded murders

---

6. Israel Today, "First Messianic Jewish synagogue."

occurred in a Jerusalem synagogue on the last day of the gathering. Cowardly acts of violence rage in the city. But their focus never wavered from God's prophetic words. The land and the people belong together. The return of the Jewish people to their promised land propelled Arab and Jew to share the word of God with urgency. All agreed that he will come and faith will unify believers.[7]

God's promise of a land, known as Canaan when Moses arrived, stretched "from the desert to Lebanon, south along the Red Sea, the Euphrates River to the east, Syria's border to the north, and the Mediterranean Sea to the west (Joshua 1:4). This land has belonged to the Jewish people ever since God declared it to be so.

When God fixed the moon in its orbit, out of reach of the enemy's hands, he appointed the entire story of redemption to be told through the sky's movements in Leviticus 23. Revealed in the cycle of the seven feasts, from spring's Passover bringing the sacrifice of the lamb, through Unleavened Bread, First Fruits, and Pentecost bringing the church age into the summer solstice and months of new births and harvest. Jesus directed eyes to be watchful of the waxing and waning of the moon telling the story in the gatherings. The fall festivals are yet to be fulfilled. Trumpets foretells the sound of Messiah's return, the ten days of Atonement that speak to the coming thousand year reign, and Tabernacle that follows when he dwells with us. No matter where on earth or what battles rage, the moon is with us, reminding the entire story of redemption is moving toward earth's next immersion, the Lord's ingathering of the Jews.

The ingathering, *kibbutz galuyyot* is followed by *mizzug galuyyot*, the merging of the exiles, a day the Talmud says will be as great as the day heaven and earth were created. The return is called *aliyah*, meaning to ascend. Aliyah referenced the pilgrimage ascending to the temple in Jerusalem for the biblical feasts of Passover, Pentecost, and Tabernacles. Making aliyah is a spiritual journey, a return to God as he draws his people back to their land and himself.

Told of by Isaiah, Jeremiah, and Ezekiel, the promise is given that God will bring each individual back to the land of their forefathers. First exiled to Babylon, then again when the Romans forced another dispersal out into the world for nearly 2,000 years, the Jews are the only people who are brought back to their homeland twice after being violently scattered. More than 3.5 million Jews have returned in the twenty-first century, speaking

---

7. Lazarus, "Arabs and Jews Unite."

many languages from countries in the north, south, east, and west. Their Hebrew language is being revived to speak the words of their forefathers.

Fulfilling prophecy precisely, during the emergency lift of about 15,000 Ethiopian Jews in May 1991, five mothers gave birth on planes flying to Israel. Jeremiah told of the return including "the woman with child and the one who labors with child, together" (31:8-9).

Isaiah spoke of their coming at the end of days, first by sea and then by air. "Who are these that fly like a cloud, and like doves to their windows? For the coastlands shall hope for me, the ships of Tarshish first, to bring your children from afar" (Isa 60:8-9). The ships are in the lead, first bringing the Jews into the port of Jaffa, where Jonah had set sail. Driven out of Russia and Eastern Europe, they streamed across the Black Sea. Britain developed a port in Haifa and more Jews came out. Ships rescuing the people from Hitler ran for shore at night, sunk deliberately on sandbars as they swam for their land.

After 1948 when Israel became independent, the ingathering began bringing thousands more home by plane, into the port of Ben-Gurion Airport. God sovereignty was demonstrated, gathering with great mercies despite the world's resistance to the Jews and their homeland. He invites believers to be excited in this and share the effort toward fulfillment.

The Lord "who gives the sun for light by day and the fixed order of the moon and the stars for light by night, who stirs up the sea so that its waves roar" will not see the offspring of Israel cease from being a nation.

> If the heavens above can be measured, and the foundations of the earth below can be explored, then I will cast off all the offspring of Israel for all that they have done, declares the LORD."
> (Jer 31: 35-37).

Sailors and scientists have observed the seas for centuries from the shore and from ships that could explore the seven percent that is surface, and then from satellites. Scientists learned that they could leave instruments submerged in the ocean, secured by wires, buoys, weights, and floats. Each new attempt advanced understanding of the ocean and its interaction with the planet. The next leap will be ocean observatories—suites of instruments with long-term power supplies and permanent communication links that feed data to laboratories in real-time.[8] Motivated by advances in computing, telecommunications, and marine architecture, researchers no longer

---

8. Woods Hole Oceanographic Institute, "Ocean Observatories."

CHAPTER 9

want to just observe the ocean for short periods in small places. They will use technologies such as satellite communications, acoustic modems, and fiber-optic cables stretching hundreds of miles across the seafloor to ask questions of the planet, such as how ocean chemistry affects biology or how the geology on the seafloor affects the physics of flowing water. Observatories will allow scientists to adjust experiments and talk to their instruments from hundreds of miles away in shore-based laboratories.

But we will never know all the mysteries of sky or water before Jesus returns.

PART 4

The Sea of Glass

FINDING FREEDOM

By Sienna Woodhall

Grade 11, Little Flower Academy, Vancouver BC 2015[1]

> Run my people run.
> In the inky darkness of the night
> They move swiftly
> North East towards freedom
> Through forests, across deserts
> Away from their homes
> Little hands grab for toys left behind
> The big hands grab chain fences
> Over and under; around or straight through
> As long as they go undetected
> The only constant is their fear
> It clouds their thoughts
> It haunts their dreams.
> War has an iron grip on their country
> Everyone struggles to breathe
> Their towns are peppered with bullet holes

1. UNHCR Canada, "Refugees and Human Rights Poetry Contest."

And salted with bomb debris
So they slip away
Melting into new horizons
Being unwanted guests in unfamiliar places
Life outside is still an uphill battle
It is so easy to give up and quit
But run my child run
So yours don't have to.

Chapter 10

"Where is your faith?" And they were afraid, and they marveled, saying to one another, "Who then is this, that he commands even winds and water, and they obey him?" (Luke 8:25)

FROM HIGH IN THE crow's nest sailors first seeing the Sargasso Sea thought it to be an island. Bounded by clockwise moving currents, the Sargasso Sea is a long 2 million square mile body of salt water in the Atlantic. Its western coast is the Gulf Stream. The North Atlantic Current to its north, Canary Current to the east and to the south the North Atlantic Equatorial Current define its borders.

Canopied by a mass of floating seaweed that stretches for miles, the Sargasso is a deep blue refuge for life on the high sea. Swimming through the paths leading Emunah through the ocean, she must navigate rubbish from people's lives trapped in the gyre's cycle. Aerosols leaching lead are captured in the encircling currents for decades before spinning out into the Gulf Stream to be carried and spit out on distant shores. About 50 percent of lead isotopes concentrated in eddies on the surface of the Sargasso are from industrial and automotive contamination in America. Most is from the early 1990s, decreasing after 1992 when use of leaded gasoline was reduced in the states.

The currents are trashed with tons of plastic swept into the ocean every year, equivalent to five big trash bags piled onto every inch of coastline around the world. Fish, dolphin, crustaceans, all of sea life swim through the human garbage, getting cut, drowned, or slowed by being tangled and dragging its weight. The garbage is swept into the most remote locations of the ocean, fouling the bottom of the sea floor, suspended in water columns, floating on the surface, lying on beaches.

Sofas, clothing, and computers made with chemicals to prevent them from catching on fire are thrown away and traces of the chemical leach into landfills. The rain comes and the winds, carrying the chemicals into streams and rivers that flow into the ocean. Filter feeders like mussels and oysters that live in both saltwater and freshwater draw in the surrounding water to feed on microscopic food. They expel filtered water and waste back out, leaving the hundreds of chemicals to build up in their tissues.

Plastic is not biodegradable but ages in the light and heat of the sun breaking it into tiny pieces that are perceived as food. Birds mistake it for plankton or fish eggs and feed it to their young, filling their stomachs as they starve and die. Deep sea fish eat the bits of plastic. It's also on the route for migratory birds dependant on the region for food.

The endangered Bermuda petral and the cahow fly throughout the Sargasso feeding on squid and fish. White-tailed tropic birds, masked boobies, and bridled terns concentrate near the patches of seaweed drawing global conservationists to converge with interest. It's a place of great beauty bestowed on all countries, where the ocean quiets its waves to offer a placid nursery to the young. Endangered eels return to breed swimming in from North America, Europe, and North Africa, as well as white marlin, porbeable shark, and dolphinfish (mahi mahi) coming here to spawn. Humpback whales swim through the sea every year on their way to and from the Caribbean and North Atlantic. Basking sharks come in winter.

Hatchling loggerheads leave their sunlit natal beaches in the south to come to the tranquil water, entering the Gulf Stream where they'll grow to 200 pounds crushing lobster and shellfish in their jaws. One of two species in the genus Lepidochelys, Emunah's relative is the olive ridley sea turtle which has an estimated nesting population of 800,000 females. Kemps's has declined to a known 1,000 nesting females.

After Emunah hatched she swam to the calm warmth of the Sargasso Sea and floated amid the beds of seaweed. Sargassum are clumps of algae the winds and currents concentrate into a faith haven for the newborn. The small yellow grapes of the sargassum are air bladders that keep it floating in the middle of its sea. The seaweed needs no support from rock or land. The ocean is its roots as the seaflowers let go of material desires to live and move and have their being by propagating by fragmentation. Other seaweeds begin life on the floor of the ocean. Species ready to flower reach up to the light, flower, birth its fruit, and sink down again blooming in shades of purple and red.

Chapter 10

God provided the sargassum community with layered places for each life. Each has need to be still and allow growth before swimming out. Smaller fish like filefishes and triggerfishes hide safely in the algae. Larger members such as young jacks, amberjacks, tuna, and dolphinfish are found under the algae. Big predators such as dolphins swim deeper in the water column.

Sea turtles spend nearly all their lives submerged beneath the curtain of water. A single exhale and quick inhale replaces the air exchanging oxygen in their lungs and preventing gasses being trapped during deep dives. Emunah occasionally catches a Portuguese man-of-war as the jellyfish sails past.

Even in its stillness the clear blue water is imposing, awesome even when a small white sun renders faint light on a bleak day. Coastal creatures find habitat here. Shrimps, crabs, worms, and fish, many who are camouflaged with matching colors, use their fins to crawl through the seaweed forest. Young tuna hide from a clamor of sea birds circling overhead. The planehead filefish is abundant.

Turtles use the sargassum as nurseries for the young to spend years in the pool of calm away from storm-tossed waves, just finding food and shelter, learning the currents, the light from the sky, and recognizing the predators in the darkness, here where the boundary of the sea is water, not land. Growing strong in the Sargasso community, Emunah's shell turned greener on a diet of swimming crabs.

> Stand therefore, having fastened on the belt of truth, and having put on the breastplate of righteousness (Eph 6:14).

Sin's shadows reside in the world around us like water laden with toxins that continue its currents despite the trash. "But you were washed, you were sanctified, you were justified in the name of the Lord Jesus Christ and in the Spirit of God" (1Cor 6:11). Stepping in to catch the wind in the sails, unwilling to stay on shores of unrest, the colors of faith nailed to the mast, waves of sanctification wash over what lies behind and strains forward to know more of God. It led John into captivity on the hilly island of Patmos hemmed by the Aegean Sea. Wearied and dusty, John was graced with a vision of where he would soon be. Sitting in a cave, wearing worn stained clothing, he sees the gloriously pristine white robes of every person in heaven who struggled through the world. The robes had all been cleansed, washed clean in the blood Jesus shed on the cross. Every person had left behind the days of unsolved problems and filth in the world to be brought into the presence of God. Not letting even the betrayal of Judas occupy their words, the disciples looked forward to how God is molding the kingdom, teaching, learning, and hearing. "I press on toward the goal," Paul said. The more he tasted of the living waters, the more Paul thirsted as it transformed him with satisfaction. Although all the currents of the world would become unclean, Paul saw the sea as a way for the word to bring drops of cleansing water into the world. If by the spirit you put to death the deeds of the body you will live (Rom 8:13).

The result is eternal life (Rom 6:22).

Describing heaven in a way we could understand, the patriarchs said the throne transcends every created thing with sovereign power. God reigns over the nations. He is seated on his holy throne (Ps 47:8). In heaven everyone stands in attendance (2Chr 18:18) and even angels are accountable (Job 1:6). The throne room is the source of created life and eternity (Rev 22:1). It is a place of justice as well as a place of mercy (Heb 9:24). Only the purified will be able to stand here, where Jesus sat down at the right hand of the throne of God (Heb 12:2). It is a place filled with praise for the one who occupies the throne (Rev 14:3).

We move in time breathing in a vanishing world. Moses came before God with a mind trained in the significance of maintaining knowledge throughout the generations. "Lord, you have been our dwelling place in all generations. Before the mountains were brought forth, or ever you had formed the earth and the world, from everlasting to everlasting you are God" (Ps 90:1–2). Our days are swept away in the flood of time. We are turned to dust. Moses asked that God's glorious power be shown to the children and establish the work of their hands. He was grateful for this attribute of God extending beyond pain and time. He considered the treasure of every day we are given, requesting his people learn to measure their days to make a difference to eternity. Then he asked for a life satisfied with God's mercy.

Moses called the people to gather. Isaiah called the people to heal and reconcile. The Prince of Peace came with a sword, calling the people again as he gave John the warnings of the final judgment. The disciples from Galilee had more opportunity to interact with the world, living on the sea, and called people into the spiritual battle. All prepared a way for us to turn over the pages of our story.

Chapter 10

The ocean's expanse far exceeds the land that emerged, retelling the mikveh that from the founding of creation brings relationship with the Creator.

In the UK the number of new churches increased by nearly 1,000 of several denominations in the years 2008 to 2013 with expectations of continued growth in Scotland, Northern Ireland, Wales, and England.[1] From here ships crossed the stormy Atlantic, carrying thousands of women, men, and children who vanished into the misty horizon. Unforgotten, survivors of the voyages built homes and towns on another shore.

In the United States in 1847, at the height of Ireland's famine, Congress passed a bill declaring overcrowded ships or ships with even one fever would not be allowed to enter the country. After already being on ships for months, the passengers were redirected up the coast to Canada, which could not reject any ship from British ports. A hundred thousand fever ships came in 1847, landing in tidal currents of cold water as ground fog blew in over the rocky shore. The death rate of refugees from the Great Hunger was one in four. As the ocean carried the ships inland up the St. Lawrence River, Canada set up a quarantine island on Grosse Isle, *Oileán na nGael* (Island of the Gaels). The island hosts mass graves of an unknown number of Irish victims. Estimates range from 3,000 to 30,000 people buried here. Among them was a four-year-old, Ellen Keane, the first to die that year. The casualties became so overwhelming that eventually the names and the numbers were no longer recorded.

> Know well the condition of your flocks, and give attention to your herds (Prov 27:23).

The words of Christ prevailed and took anchor in North America. The slow silent drift of erosion wore away boundaries as time slipped into a new century. Neighborhoods of the churches no longer resembled the original mandate of truth. Guidance once steadfast began a cultural decay.

Having died, beaten and crucified for our lives, Jesus now watches how the sanctity of life is weighed in the courts. By October 2015 euthanizing humans was legal in the Netherlands, Belgium, Columbia, and Luxembourg. Assisted suicide is legal in Switzerland, Germany, Japan, Albania, and in the US states of Washington, Oregon, Vermont, New Mexico, Montana, and California. Canada's Supreme Court unanimously ruled in Carter v. Canada that adults who are mentally competent and suffering intolerably

---

1. Evangelical Alliance, "How many churches."

have the right to kill themselves with a doctor's help. The Canadian Conference of Catholic Bishops and the Evangelical Fellowship of Canada stated that this compels each person to reflect on their personal response to those in need of compassion and care.

"While Canadian society continues to affirm the importance of human dignity, there is a worrisome tendency to define this subjectively and emotionally. For us, human dignity is most properly understood as the value of a person's life before her or his Creator and within a social network of familial and societal relationships. We are convinced the only ways to help people live and die with dignity are: to ensure they are supported by love and care; to provide holistic care which includes pain control as well as psychological, spiritual and emotional support; and, to improve and increase resources in support of palliative and home care."[2]

In Toronto a Muslim from London, England lay in a hospital bed dying from a virus from shingles.[3] He knew that Allah does not heal. His hope was in medicine. Barely conscious, he heard the doctors say, "His immune system has simply shut down. In a few hours he'll be dead." They left the room. He lay there alone. In a whisper he pleaded, "God, if you are real, don't let me die."

During the dark of the night he woke to see a man standing at the foot of his bed. Emanating rays of bright light, only his outline could be seen, but he knew it was Jesus. The Qur'an mentions Jesus as a prophet, but not as the son of God.

"Why would you come to a Muslim when everyone else has left me to die?" he wondered. Without words, Jesus spoke understanding into him. "I am the God of the Christians. I am the God of Abraham, Isaac, and Jacob."

When he woke in the morning, the fever was gone and he was regaining strength. The doctors released him to go home.

Humanity's communion with those who are suffering relies on the value Jesus places on sunken treasure. Jesus is drawn toward the sorrowful. Our bodies are buried in brokenness, but they will be raised in glory. They are buried in weakness, but they will be raised in strength. The trumpet will sound and his people will be transformed into imperishable bodies. The mortal will put on immortality.

Fallen standards that followed decay have root in many possible causes. The image of preachers living a life that does not line up with their

---

2. Canadian Conference of Catholic Bishops and The Evangelical Fellowship of Canada.
3. World Net Daily, "Isis Fighter Follows Jesus."

own teaching, harsh judgments on the world around us, too easy an acceptance of the immorality in the world, all leverage reasons not to worship the living God. It can take a one-time feeling of being shunned or a long history of mistreatment. If the breach is not acknowledged, a person will settle into the hurt and never return. The 2.7 million church members that leave church every year go away hurting and wounded.

A fifteen year study by the Francis A. Schaeffer Institute Church Leadership Development questioned why churches changed. By 1992 the body of Christ appeared to be culturally irrelevant. Church membership had dropped about 10 percent in the 1980s, and another 12 percent in the 1990s, and even more twenty years later. Combined membership of Protestant denominations fell by nearly 5 million members from 1990 to 2000, a 9.5 percent drop, even as the US population expanded by 24 million,11 percent. In 1900 there had been twenty-seven churches per every 10,000 people. By 2000 there were eleven churches per 10,000 people. If churches kept pace with population growth, there should have been 38,000 new churches. Yet half of all the churches did not add any new members.

In February 2015, New Life Research reported that America is launching new Protestant churches faster than church buildings are closing.[4] More than 4,000 new churches opened in 2014, compared to the 3,700 that closed. An average of 42 percent of those coming to the new churches had never attended worship or hadn't attended in many years. Among the characteristics of this success is in meeting in a public space, such as schools or other accessible places. The new churches stress outreach, offering social gatherings and children's events. They are focused outward on the community, rather than stopping growth at the focus on problems inside their buildings. The cornerstone for growth is in vision that constantly seeks the will of Jesus.

The greatest growth is in Messianic Jews, forming congregations around the world that grew from none in 1967 into the thousands.[5] "For he himself is our peace, who has made us both one and has broken down in his flesh the dividing wall of hostility" (Eph 2:14). Quietly beneath the surface, a current runs through humanity thirsting for heaven, aware how distant we've become from relationship with the Creator, wanting to have their lives restored and made strong in the light, especially for the unborn now exposed to mercury, asthma, birth defects, and cancers

4. Green, "Study: Thousands of Churches."
5. Jaben-Eilon, "Messianic Jewish Groups."

The last commandment of the New Covenant again calls the people to the water. "And let the one who is thirsty come; let the one who desires take the water of life without price" (Rev 22:17). The message of Jesus cannot be rationed or it is ineffectual. People would feel no change, never knowing the power in the body of Christ.

Building a church of disciples is wholly a reverence of God's every word. "He put a new song in my mouth, a song of praise to our God" (Ps 40:3). The song comes inexplicably musical in a gift to man and angels singing upon heaven's shores. Instruments and rhythms may change music, architecture may change from cathedrals to a storefront, but what the first believers in God spoke uncompromisingly persists in its effectiveness on the human heart. Their influence spread far beyond the temple. Prophets were seen standing alone, and there among his people, and over there he is talking among his enemies. In every snapshot his eyes are on the Lord. His ear is tuned to the one voice. The church will not lead the culture if they are not equipped by the Holy Spirit, presented to God as approved, rightly handling the word of truth (2Tim 2:15).

Have Christians forgotten the battle? The government and courts are pushing to erase Biblical principles from religious education. Forcing believers to separate from the world and band together more strongly to protect the young, California proposed Senate Bill 1146 to limit religious exemptions that colleges and universities use to hire instructors and conduct student services in their faith. The colleges would be eligible only for training pastors and theology teachers. Institutions would be constrained from requiring students to attend chapel services, keep bathrooms and dormitories male and female distinct, teach students religious ideas during regular coursework, hold corporate prayer at events like graduation, and every practice that distinguishes a religious institution from secular education. It would also impact students who depend on grants to attend the school of their choice.

California has 281 accredited four-year colleges and universities for students to choose among. Of these, only forty-two are religious. The bill is not about a lack of options or tax-payer funding. Pushed by LGBT activists, it is about changing what is perceived as acceptable.

"The most troubling provision of this bill limits the religious liberty to integrate faith and learning throughout the educational experience," said Dr. Kurt Krueger, president of Concordia University Irvine, in a letter about this bill.[6] "The bill effectively eliminates the religious exemption under current law that allows Christian colleges and universities to operate in accordance with their beliefs, including the freedom to hire only Christian faculty and staff. If passed without amendments, the new law would also very likely disqualify students attending California Christian colleges and universities from eligibility for Cal Grants, a key state-level student aid program."

"This third I will bring into the fire; I will refine them like silver and test them like gold. They will call on my name and I will answer them; I will say, 'They are my people,' and they will say, 'The LORD is our God'" (Zech 13:9). Believers have words that hold power in their nation, speaking about the impact of wrong choices, of the mercy of God to bring back Israel nationally and the church individually. Within the greatest commandment of the law is the attribute of those who can lead through every current and every wind. "And you shall love the Lord your God with all your heart and with all your soul and with all your mind and with all your strength" (Mark 30:31).

Jesus called James and his brother John "Sons of Thunder" (Mark 3:17), the sound described when heaven announces a drenching rainfall to water new growth and fill mikvehs for cleansing. Coming with the voice of God, they gave the truth that Jesus had brought from heaven. When heaven was opened for John to see, he heard a voice like the sound of many waters, like the sound of loud thunder, and a voice that was like the sound of harpists playing on harps. He saw flashes of lightning, He heard the voice of a multitude of people sounding to him like many waters, like mighty peals of thunder saying "Hallelujah! For the Lord our God, the Almighty, reigns" (Rev 19:6).

What is the way, we ask as we look around for what can save. The way has not changed. The commission to guard against erosion of God's values by planting seeds and heeding the thunderous overtures bringing rainfall has not changed (Mark 4:19).

When God saw the fall of creation, he saw the sorrow that would preside over his creation, the oil spills, the extinction of entire populations, the betrayed relationships, and decay of mankind's soul. Turmoil surrounded his beloved Israel. Syria, Lebanon, Jordan, Saudi Arabia, Iran, Hamas, Islamic Jihad, Hezbollah, and others are in conflict with Israel. An enemy rises whenever Israel exists as a nation. Throughout ages the destroying

6. Scheer, Holly, "California Bill."

angel has tried to defeat God's plan through Israel, from Sennacherib, king of Assyria, Hitler spearheading the Nazis, to Rouhani, President of Iran. ISIS is thought to have escalated out of Iraq in western Asia and Syria on a continent bounded by the Arctic Ocean to the north, the Atlantic to the east, the Southern and Indian oceans to its south, and the Pacific Ocean to the west. Troubles wash in on the waves of a tainted ocean, taking expression on February 16, 2015 when ISIS sent out a video, "Warning: Message Signed in Blood Coming Soon to the Nation of the Cross" with a picture of Christian blood staining the ocean waves.[7] Taunting the enemy to fight the battle so ISLAM can establish world rule, they stir chaos against Christians and Israel. Twenty-one Coptic Christians in Egypt had already been beheaded on a beach in Libya.

> It will be a sign and a witness to the Lord of hosts in the land of Egypt. When they cry to the Lord because of oppressors, he will send them a savior and defender, and deliver them (Isa 19:20).

Looking down at all the formalized prayers, the false words, the sacrifices, the council of heaven said this is not what is required. When the fullness of time had come, God sent his son to live on earth. Jesus said to God, "I have come to do your will." The magis, watchful of nature's movements, saw what appears to have been a comet, and went on a long journey across rough terrain because God had called them to worship Jesus. Angels flew to shepherds out in a quiet field to tell of the most magnificent change in all of history. Today across the Middle East near to where these angels announced God's grace and the magis walked, ISIS and others are announcing their oppression with force and cruelty.

But Jesus had said, "It is finished." There is nothing any people group can add or take away from his perfect obedience. "I am the way, and the truth, and the life. No one comes to the Father except through me" (John 14:6). We are justified the moment we hear Jesus call our name.

For nearly 1,400 years the call to the Muslim prayer expanded across earth with a goal to dominate. Today about a billion Muslims stand in resistance to Christianity's historic attempts to reach them. In a sudden harvest, Arabic Muslims are turning to Christ. North Africa Muslims, countries in the Gulf, in Europe, Canada, the United States and Middle East, young and old, male and female, the rebels and the peaceful, are being baptized in an immersion from heaven never before witnessed.

---

7. Shoebat, "ISIS Sends Out This Message To All Christians."

Chapter 10

In North Africa a young teenager struggling with her health began having dreams of Jesus in a white robe comforting and reassuring her.[8] Not until forty years later, when her daughter became a follower of Jesus, did she think about these dreams. She was reading the Qur'an searching for truth all the while feeling an oppression on her spirit. One day she asked Christians she knew to pray for her. She also sent an email to a televangelist asking that he pray for her. That night she dreamt it was thundering and lightning in a violent storm that lit up her room. She saw Jesus then he disappeared. She couldn't speak and couldn't move to turn on the light. Jesus appeared again and now she could switch on the light and shout thanks to God for bringing her to Christian faith. When she visited her mother and shared the story, her mother had a dream that a man was knocking at the door. She told her son to be ready for the knock and to open it when the man came, dressed in a white robe, asking, "My son, do you want light?"

Jesus, once a stranger to these other lands, has become a visitor in their dreams and now the host of their faith. Then we will no longer be infants, tossed back and forth by the waves, and blown here and there by every wind of teaching and by the cunning and craftiness of men in their deceitful scheming (Eph 4:14). Then the members of the body are joined and supported under Christ. Paul, between beatings, prisons, and shipwrecks, thought out the process as he wrote the first eight chapters to the Romans. He talked of no one being righteous before God. Salvation is received only through faith. Abraham was righteous because of his faith. Systematically Paul addresses the mystery of redemption. At the end of chapter eight he summarizes saying in all things we overwhelmingly conquer through Jesus whose love neither death nor any created thing can separate. The doctrine of eternal security is in the Messiah.

To be sanctified is to be chosen for a mission with God. "They are not of this world, just as I am not of this world," Jesus said. Declaring that Jesus has become our wisdom from God, (1Cor 1:30), the intricacies of working out sanctification is a process trusting God through each experience. Praying for us he said, "As you sent me into the world, I have sent them into the world. For them I sanctify myself, that they too may be truly sanctified" (John 17:18–19). He outpoured his Holy Spirit in abundance, an unstoppable flow that seeks out the depths and upwells praise to the throne room.

The first cup Jesus shared with the disciples at his last Passover seder is the cup of sanctification. "Take this and share it among yourselves," he

8. Ross, "Muslim Woman Receives Jesus Revelation Through Vision."

said (Luke 22:17). The second cup is the cup of judgment remembering the rescue from the plagues that God sent when the Pharoah refused to release the people. When Jesus said, "This cup is the New Covenant, ratified by my blood," he referred to the third cup after the meal of the Passover seder, known as the cup of redemption. The people lift their cups and say, "*Ba-ruch a-ta Adonai, Eh-lo-hay-nu meh-lehch ha-o-lahm, bo-ray p'ree ha-ga-fen. Amain*"

Blessed are You O Lord our God, King of the universe, creator of the fruit of the vine. Amen).

"I tell you I will not drink again of this fruit of the vine until that day when I drink it new with you in my Father's kingdom" (Matt 26:29). This is the fourth cup, which is the cup of praise.

> Now may the God of peace equip you with everything good that
> you may do his will, working in you that which is pleasing in his
> sight (Heb 13:20–21).

Gifts both natural and those God's spirit bestows equip the local body to carry out Christ's work in his global plan until he returns (1Cor 12:7). Each life brings a unique strength.

"Follow me," Jesus says, "and I will send you out to fish for people" (Mark 1:17).

It is God who remembers when we are brought low. He reaches through the rising waters of judgment to pull us up to feel the first warmth of light's touch. You now are the light, he says, in a hostile world trying to take you down again. Some will support the cleanliness of the environment, the water that allows life to thrive. Others fish for the souls to guide through smothering toxins, as if piloting a ship across every mood of the ocean. In all the destruction laying death at every door, the Lord's truthfulness and power raises gifts in an abundance of light in every generation. His men and women stand guard at his gates of the river of life ushering God's people. Each receive their gift as stewards of God's varied grace (1Pet 4:10). The salted tears that drop when a heart is moved, when it flickers like a fire laying in bed at night, lead to the ministry that calls. Jesus assures there is a plan. Jeremiah wept as he looked at his people. Jesus wept when he looked on Jerusalem. "Those the Father has given me will come to me" (John 6:37). James answered the call and admonished to look intently into the perfect law that gives freedom and continue in doing it. If anyone lacks wisdom, let him ask God (Jas 1:5–6) Paul told Timothy not to neglect the gift he was given through prophecy with the laying on of hands by a plurality of elders (1Tim 4:14). Refresh the purpose through continuous cleansing, dying daily so we don't stop the current of the spirit. It may not always make sense. Peter was freed from prison while James was put to death with a sword. It was not the plan James had begun life with, but it was he who beseeched believers, "Be patient, therefore, brothers, until the coming of the Lord." Know that for those who are called by God, all things work together for good.

Summer mornings the sun rises over Oak Island off the North Carolina coast giving its light over the Sargasso Sea for fourteen hours before lowering beyond the coast. The ocean is at low tide as the moon follows the sun with light, bringing in a high tide before setting after midnight. Emunah swam above the shipwrecks that litter the southeast coastline giving off foreboding tones beneath the ocean.

Testimony of mankind's warring litters the world's ocean. Fish swarm around the wreck of the HMT Bedfordshire, an Arctic trawler that had been converted into an anti-submarine warship during WWII and sank off the coast of North Carolina. Early in 1942 war raged off the shores in the dangerous reefs of the southern coast. The water lit up by explosions blasting the residents into constant fear of enemy soldiers landing on the beach. Four German U-boats along with Allied war ships and many merchant vessels lay capsized beneath rolling waves. The estimated 20,000 US wrecks scattered in the Atlantic and the Pacific and aircraft carriers in Lake Michigan whose waters flow to the Atlantic are a fraction of the sunken ships around the world. Often breaking apart, airplanes and ships leak fuel and chemicals into the water, washing through the currents. Hazardous materials smolder with potential threat to a healthy system supporting healthy life. Ships of antiquity lay on reefs and ocean bottoms in a jungle of sea animals, hundreds of feet down where surgeonfish glide among sea whips. A ship from the third century that held gallon wine jars from Rome 2,200 years ago now grows coral bouquets and hosts fish among its crevices. Ships by the dozen found from thousands of years ago, laden with furniture, pottery, bronze statues, busts of philosophers heads, and marble pillars. Merchant ships hold bags of coins, wine, Etruscan helmets from 120 BC, one with a skull still inside, astronomical instruments from 50 BC, warships from the time of Antony and Cleopatra, sunk to the depths to be discovered by scuba divers and sponge divers.

The Sea of Glass

At the crossroads of the Aegean and Mediterranean seas the remains of a first century Greek trading ship was discovered near Crete.[9] An excavation in 1902 brought up a wealth of discoveries. Three life-size marble horses, jewelry, coins, glassware, and hundreds of works of art, including a seven-foot-tall statue of Herakles were discovered. More than seventy years later, Jacques Cousteau was invited to explore the wreck. His team recovered hundreds more artifacts plus the remains of four people. A hunk of bronze was found to be a complex set of interlocking gears capable of predicting the movement of the sun, moon, and several planets, as well as the timing of solar and lunar eclipses years into the future. Named the Antikythera Mechanism, it is believed to be an early computer used to plan important events including religious rituals, the early Olympic games, and agricultural activities.

The water is an infinity of stories and light, sound and scent whispering of an unknown place able to dissolve all our pain, our tears not even a drop in this magnitude of power. The ocean bids in rising, falling waves like flickering doorways that open to the paradise of God. Again the tree of life is attainable and melancholy songs change tempos into dancing. The glimpse of this glory filled with brilliantly colored stones and crystal jasper is so beyond our ability to describe that John could not tell us more. We long to cross this gap and be face to face with the Lamb of God (Rev 21:12).

Heaven's piercing light shines all the way to the buried who lay beneath the water, lost at sea, farther than our natural light can reach. In a twinkling of a moment, even here God's children from all the ages will be lifted and transformed to be like him (Phil 3:21). When Jesus calls, "rise up," there will be no pollution or toxic oil covering then. They will see face to face, the king of glory, mighty in battle (Ps 24:8), his eyes blazing with flames, his hair white like snow, his feet like burnished bronze, wearing a robe that reaches his feet, and a golden banner across his chest (Rev 1:13–15). His voice is the sound of many waters as he says, "Well done good and faithful servant." Even in the deepest places of the ocean's trenches he says, "Follow me." "Come, blessed of my father, inherit the kingdom prepared for you from the foundation of the world" (Matt 25:34).

---

9. Woods Hole Oceanographic Institute, "The Antikythera Shipwreck."

Chapter 11

Here is the sea, great and wide, which teems with creatures innumerable, living things both small and great (Ps 104:25)

THE OCEAN WEARS THE sky's moods, morning's violet, moon's luminous glow, or the jeweled sapphire of midnight, breathing upon the land, and taking commandment only from heaven. Sunrise pours new hopes upon her, winds carry the enchantments with the tears of the drowning, fed from the deepest calm, foaming with the torrent of restlessness. Ocean mineral water blends the countless lives within sending out wave upon wave of their longing at the steps of our souls. Fresh wind exhales fragrance from the sea, knowing no boundary where yesterday and tomorrow meet. Unfathomable depths descend into nightfall where God's care alone is able to sustain.

Buoyed on the surface, ships carry passengers across the mysteries beneath as they find their way home. Underwater crop circles made by male pufferfish to attract a female decorate the bottom; nautical rivers of fresh water meet salty and the differing densities separate into layers; thousands of active volcanoes spitting out steam erupt every year to create new islands; maelstroms in devouring whirlpools that suck down everything in reach; brinicles that are ice stalactites on the sea floor caused by cold sinking brine freezing and extending outward killing anything in its path; and red tides of algae bursting into blooms excreting toxins that affect the central nervous system of fish, mammals, birds, and humans.

Faith is the perfectly designed ark instructed by God to Noah 4,000 years ago, built to float but not to be steered by man. The word used for ark was the same word used for the basket that held the infant Moses safely in the water while he waited to be lifted out (Exod 2:3–5). Sailing upon an ocean gathered when the flood abated, passing frost flowers forming on thin ice, all of creation is in waiting to be saved from a world of tyranny. Voyagers stand witness to the hand of God, impressively striped icebergs around Antarctica created when an iceberg falls into the sea and a layer of salty water freezes underneath, green stripes if it's rich in algae, blue when ice melt fills a crevice. The underwater waterfall in the Indian Ocean as sand and silt run off the island of Mauritis and waves draw it out and pull it downward off the shelf build a new stretch of land for the searching to gaze out upon the sea. Currents criss-cross where waves traveling different directions are sent toward shore in a lattice of anxiety crossing with words of assurances. The same source that brings songs of victory troubles the waters with warnings to take heed, be faithful unto death.

God's words accomplish what he sends them to do, however long in his time. It may take hundreds of years, like the huge spherical stones called moeraki that stand on the southeast shores of New Zealand. The ocean forms the boulders on its bottom over centuries, lifted in its embrace to display on the beach. Magical new worlds are experienced, green flashes on the horizon, optical phenomena of light after a sunset. Or a rogue wave suddenly rising in open water when high winds merge with strong currents into a single force disrupting our seafaring days with an unexpected threat. Waterspouts cross paths as ghostly spirals of wind skimming across the sea surface. Others pull the water up into a funnel climbing toward the sky and go inland as tornadoes.

The tidal flow slacks as the water decides to change direction and ebb back out. Rolling with light, the waves settle silt on the floor as a groundswell of memories bring up the storms of struggle. Overlapping washes of blues and reds creating history move toward the sound of a trumpet splitting the sky as God's people are gathered to Zion, the city of the living God where countless angels will be in joy with the firstborn.

The number of people on the Mediterranean Sea fleeing war and poverty in Africa and the Middle East is surging. In 2015 an estimated 1,800 migrants drowned making the trip in overcrowded and unseaworthy vessels. By 2016 nearly 22 million Syrians had left their homes. More than six million sought refuge in the neighboring countries of Turkey, Lebanon, Jordan, and Iraq. Forced displacement in Europe rose from 4.4 million at the end of 2013 to 6.7 million a year later, largely Syrians in Turkey and Ukrainians in the Russian Federation. Seeking asylum, most make their way to Germany and Sweden.

Chapter 11

As Germany tries to sustain the 1.1 million who sought shelter there in 2015, food scarcity and the volume of reports of violence and sexual abuse of women, children, ethnic groups, and homosexuals multiplied in the temporary shelters.[1] Iraqi refugees choosing to risk the return home grew to more than 200 by year's end. Rape and abuse had become a culture that is thought to be widespread in asylum centers everywhere.

The UN calls the crisis in the Mediterranean "a tragedy of epic proportions" and calls on the European Union's response for protecting victims and bringing compassion and aid to an unprecedented number of dispossessed people. Many refugees begin their journey in the backs of trucks which smugglers use to transport them through the desert and into Libya. They are left to wait in small houses where they may be vulnerable to abuse, especially the women and children. Some are held in detention until they can pay for the crossing. Others don't survive their search for safety, their lives streaming behind them in a splash of tinseled blue light and turbid shadow. Three-year-old Aylin was found dead, face-down on the rocky surf after a boat capsized on its way to Greece to find a way to Canada.[2] His mother and five-year-old brother drowned.

Children sleep on train station floors and sidewalks, fearing Hungary will intern them in camps. Greek towns fill with tents and humanitarian workers waiting for the rickety boats that arrive daily at the shores. Every day more join the millions who already fled their home countries knowing they may never return. In Syria, nearly 5 million people, nearly a fifth of the country's population, have left since war began in 2011 when Bashar al-Assad's regime began targeting civilians with chemical weapons and barrel bombs. ISIS enslaves their lives with murder, torture, crucifixions, and sexual slavery. Jabhat al-Nusra tortures and kills them. The UNHCR details how in region after region, the number of refugees and internally displaced people is on the rise. Since 2010 at least fifteen conflicts have erupted or reignited on the continents: eight in Africa; three in the Middle East; one in Europe (Ukraine); and three in Asia (Kyrgyzstan and several regions of Myanmar and Pakistan). Two United Nations agencies, the UN High Commissioner for Refugees (UNHCR) and the UN Relief and Works Agency (UNRWA), safeguard their rights and well-being. Many are women and many are children. Arriving at overcrowded reception sites, gathering

1. Justice, "Germany: Iraqi migrants."
2. Moyer, "Aylin's story."

in parks, train stations, bus stations, and roadsides, children are forced into sex to survive and pay smugglers to continue their journey.

In the past century alone tens of millions have been made homeless and countless left injured and bereaved. Three out of four fatalities of war are children and women. In year 2016 there were 300,000 children forced into being soldiers around the world.[3] Landmines have killed or maimed at least 10,000 of them. About 5,000 nuclear weapons are on hair-trigger alert around the world to launch at a moment's touch. Governments have killed about 360 million people in the 20th century. Genocide has destroyed 80 million.

The world advances with increasing danger for both the young and the old. In January 2016 Iraq ISIS gunmen executed ten boys younger than twelve after they tried to escape a training camp in Fallujah. A photo showed five of them kneeling on the sand with their executioners behind them holding guns to their heads. ISIS then went on a hunt for a thirteen-year-old who shot several ISIS members with one of their own AK-47s after they killed seventy of his birds he was breeding and beat his father for letting him. The city is quiet with the residents under siege and resistance met with unspeakable brutality. The schools now are strictly teaching about how to use weapons and the Islamic doctrine. Friday mornings in the square there are mass executions including locking people in cages, setting them on fire, and driving over them with armored vehicles. Homosexuals are thrown from rooftops. Women thought to have committed adultery are beheaded. All families are told to hand over at least one child to ISIS, with a mandatory registration of all boys after they reach fourteen years.[4]

Gunmen stormed a retirement home in the southern city of Aden in Yemen, killing sixteen people, including four Indian nuns.[5] The officials say that the gunmen raided the home for the elderly on a Friday, separating the nuns from the others and then shot them. They then handcuffed the elderly people and opened fire. Yemen, in a state of civil unrest between the government, ISIS and AlQaeda terrorists trying to make the state a base of operations, fills with the sight of Christians crucified in public as children riding bicycles stop to look at them.

In Central America gang violence and lawlessness compelled thousands of desperate families to find safety for their children, sending them

---

3. The World Revolution, "The State of the World."
4. Mamanglue-Regala, "ISIS executes 10 boys."
5. Associated Press, "Gunmen storm Yemen."

on perilous journeys north to an unknown future in the US. The US, European Union, and Kuwait pledged aid to refugees but the UN says millions of dollars more are needed. Camps are overcrowded and undersupplied. People are cold, hungry, and susceptible to disease. UNHCR estimates 2,500 people died in one summer trying to cross the Mediterranean where eddies spin salty water into the Atlantic.

Fifty-three Christians willing to risk the perilous voyage were hurled overboard in October 2015 still professing their faith after Muslim migrants became angry at a boy praying to God. The bodies of twenty-four migrants were recovered from the sea in April 2015 after a shipwreck off the coast of Libya grounded with at least 700 people on board, some locked in the hold. Migrants who survived crossing came on land still tasting the salt. They told police that twelve Christian refugees had been thrown from the boat and killed by fifteen Muslims who included a seventeen-year-old.[6]

Malta and Italy are closest to the Libyan coast, receiving the migrant tide that carried 219,000 people from Africa to Europe in 2013. About 3,500 died or were missing along the way. Believers living in Egypt carried Jesus' words into Africa in the middle of the first century. Africans began evangelizing other Africans. By the twentieth century the continent was predominantly Christian and Muslim. Islam spread, reducing Christian congregations. Only the Coptic Church in Egypt, the Ethiopian Orthodox Twahedo Church, and the Eritrean Orthodo Tewahedo Church in the Horn of Africa remained strong.

And it shall come to pass afterward, that I will pour out my spirit on all flesh; your sons and your daughters shall prophesy, your old men shall dream dreams, and your young men shall see visions (Joel 2:28). The spirit was promised to immerse mankind as the great and terrible day of the Lord nears. The time will also be marked by the Jews turning to God (Joel 3:16–17).

As a young woman in 1942, Rose Becker dreamt she was being chased by a giant, running over hills and mountains, chasing her with a sickle.[7] Then the sky opened in colors of blues and pinks. A tall man with white hair clothed in a white robe stretched his arms out to her and she ran to him. "I'll save you," he said. The giant disappeared.

Waking, she said to herself, *"Zohl zein tzu gutz"* (Let it be good), which her grandfather had taught her to say. But when she closed her eyes,

---

6. Mezzofiore, "Libya migrants."

7. Becker, Rose, "The Man of My Dreams."

she kept seeing the man in white. Sometime later she told a Christian friend about it. "You dreamt of Jesus," her friend told her. In her thought Jesus was for the gentiles. She was Jewish. But the dream continued. Then she dreamt of her son dying. When it came to pass as she'd seen in her dreams, she realized the dream of Jesus must be true. Years went by and she obtained a Bible and began searching. One day she agreed to go with her Christian friend to a dinner at a church. A Jewish man was the speaker that night. As she listened, she heard familiar words she knew as a child about the *kaporeh*, the sacrifice at Yom Kippur. When he said that Jesus was their sacrifice, she knew her entire being had been waiting to serve the Messiah.

The flurry of dreams stirring the media resonate with the Bible. In Iran a child wondered, what's beyond the stars? As a teenager his life felt meaningless.[8] As he passed the Assyrian church he had walked by many times before, he decided to go in. The pastor gave him a stack of books. Among them was a New Testament. He read it from cover to cover but felt no change. In despair he went to his room and cried for God to reveal himself. A man appeared suddenly in front of him, extending his hands, saying, "Give me your hand and your life will change." Kneeling, he began to weep, the first time his parents had heard him crying for many years. He became a restored human being. Growing in grace he married and had two children. But the persecution of Christians in Iran forced them to flee to Turkey, then flee again to Austria in the bitter cold of winter.

Young Joseph had a vision of binding leaves in the field, and his brother's sheaves gathering around to bow to his sheaf as it arose (Gen 37:5–10). Later he interpreted the dream of the Egyptian Pharaoh (Gen 41). Peter was given a vision from God while praying on a rooftop (Acts 10:9–16). A Muslim dreamt he jumped into the river where there was danger and swam to Jesus.[9] When he got on the boat with Jesus, he asked many questions. When he woke from the dream, he sought out a Christian and wanted a Bible to read.

The crossing to other lands passes above a bewildering world of new discoveries—strawberry anemones on the Atlantic's shorelines from Norway to North Africa, little hermit crabs carrying their shells, sea spiders walking about the deep of the Arctic and Mediterranean, and scallops jet-propelling around the substrates of the Indo-Pacific waters. Starfish in every color live on the beds of all the world's ocean, amid eels, flying fish, great

---

8. More Than Dreams.
9. Wellman, "Christian Dream Interpretation."

white sharks, choral nations of whales, seals and sea otters that emerge to show themselves on land, penguins and murrelets, algae in browns, reds and greens, and tiny zooplankton.

Above the ocean the wind and waves wash over the symphonies. Salt, depth, and temperature alter the speed sounds travel from the orchestra of little fish and huge cetacea. The whales communicate with each other across entire basins, but as the decibels of noise from man tear the water apart, cetacean species are becoming unable to hunt for food or talk to each other, find mates, or warn each other. Sound dissipates for thousands of miles.

Humpback whales are especially attuned to their sonar abilities, singing beautifully complex melodies in the ocean world. Unable to hear each other, breeding new generations is impeded. Boat traffic intrudes with horrifically loud noise. Supertankers cruise the oceans pulsing sound at 190 decibels or more. Smaller tugs and ferries create sound waves of 160 to 170 decibels causing a wall of constant white noise that chases marine life into small areas, away from feeding grounds and each other. Gray whales break away from their natural migration routes to get away from the blare.

Stellar sea lions and California sea lions eco-locate their world underwater. The noise permeating their conversations and ability to identify objects is making it harder to find food and each other.[10] Pingers emit shrill sounds to scare away marine life from fishing boats. Ringers are louder, causing physical pain to animals, emitting a 190-decibel nerve wracking sound to send seals and porpoises away from aquacultures. They are capable of deafening an animal.

Man has explored the ocean for metal ore, gold, and silver for thousands of years, but since the twentieth century mining the floor for diamonds, gold, silver, and gravel has brought enormous disturbance. The world's ocean contains a staggering resource of diamonds compared to that on land, deposited by water in the ocean floor. But obtaining them requires dredging that brings up sediments with machinery separating diamonds from the gravel. The industry is growing, bringing more machinery into oceans as well as for coal, metal compounds, and gas.

Repairing the deep sea is nearly impossible. Sediment plumes cloud the water when sediments are returned to the ocean floor, blocking sunlight for photosynthesis for plants marine life depend on andstirring heavy metals into the currents that accumulate in the food chain.

10. Firestone, Jarvis, "Response and Responsibility."

Sound from loud machinery deafens creation, causing tissue damage, resulting in temporary or permanent hearing loss. The fish of the ocean are disoriented. Stunned. Man-man noise is loud. Fish try to swim away from the source as they would from the low frequency sounds of a predator. Higher frequency and weak sounds sometimes attract fish, who relate it to prey and feeding sounds. Behaviors are disturbed. The result is death.

Whales and other marine mammals depend on their hearing as their song goes out before them finding food, friends, a mate, and their way through their world. On the seafloor 2,237 feet deep, south of New England's Georges Bank, unidentified sounds were recorded in among the dolphins and humpback, fin, and pilot whales. Drumming and calling like ducks, they are thought to be communications of deep-sea fish who hear and make low frequency sounds in perpetual darkness. In pitch dark caves fish swim around with no eyes or dim eyesight. But they do have ears for hearing. Researchers hypothesize the noises are elicited to attract at times of reproduction, chase away competitors, or warn when there's a predator in their midst.

Sound waves vibrate from whale song, oscillating along waves, troughing and cresting as they use echolocation to interpret their environment. Deep under the ocean, sound travels very slowly. In the zone known as the Sonar Fixing and Ranging Channel, low frequency waves can travel thousands of miles before fading. Humpback and baleen whales sing to other whales many miles away.

Humans are less able to hear it because the eardrum does not vibrate under water. In fish the inner ear consists of calciferous structures called otoliths that feel movement. The otolith is sensitive to what surrounds the fish's body. The fish rocks back and forth and the hair cells bend to register motion. The fish can hear very low frequencies, sometimes below 0.1 Hz.

Fish with a swim bladder have improved hearing, not only detecting motion, but also the fluctuating pressures of sound. The swim bladder starts to pulsate in response to increasing and decreasing pressure of sounds. Some fish species have specialized structures such as bones or air canals passing the signal through the entire fish to the swim bladder to the inner ear. Others have air-filled structures close to the inner ear that improve hearing. Carps and cat fish are hearing specialists. Only the Alosinae, a relative of the herring swimming in all the world's seawaters, are known to detect ultrasound.

Chapter 11

Ridley turtles have eardrums covered by a ring of scales called the cutaneous plate. Under the skin is a layer of thicker skin conducting underwater sound to the inner ear. Sea turtles seem to hear low frequency sounds between 200 and 750 Hz the best. Hearing is used to understand the world they are in and what is going on in their surroundings.

Does not the ear test words as the palate tastes food? (Job 12:11).

The vulnerability of children's perceptions and short-term memory are acutely affected by noise disruptions, revealed in studies of long-term exposure to the noise of the world.[11] Much more impaired than adults by exposure to noise, children's listening comprehension, reading, and writing processes absorb chronic and cumulative effects. Vibrating through the developing nervous system and the water contained by the body, over time the noise weakens immune systems. Numbing to sound, the words of the Lord get lost in the world. Encountering the voice of the Lord gives a sense of where we are with God. The words slash through the darkness, shining weapons that open the narrow gate into his presence.

Alarm calls out through the deep, calling for one of its kind, isolated, asking where did family go. In the ocean an answering call comes, then, reconciled, they swim together. On land washed by the one water, incorporated into Christ's resurrection, the covenant asks that we emerge from baptism keeping our face turned toward Jesus and forget the world. This prepares us to hear him.

Taken into our minds his words guide in the current that becomes our story. Jesus stressed listening. Take heed what you hear (Mark 4:1–25). Paul gave ceaseless thanks because hearing the word of God brought truth he could believe. What we hear identifies the enemy, reveals our sustenance, and shows us our community in a world bombarded with noise saturating the sound waves.

Sound thousands of times stronger than a jet engine assaults the ears of the ocean community, whether airguns used in oil exploration or submarines and ships emitting sonar, drowning out their world. Some systems send out more than 235 decibels, traveling across hundreds of miles of ocean, a hundred times more intense than levels known to wound large whales and kill dolphins. The Navy's most widely used sonar operates at a mid-frequency range that strand whales of four different species on the beaches of the Bahamas. The population of Cuvier's beaked whales nearly vanished, either abandoning their habitat or dying at sea. Suffering physical

---

11 Klatte, Bergstrom, and Lachmann, "Does noise affect learning?."

trauma, they are bleeding around the brain, ears and in their tissues, with larges bubbles in their organs akin to a severe case of the bends that can kill scuba divers who surface too quickly from deep water.

Stranded whales are a visible symptom of man affecting life, disrupting behaviors vital to survival and reproduction, causing panic and fleeing. Without protection, the Navy's increased sonar training will blast marine life more than 10 million times during five years off the US coast alone.[12] Reverberating through the ocean, the piercing noise slams against hundreds of thousands of sea creatures every ten to twelve seconds for weeks or months on end. That is what oil companies plan for seismic surveys to look for oil and gas deposits deep below the ocean floor in the Atlantic, from Delaware to Florida. Risking the lives of more than a hundred thousand marine mammals, it disrupts sea life more than 13 million times in the search for oil and gas.

The Atlantic Ocean is habitat for the critically endangered North Atlantic Right Whale. Only about 500 remain. The mammals breed off the coast of Georgia and give birth in the Mid-Atlantic, both proposed blast zones. To escape extreme noise, Right Whales swim up and hover like shadows just beneath the surface where they become vulnerable to collision with ships. The loud blasts also drastically impact the fish stocks that commercial fishermen and tribal fisheries depend on. Fish densities drop rapidly and have not rebounded.

Billowing over two thirds of the world, a paradise fathoms deep dominates the earth, whispering a lullaby heard into the sleeping night, then rolling its mountains of waves in crescendos of waking cymbals. The voice of the water carries one sound of all its members, worshipful, enrapturing the listener led to confess we know nothing of God's depths. This is the mark of God's hand. Acres of fluid bow to rising worship, directed to his plan to repair the world.

Emunah's colors changed as she grew and strengthened each day. Her dark shell matured into a gray-green carapace. Her belly became yellowish white. Only a few years old now, she heads toward shore, swept up the eastern seaboard with the Gulf Stream current. Assigned a mission, Emunah turned her direction home, the sole plan of her generation, called by the story of her birth. She sought Cape Cod's sheltered harbors where she found rich feeding grounds through the summer. Although she had no daily need

---

12. Morell, "US Navy to limit sonar testing."

CHAPTER 11

of socializing, here she congregated with her relatives to feed on the abundant seagrass in the shallows to become ready for her responsibilities.

As night settled, the constellations came out to wade in the ocean's surface. The word praise in the language of the Hebrew people, *halel*, is also translated as "shine" (Job 29:3). The original meaning is contained in "North Star," a star unlike others, remaining constant in the sky as a guide and marking the beginning of morning on the Hebrew lunar calendar. It is a word that raises eyes toward the direction of greatness, like the dreams about Jesus, a light that causes those who see it to look for those who will tell them what it means.

As summer changed to fall the temperature dropped. Sea turtles were to move south but the Cape jutting into the Atlantic confused Emunah. She didn't know she had to follow the shore north to reach the waters that take her south. Being a reptile she could not make her own body heat. She was trapped at the mercy of the winds and waves.

Disoriented, the sea turtle becomes cold stunned at temperatures falling below 60 degrees Fahrenheit. Emunah floated with the waves. The tide carried her onto the beach and left her exposed to the coming winter's cold. She had no chance of survival. Wellfleet Bay Audubon has been patrolling the beaches since the 1970s, wearing jackets, gloves, hats, comfortable shoes for walking miles, and carrying cell phones to call the Wellfleet when one is spotted on a cresting wave. The Sea Turtle Rescue coordinates volunteers spread out along the sand, watching as the ocean turns the high tide twice a day to see if there's a turtle washing in. Moving Emunah above the high tide line so the ocean won't carry her out again, they cover her with seaweed to protect from exposure. The stunned turtles are taken quickly from the Wellfleet Sanctuary on the serious transport to the Marine Animal Rescue Center an hour and a half away in Quincy, Massachusetts. There they are warmed very slowly over several days.

In a life-changing moment the thought in a storm wonders will daybreak ever light the sky again. Currents run ceaselessly east, west, north, south toward shores, into straits, listening to the wind's guidance. The low moan of sky and surf has not been silent since creation formed. Without this knowledge of how currents roll, the mariner and turtle alike would be lost. Yet even the disciples were afraid after Jesus sent them into the boat out into the Sea of Galilee. The storm surrounded them. In the fourth watch, when the dark of the night still blanketed them, they sensed the light about to dawn, anticipating the first chirps of the birds. Then Jesus came, the only hope left to them.

Encountering sharks, fishing nets, poisons, and oil, yet still seeking the ocean's splendor, hearing the splash of the sea answer, life turns toward its power age after age. The distant call swells into a voice intoning all life, at once vexed with the curse that fell on creation, yearning for the redemption, yet celebrating and triumphant in luminous arrival along every shore.

> Can you fathom the mysteries of God? Can you probe the limits of the Almighty? (Job 11:7).

Is it by your understanding that the hawk soars, stretching his wings toward the south? Is it at your command that the eagle mounts up and makes his nest on high? (Job 39:26–27) We are his creation, not left without instruction.

The body of the ocean responds to the slightest motion of the wind. The waves charge, shifting across the surface, oscillating the water. Breezes freshen into a gale spraying salt water into foams. The beat of waves become irregular, resounding in a wild liberation of its energy while Emunuah dives deeper to shelter with those dwelling beneath kept alive in the undercurrents. Cresting waves respond to our actions, returning on our shores, as the spirit moves across our spirit protecting, rearranging, and guiding. God is perceived as sovereign when he provides for his people. But he told Isaiah, "My thoughts are nothing like your thoughts." We want the waves to calm, the winds to hush, but God knows what he is forming as he makes the path of faith clear.

He sends his spirit to move the body, sometimes gathering those on a lost shore, other times calming with the sound of the ocean's breath, always asking we cross through the stormy waters because the sea will never rest. God will have no pleasure in those who shrink back (Matt 8:23–27). The high winds must be learned. Waves of praise are lifted, even on the night Jesus was being betrayed. He continued giving thanks to his Father. Because of this prayer the darkness within us cannot separate us from God. Because of his prayer we call God our Father too.

To God above, who makes sure the ocean shares its sound to everyone, the voices coming in the many tongues of the ocean, the clamoring floods, trickling brooks, splashing rains, gentle dews, melting snow, all rise to his ear fully understood. Some are graced with that hearing, even hearing it in a shell held to the ear, understanding the symphony blended with their wonder into thanksgiving. Hearing will pull some from the edge of death. Words will fall on the ground in front of others.

Perils and dispiriting changes are constant in the world of the creation. Bill Larkin, a man who had a dream of the ocean in May 2012, posted his vision of the Atlantic rising to swallow the Canary Islands, the coast of the Gulf of Mexico sinking beneath the waves with much of the east coast, and an earthquake separating California, bringing in floods from the Pacific.[13] In the vision he was warned it would occur during the last week of an August summer. "You don't know when your last day will be on the earth," he said. "You don't know when you'll have to go before the Lord. Are you ready to go before Jesus? Do you know him personally? Do you have a relationship with him? Do you seek God? Does he speak to you? He is your only hope."

As Emunah made her way down the coast she got caught in a tangle of fish line. The net covered her, weighted down by a wooden pallet. Her heart beat like trapped wings. Many turtles drown when they cannot surface for air because they're tangled in fishermen's drift nets or long lines. Under stress, caught in a shrimp trawl, sea turtles quickly use up their supply of oxygen and die.

> I lift up my eyes to the hills. From where does my help come?
> My help comes from the Lord, who made heaven and earth
> (Ps 121:1–2).

The plagues of cancer causing toxins drifted in the ocean that none are immune to as Emunah floated in the night. Surely he will save you from the fowler's snare and from the deadly pestilence (Ps 91:3).

In 1990 a young man prayed for three nights asking for a dream of Jesus.[14] God answered. The young man saw himself walking into a building where the Lord stood in profile shining bright with light. "When I looked at him I immediately knew he was Jewish. He looked just like the Orthodox Jews I used to see walking to synagogue on the Sabbath." Jesus slowly turned and looked at him. "I was filled with shame and embarrassment. I turned to leave and when I did a light flashed in my eyes and blinded me. When I opened them again I was laid flat on my face at Jesus' feet." Looking

---

13. Larkin, "Vision of Tsunami."
14. The Messiah According to Bible Prophecy, "God revealed."

up in awe, he saw an indescribable look of mercy in the eyes of Jesus. It would be another seven years before he pursued Christ's words with all his heart. "He revealed himself to me through his word, the Bible. I saw in their own writings who the Messiah would be and what he would do and I saw the fulfillment of these things written in the New Testament."

In a dream, in a vision of the night, when deep sleep falls on men (Job 33:15).

After these things the word of the LORD came to Abram in a vision (Gen 15:1).

But God came to Abimelech in a dream by night (Gen 20:3).

And Joseph dreamed a dream, and he told it his brothers (Gen 37:5).

David in his youth spent hours out in nature, laying on the ground looking up at the stars that God spoke forth, watching as the moon and constellations circled. As he watched, God created worship in him. David knew he was known. He wrote, "You know when I sit and when I rise" (Ps 139:2) He delighted in God's presence and wanted to understand more. Teach me your knowledge, your ways are true, your word is a lamp to my feet. Waiting for the morning to dawn, he watched the stars of Pleiades and Orion. "Can you bind the cluster of Pleiades or loose the Belt of Orion?" (Job 38:31). Jesus would tell his apostles whatever they bind on earth is bound in heaven. Whatever they loose on earth is loosed in heaven. He had given them the keys to do the work of heaven on earth.

Beyond the flight of birds, further than the stars, heaven is advocating for us to complete our journey home. Hardships, discipline, and worries mark the journey "for now you have been grieved by various trials" but even death cannot keep us from the Lord. Death has been destroyed by the gentlest power of all, Jesus.

When wave upon wave knock down believers but those doing wrong ride the crest of prosperity, believers continue rejoicing because hardships reveal God sharing his long-term plan. The trial of faith is more precious than gold, scripture tells us, a test that forges genuine quality. Jesus will commend this faith when he returns in honor and the salvation of souls is completed. We can expect the systems of man to try to stop this. A net isolates a member from the body. No longer in relationship, they are unable to transform. The design for God's community has no place for self-dependency apart from the plan for the whole.

Chapter 11

Coming alongside the turtle, scuba divers swam close enough for Emunah to look into their eyes and see how the risen Lord moves toward the suffering. The words they spoke were little, but enough to content the turtle as the divers climbed up the ladder to their boat to find a way to lift her out. They brought her to a nature conservancy where people lugged gallons of sea water into a tank and let her float for days. She could not submerge because too much air was trapped inside her. Then the day came she swam to the bottom of the tank. She was ready to be released.

An estimated 5,000 Kemp's ridley were killed by commercial fleets every year before Turtle Excluder Devices were attached to the trawl. The device is a grid of bars with an opening that allows small animals to slip through and larger animals like sea turtles strike the bars to be ejected. Pound nets, trawls, gill nets, hook and line, crab traps, and longlines also drown the turtles, both young and old. Although the US and Mexico agreed to phase out US shrimping in Mexican waters by 1979, illegal vessels continued to operate. Mexico closed the near shore waters off Rancho Neuvo to fishing during the turtle's nesting season, but the protection is difficult to enforce.

Tamaulipas has been inhabited for more than 8,000 years by changing cultures that have come and gone. The Olmec people lived in balance with the sea turtle nesting grounds. The Aztecs came later with Montezuma's armies. The Mexican empire built from the tributaries. The nesting beach in Mexico has been protected by armed guards since 1966 but is still at risk. Development along the coast encroaches on the site that holds their eggs protected. Construction of commercialfishing facilities continued just across from the turtle's camp at Rancho Nuevo. North of the nestsLa Pesca expands plans for a fishing or dredging center of the Gulf Intercoastal Waterway all the way from Texas to south of the nesting beach.

At twenty years Emunah is mature. Sensing the earth's magnetic field a sea turtle may determine its latitude and longitude. The crust of the ocean bottom is patterned with magnetic lines running parallel on both sides of the mid-ocean ridge. Generated by rocks on the ocean floor, the pattern gives off positive and negative magnetic lines where new rock is being formed by magma cooling and aligning with the magnetic north pole of earth. The new rock pushes the older magma away from the ridge on each side.Earth's magnetic field protects the planet from blasts of solar radiation. A European SpaceAgency satellite called Swarm found it weakening since year 2000[15] in spots extending 370,000 miles over the western hemisphere and strengthening over the southern Indian Ocean. The ESA's Swarm mission manager, Rune Floberghagen, theorizes the magnetic poles are getting ready to flip. The magnetic field extends from earth's interior to where it meets the solar wind blowing from the sun. The north and south poles wander and wobble in their tilt toward the sun, changing the north pole slowly over time, reversing on average every several million years in records kept by the ocean's tectonic plates.

The imprint of Emunah's birth beach has been carried with her. She has an excellent sense of smell and the scent, sound, magnetic fields, the mix of deep water and surface currents, and celestial maps lead home.

Swimming back into their first currents, the turtles find a strange tide has entered in their absence, loading with far reaching threats of floating debris. New death traps of rubber, fishing line and hooks, tar, cellophane, rope, string, wax, styrofoam, charcoal, aluminum cans, and cigarette filters threaten to be confused with food. Polyvinyl chloride (PVC) is softened to produce cling wrap used to package food, liquids, candy wrappers, bottles, and plastic trays. Chemicals used to soften PVC, adipates and phthalates, leach into foods when heated. Of concern is an adipate called DEHA, a carcinogen found in cheddar cheese that had been packaged. Causing birth defects and tumors on the livers of mice, worried thoughts turned toward the water. PVC must be carefully recycled because it gives off corrosive fumes at lower temperatures than other plastics. Sometimes sea turtles swallow floating pieces of plastic, mistaking them for jellyfish. The plastic blocks their digestive system and the turtles slowly weaken and starve. Sea turtles are found with tumors growing on their bodies. New dredging operations further degrade the journey, pulling ridleys into their channels, ruining foraging areas with dumping, altering the current's flow and murkying the water. The ocean is in crisis. It is too late for anything but the truth.

The Atlantic Ocean received its names from the ancient Greeks, derived from Atlas, a concept meaning holding up the sky. The Atlantic is a younger ocean, thought to have formed when the seafloor spread and broke apart the ancestral continent, Pangaea. The ocean filled in an elongated S-shaped basin between the Americas bounding it on its west and Eurasia and Africa on its east, host to icebergs spotted into summer months, fog swirling the surface in springtime, and hurricanes spinning across the growing gap between Eurasia and North America. Drawing its strength from the

---

15. Dickerson, "Earth's Magnetic Field."

rivers that flow into it, now pollution seeps into the sea from fertilizers, human waste, and chemicals creating dead zones.

Globobulimana affinis, tiny shells that survive on the seafloor needing very little oxygen have become contaminated. The single-celled forams are related to amoebas. Thriving in a world with little oxygen, they clean up the ecosystem by eating decomposing plants and animals and turning it into minerals. A source of food for snails, sea urchins, starfish, and fish, forams are also indicators. Extremely sensitive to their habitat, the entire community changed when the Deepwater Horizon spilled more than million barrels of oil into the Gulf. A few months after the oil spill stopped flowing, forams were collected from the seafloor. The few forams that scientists found were taken to the lab and seen to have absorbed components of the oil. In other areas no forams were found, causing the fish and crustaceans that depend on them to disappear from the area, and in turn the fish that eat these vanished.

In the instant rivers began their flow on earth, they were blessed to benefit the world, bringing refreshment into the larger body that believers would understand. Two years after the spill, the foram community was recovering. The grasses and animals along the marshes helped filter the shoreline and offer habitat for fish, shellfish, amphibians, and migratory waterfowl.

> God's voice thunders in marvelous ways; he does great things
> beyond our understanding
> (Job 37:5).

The land's edge shifts and changes under nature's motion indenting a cove where water scours the coast for debris, carrying it away for it to settle on the seabed, causing deltas to form estuaries where it moves back and forth under the influence of currents. Emunah found the coastal land of Louisiana had lost more than 300 square miles after hurricane Katrina's 200 mph winds and Rita's surge a month later spinning through in 2005.

Already diminishing to human society, wetlands are haven to many animals, birds, fish, and support large fisheries for millions of people. They filter the water and protect from rising floods. The power of a hurricane's wind and rain rushing waters into the land, pounding surf breaking down soft sediments, reshape the coast. Channels of fast moving water create new streams where once grasses grew. Mats of grass are compacted into clumps of mud. Saltwater comes in and mixes with the fresh water marsh changing the world. Katrina stayed for twenty hours, surging the ocean sixteen feet beyond its shore, washing away the soil of decomposing plants, followed by Rita reinforcing the changes. Three years of recovering, plants began colonizing the shallow ponds, then hurricanes Gustav and Ike hit in 2008 forcefully removing the new plants.

The storm torn lands have not moved the sun or stars, the moon or heaven above. Emunah followed along the edge of the land to the northeast coast of Mexico, to southern Tamaulipas where she was born.

Chapter 12

And I saw what appeared to be a sea of glass mingled with fire—and also those who had conquered the beast and its image and the number of its name, standing by the sea of glass, with harps of God in their hands (Rev 15:2)

EMUNAH BREAKS THROUGH THE water into the day. Though clouds shroud the cerulean sky, all creation knows the light is there, unchangeable, impossible to taint its pure intent. A breeze breaks with the waves, and the sand frees her steps from its churning. Rising out of the water to bring about continuance of God's design, she arrives in mass synchronization with other female ridleys coming to nest.

The sea is his, for it was he who made it, and his hands formed the dry land (Ps 95:5).

Before God divided the waters, when earth was covered with the deep, he sent light to bring mankind into light. Then God said, "Let there be a firmament in the midst of the waters, and let it divide the waters from the waters" (Gen 1:6). The waters above the firmament, a crystal platform supporting an emerald throne high above, are spoken of in Psalm 148. "Praise him, you highest heavens, and you waters above the heavens." Reborn out of salvation's waters, the immersion of Jesus lifts us above the expanse that separates us from heaven. We are translated into timeless light, as Jesus had been light and translated into a physical being, birthed from the sound of water that rushed when the new life came, pushed by God's blessing.

We rise from the immersion dripping with grace, baptized into his body to carry the grace to others. The word *tal* means "dew" and the word *tallit*, a prayer shawl, alludes to the morning dew that brought manna in the wilderness (Exod 16:3–4). The unity of brothers is compared to dew (Ps 133:3), and entering into the rest of the favor of God (Prov 19:12). The talmidim (disciples), had the traditional responsibility to learn everything that Jesus would teach, celebrating the holy holidays, praying, fasting, keeping commandments, and following their teacher everywhere. They were to reflect each dewdrop his life carried. It would not mean they would not grow weary.

Chosen by God, even Moses reached the end of himself when the people of every family were wailing and complaining at the entrance to their tents. Moses comes and opens his heart to God. He asked the Lord, "Why have you brought this trouble on your servant? What have I done to displease you that you put the burden of all these people on me? Did I conceive all these people? Did I give them birth? Why do you tell me to carry them in my arms, as a nurse carries an infant, to the land you promised on oath to their ancestors?" The burden is too heavy, he said. If this is how you are going to treat me, please let me die instead of facing my own ruin. In response, God consecrated seventy elders to share the burden of the people so he would not have to carry it alone (Num 11:10–17).

The last words of Moses before the children of Israel entered into the land without him, spoke to a new generation who had not seen the miracles their parents had seen. This man of the Torah, 120 years old, saw his people be gathered to be a nation of peace. He spent forty years leading them. Speaking to a desert people, he spoke of dew, drops of rain, showers in the morning. He reminds the young generation to look to their history and remember the days of old. Ask the elders about the faithful redemption of God's power. He told them to look to Abraham, Isaac, and Jacob. The generation anxiously waited to enter the promised land. "You have a choice," he tells them. "You and your children after you have the choice to follow God." He prays.

> Give ear, O heavens, and I will speak, and let the earth hear the words of my mouth. May my teaching drop as the rain, my speech distill as the dew, like gentle rain upon the tender grass, and like showers upon the herb. For I will proclaim the name of the Lord; ascribe greatness to our God! (Deut 32:1–3).

Water continuously offers riches on our shores. We're irresistibly drawn to see what is left after a storm blows through. But when the waters rise over us and we are overwhelmed, there is no salvation other than God lifting us out, the guarantee in his words of care for us. We will never be the same.

Chapter 12

Who made heaven and earth, The sea and all that is in them; Who keeps faith forever (Ps 146:6).

The sea turtles coming up the beach share nesting space with the gregarious sandwich terns and pelicans. Laughing gulls, royal terns and wilson's plovers also nest the salt marshes and sandy beach for their young to continue their generations. Migratory birds coming in on the flyway when earth begins its tilt away from summer depend on the Gulf. The little blackpoll warblers lift off from forest in the Maritimes of Canada and New England to fly nonstop for three days across one of the longest flights of songbirds, 1,700 miles above the western Atlantic to the northeastern coast of South America. Weighing just half an ounce, the warbler lands on coastlands for a few days of refueling. When bad weather disturbs the Atlantic skies, the birds take rest on ships.

Our Lord is an avid birdwatcher. When the creation was made, he filled the air with their songs, an abundance of birds everywhere we look. Flying over the mountains, down in the desert, out in the forests, flocks of every color and size have chirped and tweeted through the generations.

Wanting to share his delight in his ornithological world with us, Jesus refers us to the birds to teach us not to be afraid with worries. "Look at the birds of the air; they do not sow or reap or store away in barns, and yet your heavenly Father feeds them" (Matt 6:26). He wants us to understand how the kingdom of heaven offers provision the way a seed of faith no matter how small brings us to find our place of rest. "Yet when it grows, it is the largest of garden plants and becomes a tree, so that the birds come and perch in its branches" (Matt 13:32).

But we are prone to wander. "Like a bird that flees its nest is anyone who flees from home" (Prov 27:8). Our eye is lured to the tree of knowledge, seeming to have branches that we could land on and twigs that would weave good nests. Instead we find this tree lacks the living water that sustains the tree of life. It dries up and we are empty handed. We find ourselves at a loss. "I lie awake; I have become like a bird alone on a roof" (Ps 102:7). "I cried like a swift or thrush, I moaned like a mourning dove. My eyes grew weak as I looked to the heavens" (Isa 38:14).

With society tempted to redefine good and evil by re-writing God's instructions, God compares us to his birds. "The stork in the sky knows her appointed seasons, and the dove, the swift and the thrush observe the time of their migration. But my people do not know the requirements of the Lord" (Jer 8:7). Caught in the snare, tears fall. Regret settles in to become the only reality. The sense of loss weighs us down, earthbound, apart from the soaring joys of heaven. And we say, "Oh, that I had the wings of a dove! I would fly away and be at rest" (Ps 55:6).

Although the tree of life had become inaccessible, God instructed the words be written on the tablet of our hearts and never lose sight of the tree of life. The word is a fountain, a wellspring of living waters sourcing life for all the world. Jesus conveyed being the river of living water during the Feast of Tabernacles that commemorates the forty years in the wilderness. He was relating himself to God in the wilderness with Israel and foretelling the day he would return to dwell with his people.

Through our wilderness times we know this, we hear these words yet guilt and heartache distance us. Suffering, unable to speak without thinking we appear to be "bad" Christians or elicit generic comments to "have faith," we remain yearning for the words that promise, "Those who hope in the Lord will renew their strength. They will soar on wings like eagles" (Isa 40:31).

The words that call wanderers back from the brink of death are not ours to change. "Through the encouragement of the scriptures we might have hope" (Rom 15:4). The message may appear to be the smallest of currents trickling through a world blasting torrents of loudness drowning out the singing praise. But God's word contains the flights and falls of entire nations. From the depths of failure to heights praising his deliverance, from the decay of the world to his eternal redemption, each drop builds into a cascading truth. We discover how we are scripted in God's heart. We ourselves are revealed.

God tells us to "ask the animals, and they will teach you, or the birds in the sky, and they will tell you" (Job 12:7). "I know every bird in the mountains, and the insects in the fields are mine." (Ps 50:11). As noise from the world's selfish greed and false teachers drown out the sounds of nature, birds do not sing louder to be heard. They chirp and tweet and chime their songs with soft melody as they always have done. Over the ocean flying back and forth they follow a wind high above the perpetual waves.

Though the promises of heaven may be coming from only the steadfast few, even in tears a snared bird recognizes the voice of its flock calling to look beyond the wearisome journey over the ocean to reach the tree. Without excusing our flaws, its sheltering branches stretch out with grace welcoming our flight home. "Not one of them is forgotten by God" (Luke

CHAPTER 12

12:6). "Who provides food for the raven when its young cry out to God and wander about for lack of food?" (Job 38:41)

Return to me, God speaks. Bring words to God, Habakkuk said.

Words were what Jesus used to make the destroyer flee. The shared word declares us redeemed. Rising up on wings exalting God to show the way to the tree where hidden shame finds a place to be honest, to be known, accepted, and loved. As we return toward our nest the light grows brighter, illuminating the truth—God sees us as he created us to be. We are fearfully and wonderfully made (Ps 139:14). We are clothed in strength and dignity (Prov 31:25). We are pillars holding up the temple (Rev 3:12).

Ephraim is like a dove, silly and without sense, calling to Egypt, going to Assyria. As they go, I will spread over them my net; I will bring them down like birds of the heavens; I will discipline them according to the report made to their congregation (Hos 7:11–12).

Discipline is part of our sanctification so that we learn to discern the bait of the enemy. Does a bird swoop down to a trap on the ground when no bait is there? (Amos 3:5) From the smallest sparrow to the crow's announcements, the seagulls cry or the eagle's soaring, the song he gives is important to God. "We have escaped like a bird from the fowler's snare; the snare has been broken, and we have escaped" (Ps 124:7). Recognizing darkness has no fellowship with light, we discern the enemy who is "from beneath" (John 8:23).

Using imagery we understand, abiding in Christ is to find the strength of the blossoming tree of life that sustains and shelters. "The birds of the sky nest by the waters; they sing among the branches" (Ps 104:12). They have carried messages. "As I watched, I heard an eagle that was flying in midair call out in a loud voice: "Woe! Woe! Woe to the inhabitants of the earth, because of the trumpet blasts about to be sounded by the other three angels!" (Rev 8:13).

Birds are servants to God. God spoke to Elijah, "You will drink from the brook, and I have directed the ravens to supply you with food there" (1Kgs 17:4).

They are invited to the final victory. "And I saw an angel standing in the sun, who cried in a loud voice to all the birds flying in midair, Come, gather together for the great supper of God" (Rev 18:17). God appointed a bird to show Noah when there was land outside the ark for his family and all the animals that were with him. "When the dove returned to him in the evening, there in its beak was a freshly plucked olive leaf!" (Gen 8:11).

The Sea of Glass

The dove became a particular messenger from God. "I saw the spirit come down from heaven as a dove and remain on him" (John 1:32). These were the only birds that could be offered as sacrifice in the Mosaic law (Lev 5:7).

Scripture compares us to the doves as we show God's devotion to his son. "Therefore be as shrewd as snakes and as innocent as doves" (Matt 10:16). The bird reveals his longing for our relationship. "I slept but my heart was awake. Listen! My beloved is knocking: Open to me, my sister, my darling, my dove, my flawless one" (Song 5:2). A day is promised to all creation when "Flowers appear on the earth; the season of singing has come, the cooing of doves is heard in our land" (Song 2:12).

From the river of the water of life flowing from the throne of God, Jesus eagerly waits for us to join him under a sky where there will be no more predators of our soul. "On each side of the river stood the tree of life, bearing twelve crops of fruit, yielding its fruit every month. And the leaves of the tree are for the healing of the nations. No longer will there be any curse" (Rev 22:1–3). The flow of the waters of life come beautifying the scorched places of ashes.

The light gathers the nations to the river. The refugees, the homeless, the displaced who have had to leave their nations, will again be a people. Everyone around them will be those who thirsted for rebirth in the heaven of Jesus and were satisfied. Our voyage is through a time the enemy strengthens the storms against the currents that circle the earth, currents blessed by the sun, renewing growth, carrying the displaced to new lands. God will bring his flock to his paradise.

Storms bring unexpected opportunity. "Woe is me!" cried Isaiah, "For I am lost; for I am a man of unclean lips, and I dwell in the midst of a people of unclean lips; for my eyes have seen the King, the Lord of hosts!" (Isa 6:1). The prophet was having a vision, seeing the Lord "high and exalted, seated on a throne; and the train of his robe filled the temple." The splendor of God made known to him, Isaiah saw himself in the truth of heaven. The seraphim called to one another, "Holy, holy, holy is the Lord of hosts; the whole earth is full of his glory!" One took tongs and lifted a coal from the altar. Touching Isaiah's mouth with the coal, he said, "Behold, this has touched your lips; your guilt is taken away, and your sin atoned for." Sealing his humanness so he didn't speak his own words, Isaiah was purified to speak God's words.

Chapter 12

God comes to the sorrowful because they will accept him. Isaiah heard the voice of the Lord saying, "Whom shall I send, and who will go for us?" Isaiah, now cleansed to be commissioned, said, "Here I am! Send me." The rush of relief in the contrite, fully known by God, is aware of the full force of helplessness. God alone restores us. Relationship with heaven is a relationship of clear knowing of who we are in our fallen state.

The heaven God has planned reflects the days when the waters abated and he came and walked with man, longing for relationship with us. As the new era of heaven began with the Lordship of Jesus, the heaven the ancients served with so much anticipation came more into focus. Heaven became attainable. We could begin to draw waters out of the well of salvation. We can speak with him heart to heart. We are no longer slaves but sons (Gal 4:7).

Heaven will unroll with the thunderous sound of ice breaking and glass doors being pushed open. God will be in our midst. We'll dream ideas again, swell with satisfactions and friends that stood with us or a child that will never again be lost. Tears will dry. He who sits on the throne said, "I make all things new." The birth pangs of a groaning creation pass away. He will tell us, you are home. You are safe now.

An orchestra of God's elaborate metre plays throughout time, every unconstrained wind and percussion in close harmony. The ocean's hymn is sung communally. Without the wind, the moon and all the songs and fish moving under its surface, the water becomes stagnant and still. It cannot be preserved as living water if separated from the body. Ocean water perishes if it is set apart from the ocean.

Jesus came to break down the differences that divided people by destroying the enmity in his own body (Eph 2:14–15). Light shone through the dark of night when he born. Dark fell on the light of noon's sun when he died. In those dark hours the terrors of judgment poured onto him as he bore the sins of every human being. As the Father turned his face away, Jesus cried out, forsaken in the agony of being separated from God's presence. Scripture brings us to the cross to see him beyond the reach of his Father's comfort, experiencing the venom of hell's torment, conscious in his suffering. Judgment and mercy met at the cross so that we will see the suffering, flee from sin, and never have to experience what Jesus endured. He entered into our hell.

Peter speaks of the abyss while condemning false teachers who introduce other thinking into the church. The word Peter used is *tartarus*, the lowest hell. Angels who left their habitation in heaven to take control of human progeny were cast into *tartarus*, held in dismal pits. (Jude 6:1–4). Peter said God did not spare even the angels when they sinned, but sends them to the deepest abyss, putting them in chains of darkness to be held for judgment. There is no tolerance of anyone leading God's children away (Matt 18:6).

Five centuries before Jesus left his place of glory to come to us, Zechariah was shown a vision. An angel was sent to show the prophet a basket that could hold three-fifths of a bushel. The angel removes the basket's lead cover to reveal a woman sitting inside. "This is the iniquity of the people throughout the land," the angel tells Zechariah. The angel seals the basket with the lid. Then two women come with a wind in their wings like the wings of a stork and lift the basket between the earth and the heavens (Zech 5:9–11). They carry it to Babylon where it will be unleashed to spread its corruption as a system called "the great prostitute," unfaithful to relationship with God (Rev 17:1).

A hundred years later God again sent a prophet, Malachi, to call the people of Israel back to God. He warns the priests they had gone astray. Sacrifices, tithes, and the sanctity of marriage were being defiled. Recorded in the final book of the Hebrew Bible, God again announced the promise of a Messiah who would come to restore the people. If the people would acknowledge they needed God's cleansing, he will return to them (Mal 3:6). Four centuries pass before God again speaks to his people. Then a voice calls from the wilderness, "Prepare the way for the Lord." (Matt 3:2). Repent, draw a line in the sand and step off those shores.

In the immersion of the age of Pentecost, God calls "return to me." Everywhere across earth and sea Jesus is saying, Follow me, carrying his Father's words who prepared earth before man and is preparing us for heaven. It may seem at times we are imprisoned by the shores surrounding us. Paul said, "As a prisoner for the Lord, then, I urge you to live a life worthy of the calling you have received." He stressed the effort to keep the unity of the spirit. "There is one body and one spirit, just as you were called to one hope when you were called; one Lord, one faith, one baptism; one God and Father of all, who is over all and through all and in all" (Eph 4:1–6).

You are the salt of the earth, Jesus said. But if salt has lost its taste, how shall its saltiness be restored? It is no longer good for anything except to be thrown out and trampled under people's feet (Matt 5:13). When those called to be salt lose their salt, just as the conveyor through the ocean would

Chapter 12

stop its course without its salt, currents won't sink deeply enough to retrieve the prisoners of darkness and bring them to the sunlit surface.

"Salt of the covenant" first appears in Leviticus 2:13, instructing the Israelites to add salt to all the offerings. The sacrifices were prophetic of the Messiah who would redeem from judgment. Salt was also used in making incense for the temple, rising to strengthen our prayers. Moses is told about the everlasting covenant of salt when God directs him to tell Aaron and the Levites that from all the holy offerings the Israelites give to God, he will give a portion to the priests (Num 18:19). The priests were to trust God for their sustenance, with no inheritance of land. Again, when the Lord gave the kingship of Israel to David and his descendants forever it was through a covenant of salt (2Chr 13:5).

The Hebrew word for salt, "*melach*," comes from the root, "*malach*," meaning to rub to pieces, pulverize, or disappear as dust. Lot's wife is turned into salt because she looked back (Gen 19:26). The agreement had been with an angel who would not destroy Sodom and Gomorrah until after Lot and his family had left. But his wife did not keep her agreement to not look back at what she was to leave behind. She became dust.

When the nation Israel was born, they had not yet been washed with water, rubbed with salt, or wrapped in clothing (Ezek 16:6). The cord that bound the people to the idolatry of the rest of the world had not yet been cut and washed. Salt was also used by Elisha to transform bitter water so it could be drinkable (2Kgs 2:21). Again, God asked for trust even when the command made no sense.

The salt of the covenant brings the idea of relationship based on trust in every detail. Without the bond of that trust, the world of God's enemies tramples and overwhelms. Looking back at the history of Habukkuk during his captivity, there was a call to wait on God. Habukkuk was given a glimpse of what lay beyond the intensifying storms. He wanted his people to have knowledge of God. Saying his people behave just like unbelievers, he wanted them to be the vibrant people of faith they were created to be. Babylon was coming. Habakkuk's heart pounded, decay crept into his bones in holy fear of God. He was standing at the end of his pier of despair, seeing the sky swell with clouds and the winds that would whip through his countrymen. God strengthened him and he stood at his post to hear what God would say. He was shown the world filled with the majestic glory of God although the victory has not yet bud. There may be no harvest to set on the table. There may be no one to sit around the table with us. The church building may be gone. Sorrow so heavy it cannot be carried from the past into our future. Yet the Lord's name remains lifted high, shining from the sky, pouring strength like a river. Death is broken. We are saved.

On the island Sri Lanka in the Indian Ocean, a seven-year-old little boy, Sunil, says, "My mother and father tell me that we love Jesus and that is why these things happened to us. But I still don't understand why." Sunil was playing in the garden with his brother when a mob arrived to attack his church. "We ran and hid," he said. "They broke open the door and came into the big hall where the church meets. There was a lot of noise. They were breaking furniture and throwing things on the floor. Suddenly we heard loud noises from above and some big rocks came crashing in through the roof. I moved closer to my brother and covered my head with my hands."

Sunil watched as the men grabbed the assistant pastor by his collar and began beating him.

"I was too afraid to scream," he said. "They were asking for my father—the pastor. He was not at home. Where was he? I wanted him to come home, but was also afraid that if he came, they might beat him up or kill him."

Sunil saw a bearded man throwing all the Bibles, hymn books, and musical instruments on the floor. He set it all on fire.

"Through the fire and the smoke I could see my mother crying," he said. "I hid with my brother for a very long time, afraid to come out. Finally they all left, laughing loudly. My mother tried to rock me to sleep, telling me that everything will be alright. But I couldn't sleep. What will happen to us now? Will people beat me up when I go to school tomorrow? What about tomorrow night? Will they return?"

Sunil doesn't play in the garden in the evenings any longer. When the sun begins to set he goes indoors to be close to his mother.[1]

Behold, waters are rising out of the north, and shall become an overflowing torrent; they shall overflow the land and all that fills it, the city and those who dwell in it. Men shall cry out, and every inhabitant of the land shall wail (Jer 47:2).

> But for you who fear my name, the sun of righteousness
> shall rise with healing in its wings (Mal 4:2).

---

1. Wickremesinhe, Roshini, "They Walk on Water."

Chapter 12

Jesus said the day and hour of his return is known by no one, not even the angels of heaven, but only to his Father. Be ready, he said. Forty days after his resurrection he ascended to the sky and a cloud received him out of the sight of his disciples. Immediately two men clothed in white said to the disciples, "Men of Galilee, why do you stand gazing up into heaven? This same Jesus who was taken up from you into heaven will so come in like manner as you saw him go into heaven" (Acts 1:9,11).

From that moment the world has watched for Christ's return.

All things are continuing as they were from the beginning of creation (2Pet3:4).Thermodynamics continue the amount of energy, space, and matter that God established in Genesis. The hydrological cycle described in the Bible continues drawing up drops of water into rain which the clouds pour down abundantly (Job 36:27–28) in just the right amount to sustain life. Entropy is described in the Bible. "Of old you laid the foundation of the earth, and the heavens are the work of your hands. They will perish, but you will remain" (Ps 102:25–26). Again verified in Hebrews 1:11, the universe is growing old like a garment. God wanted us to foresee environmental devastation of the planet (Rev 11:18). We are not yet free of illness, dangers, death, and degrading waters once pristine. We wait for the glory that is in us to be revealed, a new creation being brought from the baptizing waters into light.

Preparing the soil may mean tearing up roots in order to expose the ground to the light. Melting ice as a new spring dawns will flow, scraping the bottom, reshaping the shoreline, pulling things into it to carry away. But it is still Jesus who commands the winds and sea.

> The voice of the Lord is over the waters; the God of glory
> thunders, the Lord, over many waters (Ps 29:3).

The ocean conveyor completes its circulation moving the massive current of water around the globe, from the northern ocean to the southern, east and west, slowly turning over water in the entire ocean. It returns to where it began, surfacing in the north Atlantic, passing Ireland and the United Kingdom, spreading into the Norwegian Sea and passing Norway where, beside it, Sweden is receiving a skyrocketing number of minors from Syria.

The Sea of Glass

Hometowns in Syria are dangerous for children. The Islamic state is spreading throughout the cedars of Lebanon and over towns built around courtyards where fountains pour spring water, surrounded by citrus trees and flowers. On the outskirts, houses of unpainted concrete cluster in villages now a century old, passed to family members through the generations. Expressions of traditional dances mark marriage ceremonies, learned from the elders, taught to the young. Since early 2011, the youth no longer walk these streets in security because of the complex civil war in Syria, now the world's strongest push displacing people. Every day of 2015 an average of 42,500 people became refugees, asylum seekers, or internally displaced.

An estimated 388 unaccompanied children came to Sweden in 2004, leaping to 7,049 in 2014.[2] Some forty-five unaccompanied minors arrive every week in Malmö where there are thirteen homes designated for child asylum seekers. The homes employ 200 social workers paid by government funds. They help youth with school work, laundry, and teach them how to take care of themselves. It is not always easy to know where the youth come from or their ages. They are asked about landmarks in their homeland. Language experts assist the 122 migration officials. Doctors and dentists are asked to help establish a teenager's age, especially around eighteen years, when the error of margin is around two years.

Children arrive at all times of day and night, making their way through Turkey by paying smugglers about $10,000, money pooled by entire families and extended family just to get one child to a safer place. They make it to Italy, then travel north by train or on a plane to Denmark. Sweden is an easy trip from Copenhagen. Once a youth gains asylum, they can sponsor their families with the help of immigration officials. In 2015, 943 adults were granted asylum based on their relationship with unaccompanied minors.

The migrant crisis deepens in Sweden, home to 9.8 million people. Foreign Minister Margot Wallstrom said Stockholm needs to pressure the European Union to push member states to share the burden.[3] Sweden took in around 190,000 migrants by the time 2015 ended. The system is straining. Arsonists attacked a house where fourteen refugees were staying in a small town of Munkedal, in southern Sweden. They were quickly relocated. Fifteen arson attacks targeted refugee centers and apartments throughout the country in 2015. Some places were reduced to cinders. A Christian cross was set ablaze on August 16 near a migrant center. That same day a

---

2. Braw, Elisabeth, "Sweden's child refugee boom."
3. Traub, "The Death of the most generous nation."

Chapter 12

bag containing flammable liquid was found at another center in the town of Arboga where two Eritrean migrants had been accused of a knife attack.

In a square brick building at the far edge of town in Malmö, the southern port city on the border with Denmark, the Swedish Migration Agency processes hundreds of refugees lined up outside or sitting inside waiting for a place for the night. White tents stand in rows on the parking lot for those who find no shelter. Hundreds are put up in a nearby hotel. Others sleep in an auditorium.

The refuge opened in summer 2015 with about 1,500 people coming in every week seeking asylum from Syria, Iraq, and elsewhere. The agency has run out of places to offer for shelter. Sweden, which had taken in Jews of Denmark, saving many people during World War II, is at capacity. WWII had created 40 million refugees making dangerous journeys from their shattered towns in Central and Eastern Europe. When Europe came together after the war, the universal need for humanitarian efforts to be acknowledged was documented as the Convention on Human Rights, the Refugee Convention, and the Universal Declaration of Human Rights. Signatories pledged not to turn back refugees with a "well-founded fear of being persecuted." Organizations like the UN High Commissioner for Refugees were founded to ensure that states honored thosecommitments. Hundreds of thousands would flee from communist oppression in eastern Europe. Half a million people would flee Vietnam into the US when the south fell in 1975. Mass migrations in the air above, along the ocean's countenance, past the boundaries of nations will be unending until the trumpet sounds and the Spirit of Holiness lifts away the darkness.

After more than 1,000 years, the ocean conveyor has shared with all the world's waters as it returns to the north where the sky is night for half the year. Here again it sinks as the Arctic air cools it around the island of Iceland. The people of Iceland began hearing of Jesus after the news left the Mediterranaean to reach Norway and go out across the sea in search of the lost. Around the year 1000, Icelanders convened to discuss whether they should practice Christianity. A priest and *gothi* (chieftain) among them, Thorgeir, went into solitude for a day and a night of meditation under a fur blanket. He emerged with the decision that Christianity was to be followed, but old traditions could be retained. Among the archives of Iceland kept from that year, it was recorded that Jón, bishop of Hólar, dreamt he was praying before a large crucifix. Jesus bent down and whispered something in his ear, but he did not understand the words.[4]

After making the decision for Christ, Torgeir is said to have thrown his statues of the Norse gods into the Godafoss, a waterfall flowing from a height of forty feet as it finds its way back into the ocean. A window in the Cathedral of Akureyri, a city in northern Iceland, illustrates this story.

The country's language has twenty-seven different words recognizing different kinds of spirits. Everyone still knows what the ancestors talked about and the names of those who had lived before them. The Evangelical Lutheran Church became the state church of Iceland, with 140 ministers being supported by the government. There are also Catholic, Baptist, Pentecostal, Mormon, Jehovah Witness, and other groups freely worshiping. About 85.5 percent of the 281,000 people are members of Christian congregations, most of whom belong to the Church of Iceland. Yet church attendance is low. Only 10 percent of Icelanders go to church once a month or more. Forty-three percent say they never attend church. In the 1970s Iceland began to see a growing Muslim population both through immigration from the Islamic world and converts on Iceland. As of 2015, 875 Muslims were registered with the official Muslim organizations in the country.[5]

The north current turns and once more cascades over the underwater waterfall between Iceland and Greenland and another generation feels the tectonic shifts in their lives as God asks them to decide about his son. None of the Iceland youth twenty-five or younger believed in God who were asked in 2015.[6] The poll was commissioned by the Icelandic Ethical Humanist Association, an association of atheists. It found 61.1 percent of Icelanders do believe in God, decreasing the younger the age.

Paul wrote, "For the Lord himself will descend from heaven with a shout, with the voice of an archangel, and with the trumpet of God." (1 Thess 4:16). This splendor, this rescue will come unexpectedly, with the heavens passing away in a noise so great that it will penetrate the entire creation, the elements melting in an intense heat.

Since all these things are thus to be dissolved, what sort of people ought you to be in lives of holiness and godliness (2Pet 3:11).

Since you are waiting for this, be diligent. (v3:14).

Follow me, Jesus says. "Come, Lord Jesus," we answer (Rev 22:20).

4. Weinberger, "Ísland."
5. US Department of State, "2013 Report."
6. RT News, "0 % of Icelanders."

Chapter 12

Behold. He comes.

He is coming with the clouds, and every eye will see him, even those who pierced him, and all tribes of the earth will wail on account of him. (Rev 1:7). John saw four angels standing at the four corners of earth hold back the four winds. No breeze moved. The ocean lay quiet (Rev7:1). The air is completely still. The sky and its stars will roll up like a scroll. The bright morning star alone is left to shine (Rev 22:16) as all the other stars fall from heaven (Rev 6:13).

> So we have the prophetic word made more sure, to which you do
> well to pay attention as to a lamp shining in a dark place, until
> the day dawns and the morning star arises in your hearts
> (2Pet 1:19)

The Lord set boundaries that not even the ocean can cross. Pulling back its surge so the dry land appeared, it leaves a fringe of sand for childhood dreams, for birds and grasses, and jagged rocks to stand proudly.

The sea began rising a tenth of an inch every year during the past century as the temperature in the water warms, resulting in thermal expansion of the surface water. Snowmelt finding its way into rivers that carry to sea adds to it. Mankind extracting groundwater for irrigation contributes to the flow. But the water is not changing coastlines the same way everywhere. Tides in Louisiana are rising because land is sinking. In southeast Alaska sea levels are falling more than half an inch a year because the land is rising. The haunting beauty of the Arctic's frozen ocean water can change our entire world as sea ice steadily declines. In 2015 it was nearly 50 percent smaller than it was in 1979 as sea ice melted an area three times the size of Texas. The temperatures are rising more quickly than ever before in history.

In the glorious glimpse of heaven John saw the multitude of those redeemed dressed in white robes, not a hint of a spot on any of them. They have been extraordinarily purified by the power of Christ's love. John is asked, "Who are these, where do they come from?" (Rev 7:13). The elder tells us these people have been crushed coming through great tribulation, the hardships Jesus spoke of when he said while in this world we will have tribulation. The power of that pain has been broken. The multitude is full of joy. Thousands and thousands of voices rise in harmony singing worthy is the lamb who was slain to receive power and riches and wisdom. It's a song sung by souls who have been restored. Its notes are the melodies of every promise God had made, now completed through the cleansing of his immersions.

The Sea of Glass

More than the sounds of many waters, the ocean is the black Atlantic in its role of slavery. It is the green Atlantic to Irish immigrants crossing from its eastern coast. To linguists the Pacific is the contributions brought to languages. Oceans sway with sunlight and rock with whispers of heaven in the stories of explorers of the Southern Ocean. The currents of sea water are the conveyance of historic change to indigenous peoples and a life-giver to peoples who are sustained by its seasonal gifts of food and shells. To poets it is a song to be translated, to scientists it holds answers. To believers it is the signature of God.

> The Lord reigns; he is robed in majesty;
> the Lord is robed; he has put on strength as his belt.
> Yes, the world is established; it shall never be moved.
> Your throne is established from of old; you are from everlasting.
>
> The floods have lifted up, O Lord, the floods have lifted up their voice;
> the floods lift up their roaring.
>
> Mightier than the thunders of many waters,
> mightier than the waves of the sea, the Lord on high is mighty!
>
> Your decrees are very trustworthy; holiness befits your house, O Lord, forevermore (Ps 93).

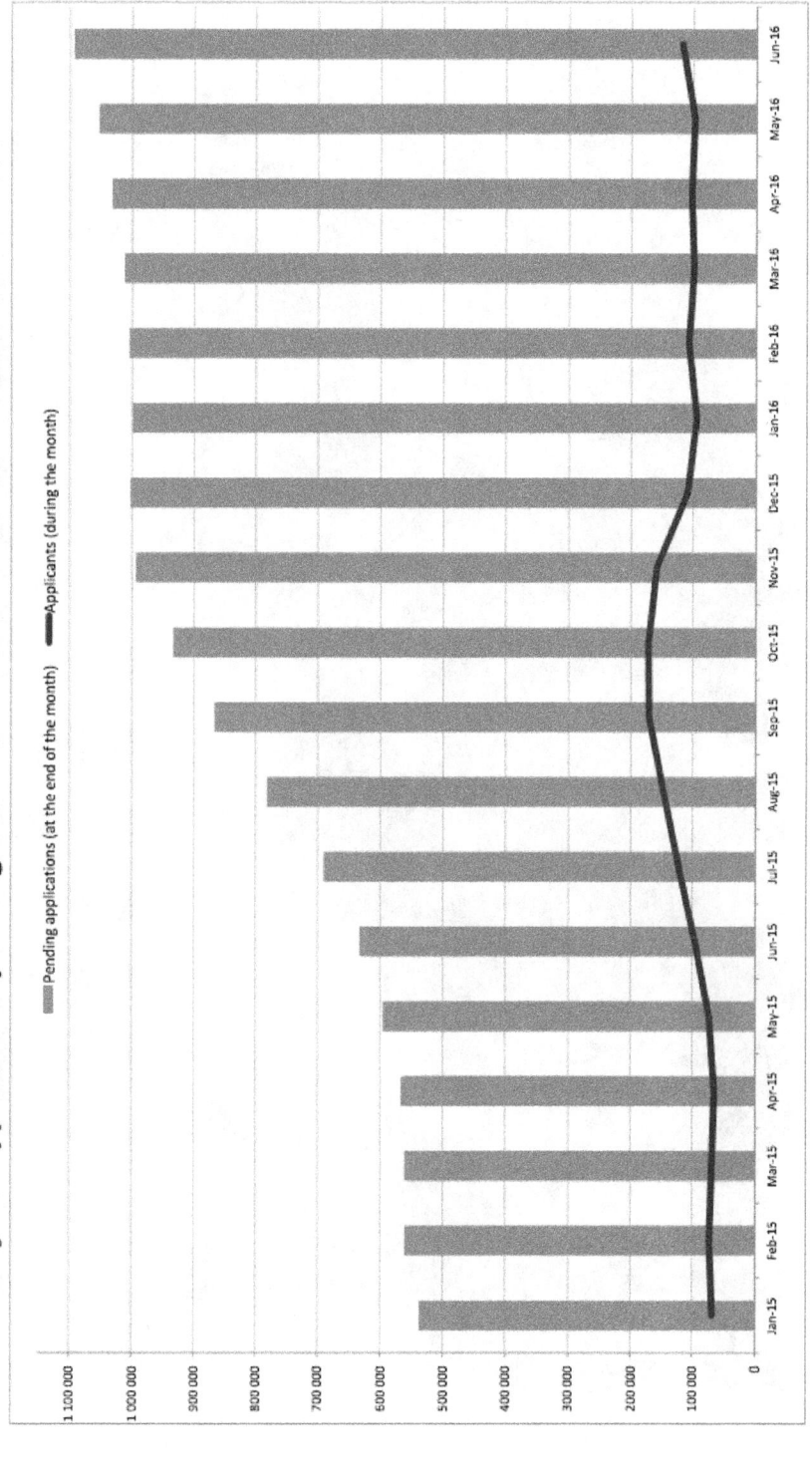

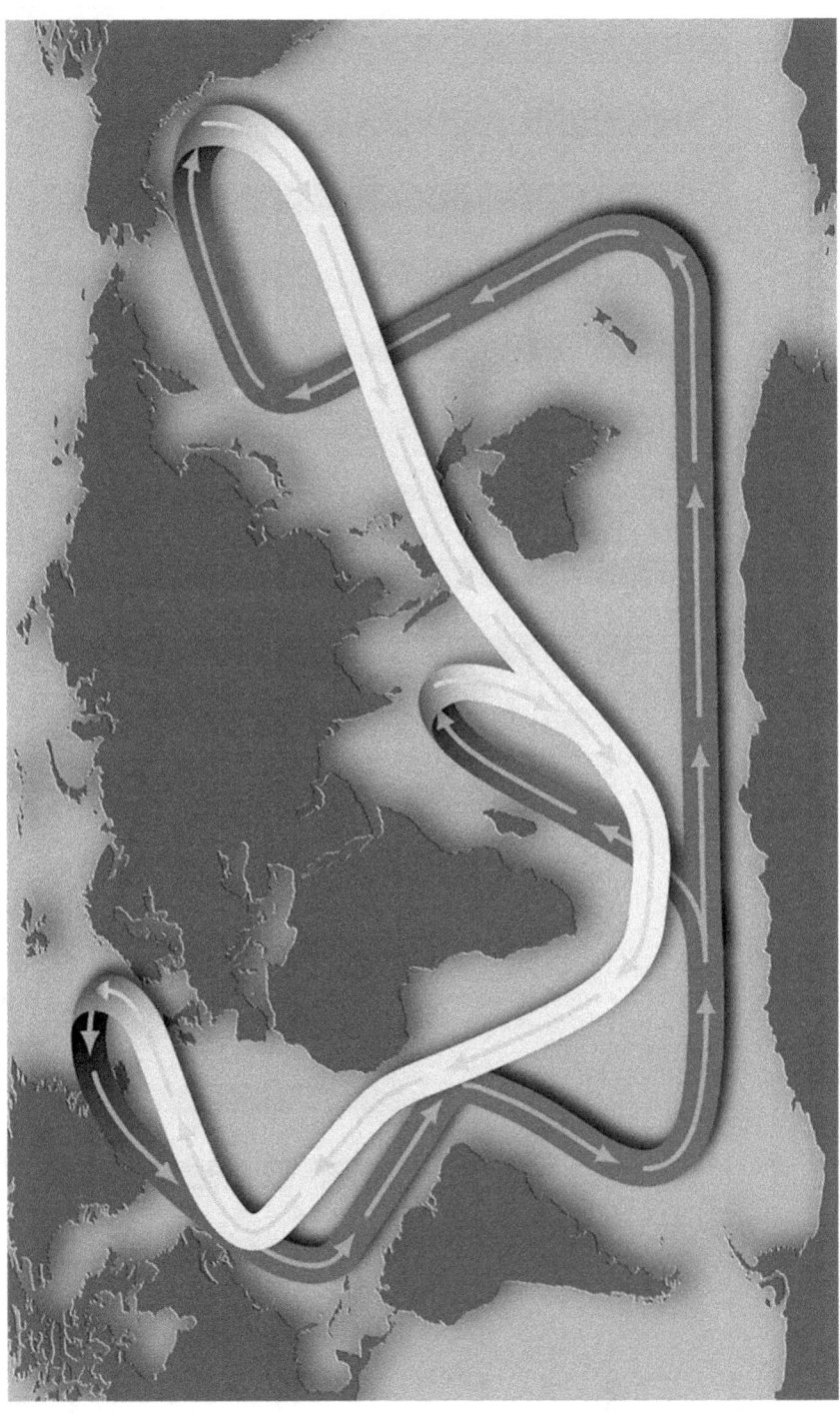

Bibliography

A MightyWind.com, "Accounts Multiply Of Muslims Who Have Encountered YAHUSHUA (Jesus Christ) In Unusual Dreams," Web. http://www.amightywind.com/fastfood/dreams/040723muslimdreams.htm

Arab Forum for Environment and Development, "Natural disaster warning," August 5, 2015, Web. http://www.afedmag.com/english/NewsDetails.aspx?id=2788

Associated Press, "Gunmen storm Yemen retirement home, kill 16 including 4 nuns," March 4, 2016, Web. http://www.nydailynews.com/news/national/gunmen-storm-yemen-retirement-home-kill-16-including-4-nuns-article-1.2552611

Barnabas Aid, "Barnabas Helps Christian Girls Escape Abuse in Kenya," January 14, 2011, Web.https://barnabasfund.org/US/News/Archives/Barnabas-helps-Christian-girls-escape-abuse-in-Kenya.html

Becker, Rose, "The Man of My Dreams," Jews for Jesus, Web. http://jewsforjesus.org/publications/issues/v02-n09/manofdreams

Bible Prophecy Tracker, "Turkish Leader: Hitler's Presidential System Is Worth Emulating," January 2, 2016, Web. http://prophecytracker.org/2016/01/turkish-leader-hitlers-presidential-system-is-worth-emulating/

Braw, Elisabeth, "Sweden's child refugee boom," Aljazeera America, May 11, 2015, Web. http://america.aljazeera.com/articles/2015/5/11/swedens-child-refugee-boom.html

Canadian Conference of Catholic Bishops and The Evangelical Fellowship of Canada, "Declaration Against Euthanasia and Assisted Suicide," October 30, 2015, Web. http://www.euthanasiadeclaration.ca/declaration/

CBN, "Islam Faithful See Jesus" After Ramadan," Web. http://www1.cbn.com/onlinediscipleship/islam-faithful-%22see-jesus%22-after-ramadan

Compass Direct News, "Pakistani Muslim Forces to Convert, Marry Him." November 10, 2011, Web.http://www.compassdirect.org/english/country/pakistan/4229/

Culture Change, "No Offshore Oil Drilling: Committee Against Oil Exploration," April 3, 2010, Web.http://www.culturechange.org/cms/index.php?option=com_content&task=view&id=637&Itemid=1

Dickerson, Kelly, "Earth's Magnetic Field is Weakening 10 Times Faster Now," Live Science, July 8, 2014, Web. http://www.livescience.com/46694-magnetic-field-weakens.html

Ehntholt, Kimberly A.and Yule William, "Assessment and Treatment of Refugee Children and Adolescents," Journal of Child Psychology and Psychiatry 2006, p. 1199, Web.

Bibliography

http://tartarus.ed.utah.edu/users/daniel.olympia/prelim%20readings/Articles/Practice/Ehntholt%20and%20Yule%202006.pdf

Encyclopedia of Life, "Kemp's Ridley Sea Turtle," Web. http://eol.org/pages/1056176/details

Evangelical Alliance, "How many churches have opened or closed in recent years," September 18, 2014, Web.http://www.eauk.org/church/research-and-statistics/how-many-churches-have-opened-or-closed-in-recent-years.cfm

Evangelical Environmental Network, "Evangelical Declaration on the Care of Creation," Web. http://creationcare.org/creation-care-resources/evangelical-declaration-on-the-care-of-creation/

Firestone, Jeremy; Jarvis, Christina, "Response and Responsibility: Regulating Noise Pollution in the Marine Environment," September 2007, Journal of International Wildlife Law and Policy. Web.https://www.ceoe.udel.edu/File%20Library/Research/Wind%20Power/Publication%20PDFs/FirestoneJarvis-acoustic-pollution-reg-07.pdf

Graef, Alicia, "Good news for our oceans: US and Chile announce new marine reserves," Care2.com, October 2, 2015, Web. http://www.care2.com/causes/good-news-for-our-oceans-u-s-and-chile-announce-new-marine-reserves.html

Green, Lisa Cannon, "Study: Thousands of Churches Closing Every Year But There Is A Silver Lining," Charisma News, December 9, 2015, Web. http://www.charismanews.com/us/53715-study-thousands-of-churches-closing-every-year-but-there-is-a-silver-lining

Hearth, Katey, "Child soldier recruitment continues amid reform," Mission Network News, February 12, 2016, Web. https://www.mnnonline.org/news/child-soldier-recruitment-continues-amid-reform/

Ingraham, Garry, "Who We Are," Love and Truth Network, Web. http://www.loveandtruthnetwork.com/who-we-are/

Intercede International, "Vietnam for Christ," Web. http://www.intercedenow.ca/report/740VFC_2315.pdf

International Day of Prayer, "IDOP 2010: Hearing Their Cry: Children's Material," p. 5, Web http://idop.org/media/pdf/children.pdf

Israel Today, "First Messianic Jewish synagogue found?" January 15, 2013, Web. http://www.israeltoday.co.il/NewsItem/tabid/178/nid/23621/Default.aspx?article=related_stories

Jaben-Eilon, Jan, "Messianic Jewish Groups Claim Rapid Growth," Jews on First! June 4, 2012, Web. http://www.jewsonfirst.org/12a/messianic1.aspx

Justice, Adam, "Germany: Iraqi migrants despair bureaucracy," International Business Times, January 28, 2016, Web. http://www.ibtimes.co.uk/germany-iraqi-migrants-despair-bureaucracy-far-right-hatred-heading-home-1540594

Klatte, Maria, Bergstrom, Kirstin, and Lachmann, Thomas, "Does noise affect learning? A short review on noise effects on cognitive performance in children," National Center for Biotechnology Information, August 30, 2013, Web. http://www.ncbi.nlm.nih.gov/pmc/articles/PMC3757288/

Krejcir, R.J., "What is Going on with Pastors in America?" Into Thy Word Web. http://www.intothyword.org/apps/articles/?articleid=36562

Larkin, Bill,"Vision of Tsunami on East Coast, Florida, New Jersey underwater," Youtube, August 3, 2014, Web. https://www.youtube.com/watch?v=mrFDA65AjPY

Bibliography

Lazarus, David, "Arabs and Jews Unite to Proclaim Messiah's Return," Israel Today, November 26, 2014, Web.http://www.israeltoday.co.il/NewsItem/tabid/178/nid/25575/Default.aspx

Lee, Esther Yu-Hsi, "US Agrees To Take In More Central American Refugees, But It May Come At A Cost," Think Progress, January 14, 2016, Web. http://thinkprogress.org/immigration/2016/01/14/3739403/us-refugee-resettlement-central-america/

Luft, Stephen, "Mikveh," Kehilah Portland, Web. http://www.shalommaine.com/sermon_notes_pdf/Mikveh.pdf

Mamanglue-Regala, Shianee, "ISIS executes 10 boys for trying to escape training camp, boy shoots militants who killed his pet birds," Christian Today, January 23, 2016, Web. http://www.christiantoday.com/article/isis.executes.10.boys.for.trying.to.escape.training.camp.boy.shoots.militants.who.killed.his.pet.birds/77462.htm

Marine and Environmental Research Institute, "Oil Spill Response," Web. http://www.meriresearch.org/focus/oil-spill-response

The Messiah According to Bible Prophecy, "God revealed to me that Jesus is the Messiah," Web. http://www.spirituallysmart.com/Messiah.html

Mezzofiore, Giauluca, "Libya migrants: Muslim refugees arrested Italy Throwing Christians into sea after fight," International Business Times, April 16, 2015, Web. http://www.ibtimes.co.uk/libya-migrants-muslim-refugees-arrested-italy-throwing-christians-into-sea-after-fight-1496777

Miller, Leila, "Local rabbis speak up about the drought," Jewish Journal, July1, 2015, Web. http://www.jewishjournal.com/los_angeles/article/local_rabbis_speak_up_about_the_drought

More Than Dreams, Web. http://morethandreams.org

Morell, Virginia, "US Navy to limit sonar testing to protect whales," Science Magazine, September 16, 2015, Web. http://www.sciencemag.org/news/2015/09/us-navy-limit-sonar-testing-protect-whales

Moyer, Justin, "Aylin's story: How desperation left a 3-year-old boy washed up on a Turkish beach," Washington Post, September 3, 2015, Web. https://www.washingtonpost.com/news/morning-mix/wp/2015/09/03/a-desperate-refugee-family-a-capsized-boat-and-3-year-old-dead-on-a-beach-in-turkey/

National Christian Evangelical Alliance of Sri Lanka, "About NCEASL," February 2012, Web. http://www.nceasl.org/NCEASL/aboutus/aboutnceasl.php

National Oceanic and Atmospheric Administration, "2015 Gulf of Mexico dead zone above average," August 4, 2015, http://www.noaanews.noaa.gov/stories2015/080415-gulf-of-mexico-dead-zone-above-average.html

NOAA, "Scientists Discover and Image Explosive Deep-Ocean Volcano," December 17, 2009, Web. http://www.noaanews.noaa.gov/stories2009/20091217_volcano2.html

Ocean Today, "Medicines From the Sea," October 22, 2014, Web. http://oceantoday.noaa.gov/medicinesfromthesea/

Odden, Cheryl, "Facing Death, Yet More than Conquerors," Voice of the Martyrs Canada News Letter, March 1, 2011, p.19, Web. http://files.efc-canada.net/si/Religious%20Freedom%20Internationally/RLC/The_Overlooked_Demographic_-_A_Report_on_the_Impact_of_Religious_Persecution_on_Children.pdf

P Janelle in Africa, "After Dreams of Jesus, Imam Renounces Islam," Open Doors USA, August 7, 2015, Web. https://www.opendoorsusa.org/take-action/pray/tag-prayer-updates-post/after-dreams-of-jesus-imam-renounces-islam/

Bibliography

Pew Forum on Religion and Public Life, "Global Restrictions on Religion," 2009, p. 1, Web. http://pewforum.org/newassets/images/reports/restrictions/restrictionsfullreport.pdf

Pew Research Center, "US Public Becoming Less Religious," November 3, 2015, Web. http://www.pewforum.org/2015/11/03/u-s-public-becoming-less-religious/

Pruthi, Priyanka, "Grace Akallo comes back from the last place on earth," UNICEF, July 20, 2013, Web. http://www.unicef.org/protection/57929_69985.html

Reed, Anne, "The real threat to marriage," AFA Journal, January 2015, Web. http://www.afajournal.org/recent-issues/2015/january/the-real-threat-to-marriage/

Research Gate, "Long term stratification changes in the Sea of Galilee," April 2009, Web. https://www.researchgate.net/publication/252886637_Long_term_stratification_changes_in_the_Sea_of_Galilee_Israel_-_climate_change_or_water_usage_pattern_change

Ross, Megan, "Muslim Woman Receives Jesus Revelation Through Vision," Charisma News, September 5, 2013, Web.http://www.charismanews.com/world/40892-muslim-woman-receives-jesus-revelation-through-vision

RT News, "0 % of Icelanders aged 25 or younger believe world was created by God – poll," RT News, January 15, 2016, Web. https://www.rt.com/news/329107-iceland-poll-religion-god

Scheer, Holly, "California Bill Would Ultimately Erase Religious Schools," The Federalist, June 21, 2016, Web. http://thefederalist.com/2016/06/21/california-bill-would-ultimately-erase-religious-schools/

Schiele, Edwin, "Ocean Conveyor Belt Impact," NASA Ocean Motion http://oceanmotion.org/html/impact/conveyor.html

Schwartz, Matt, "Orthodox Jew in Tel Aviv, Israel Has Recurring Dream About the Messiah," Christians Together, June 18, 2007, Web. http://www.christianstogether.net/Articles/82529/Christians_Together_in/Esther_4_14/Orthodox_Jew_dreams.aspx

Shoebat, Walid, "ISIS Sends Out This Message To All Christians: 'You Will Soon See An Ocean Of Blood For All The Nation Of The Cross,'" Freedom Outpost, February 16, 2015, Web. http://freedomoutpost.com/2015/02/isis-sends-message-christians-will-soon-see-ocean-blood-nation-cross/#IseTLeUgRm2iiFdY.99

Smithsonian Institute, "Gulf Oil Spill," Web. http://ocean.si.edu/gulf-oil-spill

Smithsonian National Museum of Natural History, "Temperature and Chemistry," April 30, 2015, Web. http://ocean.si.edu/planet-ocean/temperature-chemistry

Traub, James,"The Death of the most generous nation on earth," Foreign Policy, February 10, 2016, Web. http://foreignpolicy.com/2016/02/10/the-death-of-the-most-generous-nation-on-earth-sweden-syria-refugee-europe/

UNHCR, "10,000th Syrian refugee arrives in Canada to rebuild life," January 14, 2016, Web. http://www.unhcr.ca/news/10000th-syrian-refugee-arrives-in-canada-to-rebuild-life

UNHCR Canada, "Refugees and Human Rights Poetry Contest 2015 edition," Web. http://www.unhcr.ca/news/2015-poetry-contest/

UNHCR, "Red Sea tragedy leaves 62 people dead in deadliest crossing of the year," June 6, 2014, Web. http://www.unhcr.org/5391c1e56.html

UNHCR, "Refugees continue to reach Yemen by sea despite conflict," October 27, 2015, Web.http://www.unhcr.org/562f882b9.html

Bibliography

UNHCR, "Worldwide displacement hits all-time high as war and persecution increase," June 18, 2015, Web. http://www.unhcr.org/558193896.html

UNICEF, "State of the World's Children 2011: Adolescence – An Age of Opportunity," 2009, Web. http://www.unicef.org/publications/index_57468.html

UNICEF Status and Progress, "Undernutrition contributes to nearly half of all deaths in children under 5 and is widespread in Asia and Africa," October 2015, Web. http://data.unicef.org/nutrition/malnutrition.html

UN Joint Framework Initiative on Children, Youth, and Climate Change, "Youth in Action on climate change," May 2013, Web. https://www.wmo.int/youth/sites/default/files/youth_pub_2013_en_m.pdf

United Nations News Center, El Niño has put world in 'uncharted territory,' January 7, 2016, Web. http://www.un.org/apps/news/story.asp?NewsID=52959#.VprNV6P2Zjo

UN Resources for Speakers, "Refugees: Overview of forced displacement," Web. http://www.un.org/en/globalissues/briefingpapers/refugees/overviewofforceddisplacement.html

UN Resources for Speakers, "Refugees: The Numbers," Web. http://www.un.org/en/globalissues/briefingpapers/refugees/index.shtml

UN Resources for Speakers, "Youth: Vital Statistics," Web. http://www.un.org/en/globalissues/briefingpapers/youth/vitalstats.shtml

United States Commission on International Religious Freedom, "Annual Report of the United States Commission on International Religious Freedom: May 2010," p. 1, Web. http://www.uscirf.gov/images/annual%20report%202010.pdf

USCIRF Annual Report 2010, p. 42 Sustainable Measures, "Ecological Footprint," Web. http://www.sustainablemeasures.com/node/102

US Department of State, "2013 Report on International Religious Freedom," Web. http://www.state.gov/j/drl/rls/irf/2013/eur/222225.htm

US Department of State, "Remarks at the Opening of the 2015 Our Ocean Conference," October 5, 2015, Web. http://www.state.gov/secretary/remarks/2015/10/247875.htm

Voice of the Martyrs Canada: Bold Believers Magazine for Students, "Escape from Kidnappers," 1st Quarter 2009, Web. http://files.efc-canada.net/si/Religious%20Freedom%20Internationally/RLC/The_Overlooked_Demographic_-_A_Report_on_the_Impact_of_Religious_Persecution_on_Children.pdf

Voice of the Martyrs Canada Newsletter, "My Faith Was Never Shaken: The Testimony of Nankpaqk Kumzwam," April 13. 2008. p. 6 Web. http://files.efc canada.net/si/Religious%20Freedom%20Internationally/RLC/The_Overlooked_Demographic_-_A_Report_on_the_Impact_of_Religious_Persecution_on_Children.pdf

Voice of the Martyrs, "Coptic Student Murdered by Classmates for Wearing Cross," Web. http://www.persecution.net/eg-2011-11-10.htm

Voice of the Martyrs, "Kids of Courage," Web. http://www.kidsofcourage.com/?p=2665

Voice of the Martyrs. "Muslims Kill Christian Women and Children," July 15, 2010, Web. http://www.persecution.net/pk-2010-07-15.htm

The Weather Channel, "Saharan Dust Travels More Than 5,000 Miles to South Texas," June 22, 2015, Web. http://www.weather.com/science/weather-explainers/news/saharan-dust-africa-caribbean-gulf-of-mexico

Weinberger, Eliot, "Ísland," Jacket Magazine 1998, Web. http://jacketmagazine.com/04/paradiceland.html

Wellman, Jack, "Christian Dream Interpretation? Does God Use Dreams to Speak to Us?" What Christians Want to Know, Web. http://www.whatchristianswanttoknow.

Bibliography

com/christian-dream-interpretation-does-god-use-dreams-to-speak-to-us/#ixzz3yt8mmXsn

Wickremesinhe, Roshini, "They Walk on Water," Christian Solidarity Worldwide Response Magazine," 1st Quarter 2006, Web. http://files.efc-canada.net/si/Religious%20Freedom%20Internationally/RLC/The_Overlooked_Demographic_-_A_Report_on_the_Impact_of_Religious_Persecution_on_Children.pdf

Williams, Sara Elizabeth, "Why some Syrian refugees decline Canada's resettlement offer," The Globe and Mail, January 1, 2016, Web. http://www.theglobeandmail.com/news/world/why-some-syrian-refugees-decline-canadas-resettlement-offer/article27985618/

Wilson Center, "Environmental Change and Security Program," Web. https://www.wilsoncenter.org/about-28

Wisdom Quotes and Stories, "Miracle by Jesus to a Muslim in Toronto: Canada, A True Story," Web. http://www.wisdomquotesandstories.com/muslim-sees-jesus-toronto

Woods Hole Oceanographic Institute, "The Antikythera Shipwreck," Web. http://www.whoi.edu/main/topic/antikythera-shipwreck

Woods Hole Oceanographic Institute, "Fukushima Radiation," Web. http://www.whoi.edu/main/topic/fukushima-radiation

Woods Hole Oceanographic Institute, "Hydrothermal Vents," Web. http://www.whoi.edu/main/topic/hydrothermal-vents

Woods Hole Oceanographic Institute, "Know Your Ocean, Web. http://www.whoi.edu/know-your-ocean/

Woods Hole Oceanographic Institute, "Ocean Acidification," Web. http://www.whoi.edu/main/topic/ocean-acidification

Woods Hole Oceanographic Institute, "Ocean Observatories," Web. http://www.whoi.edu/main/topic/ocean-observatories

World Net Daily, "Isis Fighter Follows Jesus After Encounter in Dream," June 9, 2015, Web. http://www.wnd.com/2015/06/isis-fighter-follows-jesus-after-encounter-in-dream/

The World Revolution, "The State of the World," Web. http://www.worldrevolution.org/projects/globalissuesoverview/overview2/briefoverview.htm

Zaimov, Stoyan, "ISIS beheads 21 Coptic Christians in message to nation of the cross Christian Post," February 16, 2015, Web. http://www.christianpost.com/news/isis-beheads-21-coptic-christians-in-message-to-nation-of-the-cross-egypt-bombs-terror-group-in-response-134142

www.ingramcontent.com/pod-product-compliance
Lightning Source LLC
Chambersburg PA
CBHW071450150426
43191CB00008B/1300